Ceoltóirí Chualann

Ceoltóirí Chualann

The Band that changed the course of Irish Music

Peadar Ó Riada

MERCIER PRESS
Cork
www.mercierpress.ie

© Peadar Ó Riada 2024

ISBN: 978-1-78117-869-0
eBook: 978-1-78117-870-6

Cover design: Craig Carry

A CIP record for this title is available from the British Library.

This book is sold subject to the condition that it shall not, by way of trade or otherwise, be lent, resold, hired out or otherwise circulated without the publisher's prior consent in any form of binding or cover other than that in which it is published and without a similar condition including this condition being imposed on the subsequent purchaser.

No part of this publication may be reproduced or transmitted in any form or by any means, electronic or mechanical, including photocopying, recording or any information or retrieval system, without the prior permission of the publisher in writing.

Printed and bound in the EU.

Contents

Foreword — 7

The birth of a band — 9

Index of the band's list of arrangements — 55

The arrangements — 65

Discography — 212

Scores — 225

Miscellaneous pieces — 239

Index — 245

Foreword

♪

In assembling this account of Ceoltóirí Chualann, I have relied upon the extensive records of Éamon de Buitléar, Michael Tubridy and the family archives here. I have had the good fortune that Seán Ó Sé has sat by my side constantly advising and correcting the unfolding account. And until recently, I could talk to Seán Keane regularly. I was very privileged to have grown up with, and known, the band members of Ceoltóirí Chualann and to have counted them all, and their partners, as our extended family. There was a bond of love within this group that extends to this day. They were, and are, my friends.

I have assembled this account, and furnished as much detail as possible, so that ordinary people may learn of the extent of their knowledge, innovation, ability and courage. The idea that Sonny Brogan or John Kelly would take on complicated scored arrangements may surprise some today. But they were very able musicians with a wide understanding of music. They also had great faith in my father, Seán Ó Riada. He was a good teacher and could find unorthodox ways of explaining what he needed.

People should also remember that the times they were working in were very different to today's expectations. Irish music in general was referred to as diddle-dee-di music or only played in remote places. It was folklore. It was relegated to being something of value for collecting and admiring. It was not generally tolerated in public houses or in hotels. There were notable exceptions of course but they were scarce. Ireland was 'modernising'. Electricity was entering more of the country's human habitation spaces. Younger generations now looked for a more exotic or foreign spark to their entertainment. Television arrived during this period. Yet Ceoltóirí Chualann thrived and innovated their way through these 1960s with great success.

When you read the arrangements, you will see that they are far more sophisticated than mere accompaniment. I admit that I find it very hard to see anything comparable, in the last fifty-three years, since they played their last notes.

Occasionally, over the years, we have assembled and played for special events. Accordingly, as a member died and passed on, a close relative, or similar musician, has taken their seat. I sat in for my father. We always use the original arrangements when playing. I wonder if we will ever sit together again on stage, making music publicly.

I thank Mary Feehan, Dee Collins and Mercier Press for their interest and assistance. My eternal thanks to Éamon, Mick, Seán Keane and Seán Ó Sé for their help with this project, and to Eoin Ó Suilleabháin, Réamonn Ó Ciaráin of Gael Linn, D. A. Duncan, courtesy of Irish Traditional Music Archive archives for the Sonny Brogan photo, Liam O'Connor and Maeve Gebruers of ITMA, Michael Scott, DMG Property Group and Emer Twomey of UCC Archives for help with pictures and copies. I hope some of you readers find it of interest.

Beannacht Dé le h-anamnacha na mairbh.

PEADAR Ó RIADA
An Draighean, 2024

The Birth of a Band

♪

Seán Ó Riada grew up in a house where music was part of the background fabric of life. His father, a fiddle player from Clare, was a sergeant in An Gárda Síochána – the Irish police force. As a youth, he drilled and trained with Sinn Féin but joined up with the new fledgling national police force, initially as a member of the Dublin Metropolitan Police. The Irish state was in the process of setting up its own institutions and this force was amalgamated into the new An Gárda Síochána. 'Seán Ó Riada' the elder (John Thomas Reidy) 'passed out' as a member of the first class or intake on 23 June 1923. He had an uncle in the RIC, Michael Lernihan. Seán Ó Riada's mother, a concertina /melodeon player from the West Cork Gaeltacht Cill na Martra, was a nurse and worked as a surgical theatre nurse under Dr Dundon in the North Infirmary during the War of Independence in Ireland. While I think her father Dan was a bit of a Redmonite, two of her brothers had to hot foot it to Australia having been recognised during an ambush and a friendly RIC sergeant cycled out form Macroom to Dan to warn him that the dreaded Tans were coming to raid and pick them up. So my granduncles, Denis and Jim, left for Queenstown (Cobh) immediately. Denis never returned but Jim came back briefly in the late 1960s.

Both John and Julia, Seán's parents, sang around the house and danced if suitable music erupted from the radio. They were both good traditional set dancers and both came from families where entertainment was based around the household and visiting neighbours at night-time, which included card-playing, dancing, storytelling, singing and music. Both came from agricultural backgrounds and were reared on farms. Seán grew up in Adare, County Limerick where his father was sergeant for twenty-eight years. He studied music from a very young age and became a member of the Limerick youth orchestra of the time, and apparently was leader of the string section by the age of twelve. He studied violin and piano. On going to university, University College Cork, where he studied Classics first before changing to Music under Aloys Fleischmann, he developed his interest in jazz and indeed made his pocket money playing jazz in various bands.

He married at the age of twenty-two in 1953 and once qualified, that year, assumed the position of assistant musical director of radio in the national radio station – Radio Éireann. Towards the end of 1954 he went to England and then to France in search of patronage or position to allow him to compose classical music. It didn't happen and he returned in the following early summer of 1955, and assumed the position as musical director of the Abbey Theatre. Whilst in this post he was composing for orchestra and aslo composing choral settings for Radio Éireann.

His duties in the Abbey Theatre meant he was heavily involved each year in their annual pantomime in the Irish language. He also was in charge of providing interval music and all other incidental music during or indeed before or after plays on stage in this, the Irish National Theatre. At the playwright's request he assembled his first vestiges of Ceoltóirí Chualann for the play *The Song of the Anvil* by Bryan MacMahon. Bryan, an accomplished writer from Listowel in County Kerry, asked Seán to provide a group of traditional musicians, as the sound backdrop to his play, which opened for three performances on 12 September 1960. The full-length play revolved around a fantasy story MacMahon created in a world and place called the valley of Glensharon. The valley is under threat of an evil spell, that may be cast upon it at any time, by a stranger. Emerging from the mist come a visionary, a failed priest, a magician of the mysterious, two village nitwits and a sex-starved spinster. The Lucht Sí (fairy folk) element gave the play a secondary title of *The Golden Folk*. It involved fifteen dancers and Wren Boys and hence the need for traditional players. Bryan had a great cast, as can be seen below, from the listing on the play's programme. With its cast of twenty-two, one can see many famous names in the annals of Irish theatre in subsequent years:

Mooney, Ria – Director
Brogan, Harry – Actor as Mick Twin
Carroll, Bert – Stage Manager
Ó Guaillí, Éamonn – Actor as Garrett Gowa Fitzgerald
Long, Paddy – Actor as Dancers
Mac an Ailí (Fhailí), Reamonn – Actor as Dancers
Mac Anna, Tomás – Set Designer
Mac Cafraidh, Seamus – Actor as Dancers
Mac Cionnaith, Tomás P. – Actor as Fr 'O Priest' McHugh
Mac Leid, Pádraig – Actor as Crowd
Mac Seáin, Raghnall – Actor as Crowd
Ní Bhearain, Caitlín – Actor as Elenrose Schneide
Ní Bhrolcháin, Ester – Actor as Dancers

Ní Chatháin, Máire – Actor as Kitsy Carty
Ní Cheallaigh, Eadaoin – Actor as Crowd
Ní Dhomhnaill, Máire – Actor as Deborah
Ní Liodáin, Eithne – Actor as Dancers
Ní Mhurchú, Fidelma – Actor as Crowd
Ní Nuamain, Aingeal – Actor as Crowd
Ó Briain, Micheál – Actor as Paddy Twin
Ó Dubhlainn, Uinsionn – Actor as Walter Cunningham
Ó Floinn, Philib – Actor as Darby Jer. O'Shea
Ó Foghludh (Foghlú), Liam – Actor as Dancers
Ó Goilidhe (Ó Goilí), Seathrún – Actor as Crowd
Ó hAonghusa, Micheál – Actor as Crowd
Ó Luain, Peadar – Actor as Ulick Madigan
Ó Riada, Seán – Music
O'Sullivan, Clara – Actor as Dancers
Redmond, Avice – Actor as Dancers
Ryan, Patricia – Choreographer

The old Abbey Theatre went on fire in 1951 and the company moved to the Queens where they performed until 1966. The Theatre itself was demolished in 1975 and the site now is one of Trinity College's buildings.

Running on stage at the same time (opened 15 September 1960) in Amharclann an Damer (an Irish language theatre on Stephen's Green) was a play from Seán's pen entitled *An Ceannaí Glic* based on the death of the poet Eoghan Rua Ó Súilleabháin. He assembled another small group of musicians for this play and when he amalgamated both groups, he had Ceoltóirí Chualann.

Seán had become friendly with Éamon de Buitléar whilst purchasing fishing and shooting equipment in Hely's sports shop in Dame Street Dublin. He also had a pet shop of his own. When he received Bryan MacMahon's request Seán spoke to Éamon about it and he introduced him to Sonny Brogan. John Kelly from Carrigaholt in Clare was never far from Sonny and Seán already knew him through his stint at Radio Éireann.

Éamon de Buitléar became part of our lives and acted as secretary to the band members for Seán. He was married to Lally Lamb and she would baby-sit us from time to time. She was calm and quiet, very warm and gentle and I associated her with warm homely actions such as baking and knitting. She always had her hair in a bun. She was from a very famous painting family (her father was Charles Lamb) and worked in a shop selling books and painting and craft materials and would bring painting and colouring materials to us regularly. We always looked forward to her visits.

Both she and Bernie Potts were the 'advisers' to the other girls or spouses to the lads at practice sessions of the band. Éamon seemed to be always dressed in native natural materials such as tweed or báinín suits. He spoke Irish or Gaelic always and was a very interesting man and communicator. He and Seán would discuss anything from nature, fishing, history, interesting details of the Náisiún Gaelach and the weekly progress of our bee colonies.

Éamon was born in Galway where his father was stationed in Dún Uí Mhaoilíosa

(Renmore Barracks) at the time. His father Col Éamon de Buitléar was aide-de-camp to Douglas Hyde, Ireland's first president. Éamon's mother, a Waterford woman, like her husband spoke fluent Irish and thus Éamon Óg de Buitléar was raised. His father was a multi-linguist and a member of the Irish army intelligence unit. Éamon was a truly committed environmentalist long before such a person was common. He made many documentary films on Irish wildlife, published books and promoted the language and culture in pioneering ways, including cartoons for young children. He made a major contribution to Irish life and the nation during his life and will be long remembered as the man who brought nature into our living rooms through the television with his programme series *Amuigh Faoin Spéir*.

He knew Cúil Aodha pretty well having being sent there by his father to polish his Irish. He stayed in Peaití Tadhg Pheig's (Ó Tuama) house during those summers so you can see there were circles of communication and community throughout all our families and milieu.

Éamon played the accordion. In particular, my father would give him chords to play in the band arrangements. These were a new feature in Irish music at the time. I remember my father explaining the sequence required and mapping it out, on the floor in front of Éamon, in match sticks lined up in squares. I recall on one Sunday evening during rehearsal, my father came up with an unusual arrangement for a song called 'Ding Dong Detheró, buail sin séid seo' (Ding Dong Detherow, Beat this, blow that). My father had the idea that the chorus would be accompanied by strange sounds so we kids were sent off to find things that would make noise, if hit. I came back with a green bottle and we found a USA biscuit tin box lid as well. Éamon and Ronnie had to hit these items in a certain sequence to make a music 'loop' before such things were even invented. You can hear this arrangement on the band's second LP called *Ding Dong* published by Gael Linn (1966).

Éamon was one of the rocks of my life until he died in 2012. He was what we call in our own language a 'Duine Uasal' meaning a 'Noble Man'. He was instrumental in gathering the band together in the beginning and later did a lot of the organisational work when Seán had moved to Cúil Aodha in West Cork. After Seán died, Éamon formed a band called Ceoltóirí Laighean which also had John Kelly as a member.

♪

There was a hierarchy in Ceoltóirí Chualann of course. The Clare fiddle and

concertina player John Kelly appointed himself the second in command, he always sat by my father's side. He gave opinions about all things musical and had a gruff exterior. He was always right so my father listened to him and was also involved with him in other projects. John Kelly was the senior man in the band and everyone listened carefully to what he had to say.

John Kelly was from the townland of Rehy, near Kilbaha, at the very tip of the western Clare Loop head peninsula. His father Michael and mother, Elizabeth Keane, were steeped in our native culture and tradition. His mother was from Scattery island nearby and many a tune in today's repertoire originated there and arrived through John Kelly. He knew and played with many iconic figures in the past of our great tradition – his uncle Tom Keane and neighbour Patsy Geary were major influences, as were people like Nell Galvin who knew Garrett Barry, the piper. John also recorded with the great piper Johnny Doran.

He moved to Dublin in 1945 and opened a hardware shop at the end of Capel Street where you would find all kinds of useful things, including instruments – if needed. As a child I used to be fascinated by the selection of 'pen-knifes', which I coveted, but they were all under lock and key, under glass, along with a selection of mouth organs. John married a Wicklow woman Frances Hilliard and they raised a family who we became entwined with as we all grew up. Their older members were slightly older than us Riada's but we have always been close since that time. John was one of the great traditional fiddle players of the twentieth century. In his youth he diligently followed the music, no matter how difficult the journey might have been. This trait he kept to the end of his life when he could be seen at a Stephan Grappelli concert or instructing aspiring young fiddle players. His knowledge of the tradition was a constant rich source for my father, Seán. Like everyone else in the band they were good friends and he introduced Seán to many traditional musicians.

John Kelly's side kick was the Dubliner Sonny Brogan who played the accordion or box. Sonny worked as an elephant keeper in Dublin Zoo and used to complain about their noisy racket. He suffered a little and would say 'Me nerves are at me'. He must have been married to a wonderful woman. I remember her as Margaret, a small lovely friendly woman who would wave Sonny off with a gentle smile in her blue kitchen smock with its red trim and flowery pattern. She always had Sonny nattily and carefully dressed in a dark navy-blue suit. There was always a crease in the trousers that could mow a lawn. His shirt was dazzlingly white and the pinned collar was as stiff as a plank and encased a red peacock patterned tie that was carefully tied to perfection. He was a great box player but would get nervous when having to perform in the full glare of the audience or in front of the radio or studio microphone. Though born and bred in Dublin, his parents hailed from the Kildare side. John Kelly and himself were always sitting together to one side of my father who would be at the piano. I remember his sudden death in January 1965 and how it affected my father when the news arrived. The members of Ceoltóirí Chualann were like a 'Band of Brothers' and I saw Seán shed tears in our kitchen before heading for Dublin. He later wrote of Sonny:

> It was in the autumn of 1960 that I first met Sonny Brogan. I had been asked to supply music for Bryan MacMahon's play *The Song of the Anvil* at the Abbey Theatre, and had conceived the idea of using a group of traditional musicians for this purpose – the first time, as far as I am aware, that such a step had been taken. It was Éamon de Buitléar who introduced me to Sonny, who was at first rather shy and reserved, until he realised what was wanted of him. The play went on and, though it did not find favour with the public which it more than merited, the music seemed to succeed with everyone, not least of all the actors and backstage staff, who used to be entertained by impromptu concerts given by the musicians in the dressing rooms. Sonny was, of course, a prime mover in all this and one of the reels which they used play most often backstage, commonly called 'Redigan's', was re-christened by us privately as 'The Abbey Reel'.
>
> When the run of the play was over I hated the idea of parting from the musicians and so formed 'Ceoltóirí Chualann', of which, during the few years we have been functioning Sonny was a mainstay. I would not suggest for a moment that our association was all sweetness and light. Many the argument we had – it is well known that musicians argue more fiercely about traditional music than about anything else. However, we always saw eye-to-eye in the finish and each argument served only to make us better friends.
>
> Sonny's qualities as a musician were rare. He had an astounding memory, so much so that I was inclined to regard him, with John Kelly, as our living reference library. He could recall three or four different versions of a tune going back through three or four layers of time and often through three or four changes of title. He had a passion for the pure, simple essence of tunes, uncluttered by mistaken ornamentation. He was also, of

course, an outstanding accordion player, one of the very few who could make it sound suitable for playing Irish music.

As a person, Sonny was – well, he was contentious, convivial, argumentative, loyal, dogmatic, witty, utterly reliable, a tiger when his temper was roused (which was rare), and at the same time curiously gentle and courteous. He was a good friend. I shall miss him. 'Beannacht Dé lena anam'. (Seán Ó Riada)

♪

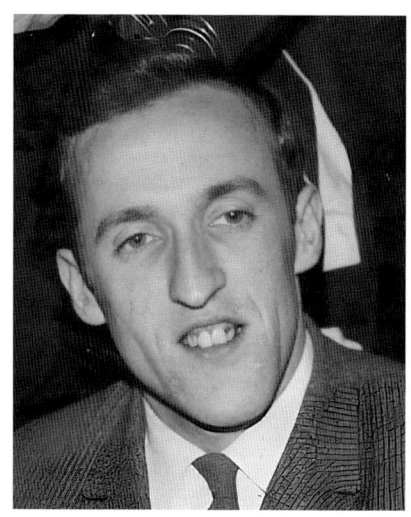

As THE BAND would sit at rehearsals in our sitting room in Galloping Green, on my father's other side or righthand side, and in the window would be the pipes and piper Paddy Moloney. He was a young wiry Donnycarney, Dublin, lad with a mop of fair hair. He worked as an accountant in Baxendales, one of Dublin's major hardware stores. He was following his father's footsteps in that his father John had also been an accountant. But it was his mother Catherine who bought him his first tin whistle and started him on his glittering musical path through life. He attended the famous Leo Rowsome, who was his piping teacher. It was at Baxendales that he met his fiancé Rita whom he later married and they both raised their three talented children.

At rehearsals he would give out about the reeds in his pipes a bit but could do anything he wanted to with the chanter, on which he was a true wizard. He also played the tin whistle and was no stranger to the melodeon. I remember him courting his wife Rita at rehearsals. He had a good musical ear so that he could be given contra melodies and rhythms, which were a new phenomenon at that time. A good example can be heard in the early track from *Reacaireacht an Riadaigh* – 'Toss the Feathers' (Ag Scaipeadh na gCleití). Paddy later went on to form the group 'The Chieftains' who have successfully travelled the world stage since then. This group initially consisted of some of the members of Ceoltóirí Chualann and was augmented as the years went by. In those early years most of their arrangements were Ceoltóirí material but since then they have gone on to do many collaborations with many famous musicians of other cultures, various genres and traditions. It is no exaggeration to say that his band The Chieftains have become world famous.

The main tin whistle player in Ceoltóirí Chualann was Seán Potts. Seán was a Liberties man, born and bred, but his people originally came from Wexford and for generations were one of Ireland's iconic traditional music families. As a kid I remember him as working for the Department of Post and Telegraphs. I used to marvel at the way his wide fingers could shape the sound of his melody by exposing only fractions of a hole on the tin whistle. It would always make and mark him, as the 'standard' on that instrument. His uncle Tommy was a particularly innovative musician. Seán's style on whistle is  instantly recognisable. But he also played the pipes. He had just married by the time I got to know him. His wife Bernie Sanfey was the boss amongst spouses at rehearsals and she and Lally (Éamon's wife) would steer or advise the others who were either courting or just married. There was always great fun around them. Bernie is an ardent Dublin GAA supporter while Seán's roots are in Wexford. My father would often give Potts the lead on tin whistle, in slow airs, because of his distinctive style. Seán Potts later formed a group called Bakerswell, after he spent some early years with The Chieftains. Once he came off the road with The Chieftains in 1979, he ploughed much of his energy into Na Píobairí Uilleann, an organisation promoting Irish Uilleann Pipe playing and music. In his time there it grew immensely and now has a fine premises and a burgeoning following all over the world. Indeed, I have heard it said that you cannot throw a stone now without hitting a piper. A very different world to 1960, when I knew of only six practising pipers in all of Ireland. His tradition carries on through his son Seán Óg who is also a good piper.

The third tin-whistle player was Mick Tubridy. The longer in my life that I know Mick, the more I am convinced he is the truest gentleman I have ever known. He was the flute player in the band. He would come armed with a paper bag of small liquorice multi-coloured sweets. He was always smiling and quite spoken and gentle. He wore glasses. He worked as a structural engineer until his retirement in 1993. He was responsible for the structural design of government buildings in Merrion Street, Dublin, and of the passenger terminal buildings at Dublin airport.

In 1994, Michael was asked to re-design the Birr telescope before its reconstruction in 1996–1997.

But his biggest task, as far as we kids were concerned, was to pass our test. As the band would rehearse, we would get to know the arrangement and when each instrument was due to join in that arrangement and play, we would wait until the last second and pop one of the small sweets onto the embrasure or hole for blowing the flute. Poor Mick would have to stick his tongue out and whip the sweet out of the flute so that he could play on cue. We never managed to catch him out. He married a fine step dancer called Celine Kelly of Gort a Choirce in Donegal.

Later in life they both developed a very strong interest in set-dancing and traditional step-dancing. They travelled the world teaching and were famous in countries as far away as Japan. Celine passed away in 2017. Perhaps one of their lasting legacies will be a wonderful book Mick published under the title *A Collection of Irish Traditional Step Dances*.

Michael acted as a recorder of the arrangements and would write them out neatly every evening as Celine went through the very extensive list. He was a founding member of The Chieftains group along with Paddy, Seán Potts and Martin. He retired from that group in 1979. I have never heard a raised voice from him or a negative comment of any kind about anyone or anything. In later life I have found him to be a fascinating companion when on dark winter nights at the end of a session he starts reading the sky as we head for home.

The second fiddle player in those initial early days was one of Seán's colleagues from the Abbey Theatre pit orchestra, Martin Fay. He worked at an electronics

firm, Unidare, but also did quite a lot of session playing for the Gaiety Opera season, Mosney and so on. He also married an Irish step-dancer and teacher, Gertie McCormack. He had the great advantage, from Seán's point of view, that he was a professional musician and a good music reader. This meant, in particular, that Seán could give him sheet music with contrapuntal melodies or harmonies. He also could play the viola, which gave a greater depth to the strings, when required. Martin also did a bit of acting for Seán in his 'movie-making' years. He was the suave, debonair member of the band with a laconic kind of humour. Martin was the font of many muttered jokes to the lads that would be inaudible to us young ones but would always result in loud guffaws from the men. He never seemed to push himself ahead of others and I have to say I was fond of him and in later years his quite manner and kind smile were always considered an oasis of friendship.

Ronnie McShane was a fellow worker in the Abbey Theatre and was a props manager/maker when Seán was musical director. He was a McShane from Dublin and as such he came from a rich theatre tradition, with both his parents working for the Queen's Royal Theatre. This theatre, called the Queens by all, was situated across the road from the Pearse Street fire station. Ronnie's father was the very popular caretaker and usher. They lived next door to the theatre. Ronnie's aunt Kitty was married to the English actor Arthur Lucan. They had a very popular mother and daughter routine called 'Old Mother Riley' which appeared on stage and screen regularly. The Queens had a who's who of famous actors passing through at the time, including the likes of Charlie Chaplin. Ronnie had two brothers and the three of them attended the local St Andrews School where Ronnie was very popular with his jokes and humour. When the Abbey Theatre went on fire on 18 July 1951, the company shifted over to the Queens.

When Seán Ó Riada arrived there in the summer of 1955 he immediately struck up a friendship with Ronnie who became family to us. He was full of tricks and funny stories and would always play and tease us. He was a kind of army style batman to my father and always came to the rescue when something went wrong. I remember at one stage a Hollywood film director, Stanley Kubrick, was coming to the house in Galloping Green to meet Seán and discuss some projects. Seán had by now been associated with the film *Mise Éire* for which he provided the score. Seán wanted to introduce Kubrick to the sound of Ceoltóirí Chualann and decided that having them nonchalantly playing downstairs in the basement, while himself and Stanley conferred in the sitting-room overhead, was the best method to engineer this encounter. But a drain flowed underneath the basement floor. The room had a big open fireplace in it and another room leading off. On the Friday of the Kubrick weekend visit it rained from the high heavens and the drain burst through the floor until halfway up the basement stairs.

Mother was not amused and Seán sent for Ronnie. Calmness itself, he arrived on his motorbike, assessed the situation, and called the fire-brigade – to pump the place out. With the water gone, we all set about cleaning up the place and my father decided that a fire should be lit to dry the damp floor and walls. No Hollywood Indian smoke signals ever produced as much smoke and the place was still choking all below decks, when Kubrick arrived the following day. The lads in Ceoltóirí Chualann played away, below in the smoky pit, as ordered with pre-arranged signals tapped by Seán's foot on the floor above. I recount the story to demonstrate Ronnie's importance to Seán, the kind of unusual mix of people that flowed through the house and the closeness of the band members to the family – they were our extended family.

Ronnie was a very true and loyal friend of Seán's and later followed him to Cúil Aodha where he worked with him as a PA/batman/fixer and long-suffering guinea pig for Seán's different projects and schemes. Ronnie was always innovative and would try anything. He had the sharpest beat on the bones of anyone I ever heard. He was a willing experimentalist with Seán. He also made and prepared his own sets of bones. A real Dubliner, always witty, he provided running commentaries for various situations and even for arrangements such as the 'Galway Races' and the 'Foilmore Drag hunt'. He married the wonderful Vera, and they had two great sons.

Seán Keane joined Ceoltóirí Chualann as a young man who my father described to somebody as being as handsome as a Greek Adonis. He had entered a fiddle competition in conjunction with the *Fleadh Cheoil an Radio* series and had come to my father's attention. On winning the competition Seán asked him to join the band.

Seán Keane was born into a musical family in Drimnagh, a Dublin suburb. Keane's mother and father were both fiddle players from musical communities in County Longford and County Clare. He had a brother James who is no slouch on the accordion as well. A brilliant musician he pioneered the idea of technique associated with traditional Irish fiddle playing. He brought another dimension to the fiddle section of the band, augmenting both John Kelly's rich traditional style, repertoire and understanding and Martin Fay's versatility and ability. This tall fair giant of a man is also a giant in the world of traditional Irish fiddle music. He has travelled the world with The Chieftains.

He was married to a wonderful convivial woman Marie Conneally from Ennistymon in County Clare but she sadly passed away in 2020. I think it is true to say that her death, during covid lockdown, knocked the stuffing out of Seán. Marie and Seán raised a musical family of their own in Rathcoole – a daughter and two sons. He joined The Chieftains in 1968 and remained with them until his death. He died peacefully and suddenly in his sleep at his home in Rathcoole in early May 2023 and caught us by surprise and shocked us thoroughly. I had had a long phone conversation with him days beforehand which started out about one of the arrangements in this book but, as usual, wandered around the world for forty minutes. He was a good friend to many traditional musicians around Dublin and Clare and further afield and always willing to play a tune. He will be missed in traditional Irish music circles for many years to come.

Peadar Mercier was the last member to join the band. He did so during the mid to late 1960s as bodhrán and bones player. I believe he was in the original group playing in the Damer for Sean's play, *An Ceannaí Glic*, in 1960 but was called Paddy rather than Peadar in the programme notes. My abiding memories of Peadar are of his extraordinary gentleness. He took over much of my father's bodhrán playing in the later arrangements as Seán concentrated on the harpsichord. Peadar was a good Gaelgóir and married Nuala McGann from Ennis, County Clare. She also sadly died in 2020. Peadar also played with The Chieftains for many years and travelled the world with Paddy and the boys. Like most of the Ceoltóirí, Peadar has been followed by his children into the world of music and stage. His son Mel takes his father's place when the band reforms occasionally for special anniversaries.

The first singer chosen by Seán for this new fledgling band was Darach Ó Catháin. Darach was born in 1922 on the Máimín in Leitir Mór west in Connemara but had been moved as a youth in 1935, to the newly created Gaeltacht in Rath Chairn, County Meath. The government of the time had bought up old estates and was redistributing the lands to small farmers. As part of the movement, they set up

 two small Gaeltacht or Gaelic-speaking areas and transmigrated indigenous Gaeltacht people from Ireland's Gaeltacht regions along the poorer west coast or mountainous regions and hoped thus to spread the Gaeltacht areas on the island of Ireland. They provided new opportunities for Gaeltacht people who would probably otherwise have emigrated overseas. It was a good idea but the continued input over the decades, to support these fledgeling Gaeltacht communities, was very rigid and these new Gaeltachts survived in spite of government support, rather than because of it. The Rath Chairn Gaeltacht is the result today.

Darach was the Ceoltóirí Chualann singer in the early days. He married and by 1963 had very little option but to emigrate. He moved to Leeds in England with his young wife Bríd and raised their loving family there. We lost touch for a decade or two but always were very fond of him and subsequent reunions were always great occasions of love and respect. He was one of Ireland's greatest sean-nós singers of the twentieth century. This was a very small group of people who still expounded the old Irish way of passing the equivalent of European art song tradition from one generation to the next. This was not a form of folksong or ballad singing in Irish. As an oral culture, information had to accurately be transferred from generation to generation, be it the Brehon laws, history, genealogy and so on, by use of mouth and ear, ratherr than eye and paper. Metered verse was the favourite way to commit this information to memory and changing one word could make a real mess of a passage of information within a generation or two. The great sean-nós songs passed on the mores of the indigenous culture – accounts of events or places, the best example of how to react in life's events, great people's contribution to the march of time and a nation, etc. Ballad song or folksong is primarily for entertainment and therefor one can change the places, names, situations, etc., to suit the audience. Irish culture favours emotional energy versus the European or Western culture's reliance on intellectual energy.

Darach was a master sean-nós singer. The times he lived in did not provide for a livelihood based on his mastery. That would be different today. Our bond with Darach was very deep.

Seán Ó Sé joined the Ceoltóirí as Darach left. He was very young and very gifted. His voice became synonymous with Cork and his repertoire was very extensive as Seán kept pushing him to greater challenges. They were extremely close and indeed there was a distant relationship through both their maternal lines being from Cúil Aodha. My grandparents always looked upon him as a second son to them and brother to my father. I know too that Seán Ó Sé had great affection for them and greatly enjoyed visiting them weekly at their home in Dorgan's Road in Cork, usually on a Monday night.

The great gift that Seán brings to people is not just his singing but also his good humour and storytelling. This was a trait from the beginning and a constant feature of Seán Ó Sé's company. Both Seáns would work on Tuesday nights in Cúil Aodha, preparing songs for the radio programmes. After the work was done, they would join my grandparents in the sitting room. Seán Ó Sé would have brought them from Cork city for the evening and there would usually be some other company – neighbours or friends. There would be great storytelling and laughter and then, when the men arrived in, songs were sung. It was idyllic and very romantic.

Seán Ó Sé is the icon for Cork. His life as a teacher in Knocknaheeny made him part of the Cork's north side's daily life for several generations. He has sung at many a great homecoming for victorious Cork hurling and football teams as they reach 'Pana' on their victorious return from a victory in Croke Park. His voice is the last heard over sixty-five years, for so many funerals of Cork's famous and not so famous. His knowledge of Irish history, especially in the more southern counties, is deep and his wealth of stories and accounts of sporting and cultural events and actions is unsurpassed. But I suppose I would say that as he is my close friend and we still enjoy making music together while breath remains in our bodies.

Seán was a born and bred West Cork man from Cúm Thóla near Bantry. Both his parents were national schoolteachers there and raised Seán and his sister Máirín completely through Irish. The Ó Sé's were a noted family of singers and folklorists and contributed much to the collected body of folklore from West Cork. His mother's people were from Kealkill and her mother from Cúil Aodha. His background was steeped in the culture of the Gaelic

Nation and his interest in these matters made him soak up the last remnants of that world as he grew up. As a young man he studied to be a teacher and also attended Cork School of Music where he briefly, but importantly, studied singing under John T. Horne. He gives those early lessons the full credit for maintaining his wonderful voice well into his late eighties.

♪

IN THE FIRST INSTANCE Seán decided that Ceoltóirí Chualann would launch themselves with a concert in the Shelbourne Hotel which was the most upmarket hotel in Dublin at the time and traditional music would not be played there. Seán hired their ballroom and a programme was prepared – all was ready. That afternoon Seán made a frantic call home to my mother, Ruth, in Galloping Green to say that he had forgotten the book of cloakroom tickets which were required to number the seats. It was decided that I would be given the book, placed on a bus into the city centre and the bus conductor instructed to drop me off across the road from the Shelbourne. The concert was part of the Dublin Theatre Festival programme 10 September 1961and I was a strong seven-years-old. Ceoltóirí Chualann been in existance for the best part of a year by then.

Their first programme consisted of arrangements made by Seán of traditional tunes and songs sung by the great sean-nós singer, Darach Ó Catháin. Seán was enthralled with rediscovering the 'Náisiún Gaelach' or the 'The Great Gaelic Nation' and Darach was, to Seán, a last lingering remnant or voice of this Gaelic Nation.

But back to Seán's interest in the old Gaelic Nation: the world of Brehon laws and poetry and heroism and legend and language. Eoghan Rua Ó Súilleabháin became his immediate hero and Aogán Ó Rathaille a person for venerating. Both these men were seventeenth- and eighteenth-century bardic poets from Sliabh Luachra on the Cork–Kerry border. Eoghan Rua was the more recent of the two and had come to depend on the ordinary people to support him as the great Gaelic houses had all gone by the time he arrived. Aogán, on the other hand, had to spend his life watching this awful demise and see his whole world, both physically and culturally, be annihilated. He was the last of the old filí or poets of the Náisiún Gaelach.

This was the material that Seán was exploring and inhabiting when he began his series of *Reacaireacht* radio programmes for Radio Éireann in the closing years of the 1950s and early 1960s. He already had Ceoltóirí Chualann performing in concert as the main stay for the radio programme. He had asked Darach Ó Catháin to join them, with the actor Eoghan Ó Súilleabháin as presenter. The format used was a mix of arrangements of music; a selection of poems or verses by the great poets and a few songs sung by Darach. Thus, one had a flavour of the different formats or representations of Irish culture as it still lived in the remnants of the Gaelic Nation of the day. Seán was quite friendly with the management of Gael Linn, having gone to college with Roibard Mac Góráin who amongst his many hats wore the hat of head of the record department. With the album *Reacaireacht an Riadaigh*, the idea or concept that is the common thread throughout this album is the idealised Gaelic culture, some of which still survived in the Gaeltacht or Gaelic-speaking areas in Ireland. These areas were stretched along the western seaboard hemmed, in by the Atlantic Ocean, with the exception of the Múscraighe Ui Fhloinn Gaeltacht, which was perched in the hills of the Cork and Kerry border. He wished to remind the people of what they were forgetting rapidly as Ireland embraced the culture and value systems of the Anglo-American lifestyle.

There is a sparsity and rigour about this album. It is a distilled presentation. The arrangements for the band are uncomplicated and straightforward, although we do see

Michael Tubridy, Éamon de Buitléir, John Kelly, Anthony Kelly (John's son), poking his head out, Sonny Brogan with whistle, Paddy Moloney in front of Sonny beside Martin Fay, with Seán Ó Riada behind with Ronnie McShane and Seán Potts.

that by the last track there is an arrangement made for the band where they accompany Darach Ó Catháin, for the first time, with the traditional song 'Peigín Leitir Mhóir'.

Seán recited the verses or poems himself and can be heard to have a pretty good command of the language. (He converted the household to Gaelic speaking sometime during the late summer of 1958 as I was starting my schooling in Scoil Lorcáin, which was an all-Irish National School.)

He was reintroducing the people to a period in our nation's history when we still had much of our indigenous sensitivity intact and this could be imbued from the sounds and ideas of those more Gaelic times. This initial series on Radio Éireann was followed by an LP or vinyl version which was published by Gael Linn under the title *Reacaireacht an Riadaigh* (CEF 010 – 1961).

Seán's recognition in the public arena had been shaped by his eponymous film score for *Mise Éire* in 1959 and be a second film *Saoirse?* released in 1961.

During this year of 1961 he was asked to provide the sound track for a film based on the 1902 play by John Millington Synge – *The Playboy of the Western World*. That film starring Siobhán McKenna was released in 1962 as was the vinyl album of the music under the title *The Playboy of the Western World* (Gael Linn, CEF 012 1962).

> The band line up at this stage was:
> Michael Tubridy – Flute
> Seán Potts – Whistle
> Paddy Moloney – Uilleann Pipes and Whistle
> Sonny Brogan – Accordion/ Box?
> Éamon de Buitléar – Accordion and Bodhrán
> John Kelly – Fiddle
> Martin Fay – Fiddle
> Seán Ó Riada – Bodhrán and Harpsichord
> Ronnie McShane –Bones

♫

Reacaireacht an Riadaigh was broadcast on Sunday nights from 1961 onwards. The earliest recorded broadcast on current lists/archive records is 12 March 1961. But changes were afoot. Darach had to emigrate to England, he went to Leeds where he and his wife Brid raised their seven children. I missed him out of my life as he was a gentle presence from which a certain feeling emanated, which I later learned to associate with Gaelic or Gaeltacht life. He returned for various Ó Riada and Ceoltóirí Chualann commemorative concerts and for a short tour in Ireland with Séamus Mac Mathúna of Comhaltas Ceoltóirí Éireann. He was still the same Darach and all in the band, and family, were very fond of him. He died in 1987.

At this time also *Reacaireacht an Riadaigh* was augemented by a new series on Radio Éireann called *Fleadh Cheoil an Radio*. Seán changed the format. This was a bilingual half hour weekly radio show and the concept was the return to rural Ireland and its music and lore. *Fleadh Cheoil an Radio* was broadcast on Saturday nights on Radio Éireann from 1963 to 1968. It was usually repeated on Tuesday nights. Sean Seán Ó Síocháin was the Fear an Tí or presenter in the first year. Songs in Gaelic nd in English were both featured. A storytelling slot was also part of the programme and this fell to Éamon Kelly who was from 'across the hill' from Seán's home in Cúil Aodha. He was also a well-known actor among friends and acquaintances from Seán's former workplace in the Abbey Theatre. Éamon developed the stage persona of the seanchaí which is the name Gaeltacht people, and indeed many from rural parts in Ireland, gave to a storyteller. Needless to say, the name became part of the *lingua franca* nationwide after its weekly appearance here. Éamon developed a huge following. It was quite a task to find a story a week.

Seán was constantly gathering them and a lot came from Múscraí via Peaití Tadhg Pheig with whom Seán had the pleasant task of spending Sunday afternoons in the local Baile Mhuirne Hibernian pub after mass until 2:00 Sunday closing time. Another provider of yarns and stories was another friend of Seán's, the local folklore collector Seán Ó Cróinín whose mother, Bess Cronin, had been a major source of songs for the famous folksong collectors of the first half of the twentieth century. Among those collectors I will name Seámus Ennis, Jean Richie, George Pickow, Brian George, Diane Hamilton, Peter Kennedy and Robin Roberts. Seán gathered more stories from friends over the border and close to Éamon's native place in Sliabh Luachra. In particular, John Spillane from Gneeveguilla was a great source. John was the gamekeeper in the Killarney estate which had not yet been passed from the McShane family onto the state at that time.

But the gathering of stories was the easy part. Éamon would then have to parse and dissect them, time the punch lines and develop them, sometimes with several stories woven in together, in one narrative, to make riveting radio. And he was good. He based his accent on our local Sliabh Luachra/Múscraí kind of dialect which contained a pretty Elizabethan vocabulary and whose sentiments, sentence structure and colour was more or

Éamon Kelly (An Seanchaí)

less Gaelic, through English. It was his own native dialect of course but one did tone one's accent down when mixing in the more 'refined' company of the capital city and its cultured inhabitants. But once the seanchaí Éamon hit the stage or the airwaves, the mouth widened, the throat opened down to the chest cavity and a flow of rhythmic fluent sentences weaved through the air, punctuated by the listeners' guffaws and chortles. His sense of timing was superb.

Seán Ó Síocháin took over Darach's slot as the band singer. He was from Cill na Martra which was the same parish as Seán Ó Riada's mother. He was a ballad singer with a fine deep voice, usually to the accompaniment of an accordion. Slightly older than the rest of the band and Seán, he fitted in well as they were all culturally cut from the cloth. Except for Ronnie, most of the band members were originally from rural Ireland or first-generation Dublin.

After the first season, Seán Ó Síocháin had to retire as he was made general secretary of the GAA and had to give all his time and concentration to this onerous job. I was present at the concert on 21 April in 1963 in St Francis Xavier Hall, the night he handed over to the new kid on the block – another Corkman, Seán Ó Sé. This was the last recording/concert of the 1963 run of the programme. The programmes were recorded as live concerts – two every night. At the end of his last programme as host Seán Ó Síocháin bade farewell and introduced the new singer Seán Ó Sé. Then they both sang 'Níl 'na Lá' together in the key of D. At the final verse and chorus, they split octaves apart and moved to the key of G. It was a really dramatic flourish and finish to the night and I remember the tingling excitement and thrill it engendered in me and will always associate that feeling first felt then, with Ceoltóirí Chualann.

The band's encore was a set of reels and Seán, Éamon de Buitléar and I think Michael Tubridy did a kind of impromptu three-hand reel dance across the stage in the glee of the moment.

The format was a Saturday night and a Sunday night concert with live audiences. Two half-hour programmes were recorded each night. On occasion there might be a third programme to record if there were five weeks in the month. These recordings took place in either the St Francis Xavier Hall (photo top p. 29), The O'Connell Hall or in the Wesleyan church in Portobello (bottom p. 29).

The routine was that Seán Ó Sé and Seán would travel up from Cork together. They

always arrived before anyone else. They would call to Rohan's across the road from the GPO and would also have broken their long drive up in O'Donoghue's of Port Laoise. Seán was in the habit of playing jazz on the piano in the rehearsal room in the GPO whilst he and Seán Ó Sé were waiting for the others to arrive. The rehearsal would follow the programme's layout and the arrangements as sent on by Seán earlier to Éamon de Buitléar in the form of a small reel to reel tape and the paper sheets containing the written arrangements. The programmes themselves were recorded as two halves of a concert. Once the programme was recorded, the engineer and the producer would listen back to ensure all was ok in case one of the items might need to be re-recorded. The engineer was usually Michael Murtagh and the producer was P.J. O'Connor. The concerts themselves were ticketed and always sold out. Proceedings usually started at six in the evening and were finished by ten o clock.

The constant recording of these programmes was a merciless animal devouring songs, tunes and stories. This eight-year period is the basis for the Ceoltóirí Chualann arrangements in this book. Michael Tubridy acted as band secretary writing down the arrangements and as did Éamon de Buitléar who presented me with the two complete volumes sometime during the late 1970s. Éamon often visited me to chat about wildlife, filming, beekeeping or music and our close friendship endured until he passed away in 2012.

Incidentally Seán would pay the musicians initially but once the show was established, proper contracts were provided by Radio Éireann to each performer. I presume Seán was paid a flat fee per programme for the band in those initial days. In relation to that end of things Seán Ó Sé informs me that when the band performed concerts as in say the two Macra na Feirme fundraising concert for their Inchees branch, Seán paid 'top dollar'.

Those two concerts mentioned by the way were held, one in the Kenmare Carnegie Hall and the other in the Millstreet dance hall. They were fund-raisers for a local hall in Icnhees near Kilgarvan. Pat and Kit Dineen were the driving force behin this project. The close friends of Sean's I was at the Kenmare concert and remember their dancer, Paddy Bán Ó Broin, going on the missing list for a while at the start of the concert along with, I think, Sonny Brogan. My father kept telling bigger and bigger lies to the audience that Paddy was backstage and would shortly astound them with his dancing prowess. Seán claims grew as the errant dancer stayed missing and just before he finally appeared I heard my father claim that Paddy would definitely make ribbons of the stage floor. Paddy was a good man. He was a teacher and played the flute. But in a time when few men step-danced in public Paddy was a star. He danced with gusto and creativity with a large range of traditional steps. Irish dancing has changed completely since those days. But there will never be another Paddy Bán. I remember him being a 'mean' mouth organ player also and his very blue version of 'An Phis Fliuch' is always in my ear. He was musical right through to the marrow of his bones. Flute player Desi O'Connor was his great musical companion when he had to perform on stage or television or such events. Desi was of the same ilk as Paddy with a style of energetic playing that pulsed out a strong rhythm. My memory of him is always as a big jovial man, any time I was in his company. I always found great fun in their camaraderie.

♫

CEOLTÓIRÍ CHUALANN ARRANGEMENTS were Seán's work. Initially they were rehearsals and the format was perfected at weekly rehearsals in the sitting room in

No. 2 Galloping Green on Sunday afternoons. But there would also be night-time rehearsals as the schedule was demanding. Seán had a Steinbeck piano in the sitting room and John Kelly would sit on Seán's left-hand side with Sonny beside him. The rest of the lads spread out from the right in a semi-circle with Paddy usually in the window nearest Seán. As the piano was placed a little out from the wall, and the sitting room fireplace, there was a space and the 'Monks Bench' placed there to the further left of Seán, John and Sonny and in this corner sat the wives and girlfriends of the band, when they came along. We kids stayed with them and enjoyed greatly their company – mostly Lally de Buitléar, Bernie Potts and Rita, Paddy's girlfriend.

Seán was demanding in his arrangements. This was completely new territory. While some people today like to quote Seán as saying his formula was based on jazz habits – i.e., ensemble playing with solo interludes interspersed in which a musician's prowess was on display, this is not quite the whole picture. As he was classically trained and educated in UCC under Aloys Fleischmann in Cork and all that rich tradition entailed, Seán was keenly aware of the craft involved in orchestration. Of primary importance is the colour of various combinations of instruments. Usually, one thinks of say 'Wind Instruments' which translate in Ceoltóirí Chualann terms as whistles, flutes and pipes or 'Strings' which in Ceoltóirí Chualann translated as fiddles and occasional viola (played by Martin Fay) or reeds as in accordions both to carry melody, usually Sonny leading, or chords and chordal progressions with Éamon leading. Ronnie supplied percussion on bones and Seán was on bodhrán. Sometimes Ronnie or Éamon occasionally filled in for Seán on bodhrán when he was playing harpsichord. When no harpsichord was available Seán would ask Ronnie or Éamon to stick a thumbtack in every hammer of the piano on stage so that it sounded a little like a harpsichord (or indeed I also did it on occasion). Playable harpsichords were not common in Ireland of the 1960s. They are demanding as far as running repairs and tuning go. But Seán was trying to get as near as possible to the harp with metal strings and plucked by finger nails and that was non-existent in the Ireland of the 1960s.

Usually dance tunes were paired off to provide a modulation half way through the arrangement but quite often the original or first tune/melody would return to finish off the arrangement. Irish tunes are usually in two or three parts. For the purpose of describing or organising the band to follow the arrangement, Seán called each part of the tune A or B or C and so on. He would then distribute the order and combination of instruments during the playing of the arrangement so that the whole duration was always changing colour and tone in rather the same way that one orchestrates in European terms. But he would arrange a solo section interspersed with the combinations of instruments as well as a tutti or Whole Band (WB).

Thus the arrangement would appear something like:

Name of tune	
AA BB	Whole Band (or W.B.)
AA	Fiddles
BB	Whistles and flute
AA	Pipes and Box drones and bodhrán
BB	Whistles Flutes and Fiddles
AA BB	Whole Band
AA BB	Whole Band

♫

Each half-hour programme would include at least a story, two songs and four instrumental arrangements.

Apart from the arrangements of traditional tunes as say in reels or jigs or hornpipes, etc., Seán began to introduce the music of the harp and also the playing and arranging of slow airs and marches. Hitherto, this was not the usual fare from céilí bands who were ostensibly there to provide music for dancing at céilithe/ceilidhs. Seán had by now delved deeply into the Petrie and Bunting (1792 Belfast Harp Festival) collections and had begun to reintroduce this body of music back into the public consciousness. One has to remember that when this music was being collected, the tools available to the collector were those of the European tradition and understanding. That is to say they wrote them down on two-dimensional paper, using the staff notation method that had evolved in Europe and was based on modes and the later chromatic scale and tempered pitch. In fact, the European ear could only hear intervals of semi-tones and tones and anything more refined was regarded as 'out of tune' and rounded up or down to the nearest appropriate note in the European ear.

One of Seán's great talents was that he was a brilliant sight-reader. He also was a bit of a polyglot and used to reading in Irish, English, French, Latin and Greek with a passing smattering of German, Italian and Russian which he taught himself for the purposes of following opera texts and scores. He regularly read periodicals and such in these languages and had a collection of teach yourself books. Indeed, he tried to get me to learn Mandarin or at least to help him by letting him practise on me. 'Fat lot of good' that did him! Urdu was another language he was interested in. The point about this is that his brain was attuned to functioning in various languages at the same time. This brain muscle or trait, when combined with his sight-reading ability, allowed him to instantly read the old collections and translate them into the music the collector probably heard rather than what the collector actually wrote down using the 'foreign' metrics at his disposal. The immediate result of this was to give a piece of music a different pulse and shape.

When Seán read and played O'Carolan pieces, from a collector's manuscript, they became alive and musical, rather than just a collection of notes played in a slightly stilted fashion in a similar way as one hears a computer playing a synthesised version of a tune loaded into its memory bank. Suddenly the music of Toirdhealbhach Ó Cearbhaláin and friends became worth playing again.

This led onto another of Seán's ideas – the *Concept Album*. He started out in 1961 with *Reacaireacht an Riadaigh* (which was the idea of the high art of the indigenous Irish Nation. In other words, it encompassed a collection of music, songs and poetry that were examples of the more refined elements of the culture rather than that which would be regarded as the folk element in the culture such as would be found in the daily lives and moments of community celebration of rural Ireland. Thus, one found examples of sean-nós with Darach Ó Catháin, seventeenth-century poetry as recited by Seán himself and a mix of slow airs and dance music arranged for, and played by, the band Ceoltóirí Chualann in a way that our music had not been presented before. In other words, the music was to be listened to rather than a background function to dancing and convivial socialising as was the norm at the time.

The track listing consisted of side A: A1 An Long Faoi Lán-tSeol (instrumental), A2 An Caiptín Ó Máille (solo sean-nós song), A3 Ní reacaireacht gan reacaire (recited by Seán Ó Riada), A4 An Buachaill sa Bhád (instrumental), A5 Liam Ó Raghallaigh (solo sean-nós song), A6 An té a mholas an éigse (recited text). And the B side consisted of: B1 Port an Deoraí (instrumental), B2 Amhrán an Taé (solo sean-nós song), B3 Caint na n-éan (recited text), B4 Ag Scaipeadh na gCleití (instrumental), B5 Sail Óg Rua (solo sean-nós), B6 Mo Ghile, m'Fhear (recited text [Chorus of the song of the same name]), B7 Spailpín a Rúin/An Lon Dubh (instrumental arrangement consisting of slow air followed by set dance). The original cover of the LP (over) was white with red lettering boldly proclaiming the

REACAIREACHT an RIADAIGH

gael-linn

Ceoltóirí Cualann
á stiúrú ag

SEÁN Ó RIADA

Amhráin : Darach Ó Catháin

LP name *Reacaireacht an Riadaigh*, Ceoltóirí Chualann á stiúrú ag (directed by) Seán Ó Riada (in bolder black lettering, followed by Amhráin (songs) Darach Ó Catháin. The Gael Linn name was reversed white on a black label in the middle of the page. The reverse cover contained the words of the songs and the full track listing and publishing information as was in those times.

    The second album was called *Ding Dong* (CEF 016) and the concept here was the music of the ordinary people of rural Ireland of the time. Songs were in Irish and English, and were also unapologetically nationalistic and patriotic. The singer by now was Seán Ó Sé. It mirrored the mood in the country as the Irish Nation strived to achieve economic independence and grew into the clothes of nationhood.

gael-linn NA hAMHRÁIN A CHANANN TOMÁS Ó SUILLEABHÁIN

1. AN RÉALTAN LEANBACH

Tá an Réaltan leanbach sa tír lastuaidh,
Tá gile agus finne le fáil 'na grua,
Tá a píob mar an sneachta agus í 'na suan,
'S gur binne liom a glao ná géim ón gcuaich.
'Sé mo léan gan mé agus í,
I ngleanntán sléibhe nó ar mhaol-chnoc fraoigh,
Mar ar bh'eol dúinn cluiche, nó stró beag imirt,
A bháibín na finne, dá dtéadh siúd linn.

'Sí an Réaltan leanbach do ghrás ar dtúis,
'S is fíor gur thugas taithneamh dí thar mhná na Mumhan,
Ó dá mbeinnse marbh is an bás im chionn—
'S a rún, ná tréig mé ach éalaigh liom.
Ná leigse chun féin mé mar chách ar siúl,
'S gurbh aoibhinn an lá bheinn sealad agus tú,
A Rós gan dearmad, beir scéala cruinn abhaile uaim,
Go n-éalóidh an cailín deas thar sáile liom.

2. CU - CÚ - ÍN

Cu-cú-ín a chuaichín, cá ndéanfam an Samhradh?
Cu-cú-ín ars' an chuaichín, ó déanfam sna gleannta é.

Cé gheobhaidh inár dteannt' ann?
Beidh an dreoilín 's a chlann ann.
An baol dúinn an seabhac ann?
Ealóimid fé chrann uaidh.

3. CUAICHÍN GHLEANN NÉIFINN

Ó éireoidh mé amáireach le fáinniú an lae ghlégil,
Agus déanfaidh mé mo dhea-rás amach faoi na sléibhte,
Agus fágfaidh mé mo bheannacht ag mná deasa an tsaoil seo,
Agus dheamhan a bhfillfidh abhaile dhom go labharfaí'dh
        an chuach i mbarr na gcraobh ann.

Tá mo ghrá mar bhláth na n-áirní 'bhíonn ag fás i dtús an
        tsamhraidh,
Nó mar na nóiníní bána 'bhíonn ag snámh ins na gleannta,
Nó mar bheadh grian ós cionn a' Charnáin ins an tsráid ag
        gabháil síos dom,
Is mar síod a bhíonn mo ghrá bán ag déanamh rámbailte
        trím inntinn.

Nach aoibhinn don áiléar a mbíonn mo ghrá geal ag gabháil
        air,
Nach aoibhinn don talamh úd a shiúileann a bróig air,
'S nach ró-aoibhinn don óigthear a gheobhas mo stóirín le
        pósadh,
'Sí réalt eolais na maidne í agus drúcht an tráthnóna.

4. THUGAMAR FÉIN AN SAMHRADH LINN

Bhí mise 's mo bhean bheag lá ag gabháil an bóthar,
Thugamar féin an Samhradh linn,
Is cé chasfaí dúinn ach gruagach an óir bhuí,
Thugamar, etc.

Curfá
Samhradh, Samhradh, bainne na ngamhna,
Thugamar, etc.

D'fiafraigh sé damhsa ar níon damh an óig-bhean,
A's dúirt mé féin gurb í mo bhean phósta í.

A' dtabharfaidh tú damhsa choíche go deo í?
Nó mura ndéanfaidh tú sin damh déanfaidh mé an comhar
        leat.

Gabh thusa na mullaí 'gus mise na móinte,
'S cé bith fear a leanfas sí bíodh sí go deo aige.

Chuaigh seisean na mullaí 'gus mise na móinte,
'Gus lean sí an gruagach, b'aige bhí an óige.

D'thill mé 'na bhaile go buartha cráite,
'Gus luigh mé síos ar mo leaba trí ráithe.

5. SEÁN Ó DUIBHIR A' GHLEANNA

Ar m'éirí dhom ar maidin, grian an tsamhraidh ag
        taithneamh,
Chuala an uaill dá casadh 'gus ceol binn na n-éan,
Bric is míolta gearra, creabhair na ngoba fada,
Fuaim ag an macalla, 'gus lámhach gunnaí tréan.
An sionnach rua ar an gcarraig, míle liú ag marcaigh,
A's bean go dúch sa mbealach ag fíreamh a cuid gé,
Ach anois tá'n choill dá gearradh, triallfaimid thar caladh,
'S a Sheáin Uí Dhuibhir a' Ghleanna tá tú gan ghéim.

'Sé sin m'uaigneas fada, scáth mo chluas dá ghearradh,
An ghaoth aduaidh am leathadh, 'gus bás ins an spéir,
Mo ghadhairín suairc dá cheangal, gan cead lútha ná
        aistíocht,
Do bhainfeadh gruaim den leanbh i meán ghil an lae.
Croí na huaisle ar an gcarraig, go ceáfrach buacach
        beannach,
Do thiocfadh suas ar aiteann go lá deire an tsaoil,
Is dá bhfaighinnse suaimhneas tamall, 6 dhaoine uaisle an
        bhaile,
Do thriallfainn féin ar Ghaillimh—is d'fhágfainn an scléip.

6. AN tAMHRÁINÍN SÍODRAIMÍN

Tá úcaire mór seang cois Banndan is long aige,
Amhráinín síodraimín siosúram só.
Gearrchaile is caidhp uirthi 's greim aige an chúl uirthi,
Amhráinín, etc.

Curfá
Máirtín cé mór liom é, trállioram, tráiléaram,
Malaí ghá fuadach le neart gaoithe, neart gaoithe,
Portláirge a's cuanta, párúram prédill,
Amhráinín síodraimín siosúram só.

Go baile Chionn tSáile chuaigh Máirtín ag píobaireacht;
Bhailigh bean agus fiche ar mhire 'na thimpeall ann.

Lean Malaí sa mbád é, a's a máthair ghá tionlacan;
Ba ghairid na dheáidh go raibh Máirtín ar crúca acu.

Tá úcaire mór seang cois Banndan is cúram air;
Beirt bhan ta tintreán a's cliabhán sa gclúid aige.

7. MO MHÚIRNÍN BÁN

Do bhí mé oíche faoi Fhéil Bríde ar an tórramh thíos ag
        an Mullach Mór,
Nuair dhearc mé an Fraoileann ar thug mé gnaoi dí, mar
        bhí sí aoibhinn deas álainn óg;
Is í go cinnte mharbhaigh m'intinn—leá na bhFiann ní
        leigheasódh mé,
'S go bhfuil mo chroí istigh 'na mhíle píosa mura bhfaighe
        mé dídean ina brollach bán.

Sé fáth mo bhuartha nach bhfaghaim cead cuarta sa
        ngleanntán uaigneach a bhfuil mo mhíle grá,
Bíonn im ar uachtar ann a's im ar íal luachair ann; 'gus i dtús
        an fhuaicht a bhíonn na bas á mbleán.
Bíonn búibín lao ann, bíonn bric na scaoi ann, 's an eala
        aoibhinn ar an linn 's í ag snámh,
'S dá mbeinn sách críonna bheadh mo shaibhreas déanta,
Agus cead agam síneadh le mo mhúirnín bán.

8. CNOCÁINÍN AERACH CHILL MUIRE

Is buachaillín mise do shiúlaigh a lán, ag cur tuairisc na
        háite is fearr ionad,
I múineadh in iompar i gclú-chirt 's i gcáil i mbéasa, i
        dtréithe, 's i miotal.
Ní heol dom aon chúige ná dún-bhaile breá, dá bhfacasa
        im shiúlta ba shúgaí le rá,
Níor luíos riamh mo shúil ar aon dúthaigh chomh breá, leis
        an áit úd a nglaoitear Cill Muire air.

Annsúd a bhíonn tionlac mion-chlóir is faoileán, an
        chéirseach fraoigh-chearca 'gus druide,
Ar ghéaga 'na slaoda ag géilleadh fé bhláth, a's gur méin
        liom le háireamh a bhfoireann.
Bíonn fuaim ag an gconairt dá leanúint chun fiaigh,
Ag traochaint an tsionnaigh is marcaigh 'na dhiaidh,
Bíonn adharca ghá séideadh 's na céadta huzza,
Ar Chnocáinín aerach Chill Muire.

But we also find the experimental as well with such tracks as 'Ding Dong Dedaró', an approach that seemed to inspire other people to imitate years later. The poetry was gone in this set of recordings. The story element was not repeated on the album either – space was limited on an vinyl LP. But otherwise, the album reflected what was present in the weekly radio broadcasts of *Fleadh Cheoil an Radio*. There were five tracks on each side of the album. Side A consisted of 1 Raca Breá mo Chinn (song as Gaeilge), 2 Cearta an Duine (instrumental), 3 The Boys of Kilmichael (song in English), 4 An Tonn Reatha (instrumental) and 5 Raithneach a Bhean Bheag (song as Gaeilge); Side B or the flip side ran as follows: B1 Táimse ar an mBaile seo (song as Gaeilge), B2 Rogha Liatroma (instrumental), B3 The Valley of Knockanure (song

in English), Ril Mhór Bhaile Chaladh (instrumental), B5 Ding Dong Dedaró (Ding Dong Detherow – children's song as Gaeilge). The LP had a cover in black with half profiles of Seán Ó Riada and Seán Ó Se's heads facing each other and the title in Blue and the artists listed as Seán Ó Riada, Seán Ó Sé agus Ceoltóirí Chualann. Track listing was on the reverse. Officially it is recorded as published in 1967.

The third concept album was called *Ceol na nUasal* (CEF 015). This is also officially recorded as published in 1967, but indeed its number is earlier than *Ding Dong* and my memory is that *Ding Dong* was released before *Ceol na nUasal*. In this album Séan Ó Riada wants to re-acquaint the Irish public of the time with the art music of their indigenous culture. This was the music of a people who were very au fait with what was happening in Europe of their time – the Renaissance. The harpers were the superstars in Ireland and were only equalled by the poets. Even though the poets no longer held the extraordinary power and hold over the many kingdoms and fiefdoms or Tuatha (clans) of the Irish Nation, they still were treated like little gods. While the English crown had overall authority, the Normans were gradually assimilated and became 'more Irish than the Irish themselves'. Art flourished and the Italian influence could be felt in various areas, even in the changing design of the harp itself, which became larger and developed a curved sound box. Changing political fortunes and the attempt by the English crown, beginning with Elizabeth I, to annihilate and exterminate the Irish obviously drove the harpers and poets out of the country. Elizabeth recognised that music and language were the bedrock of identity and with that came resistance and rebellion.

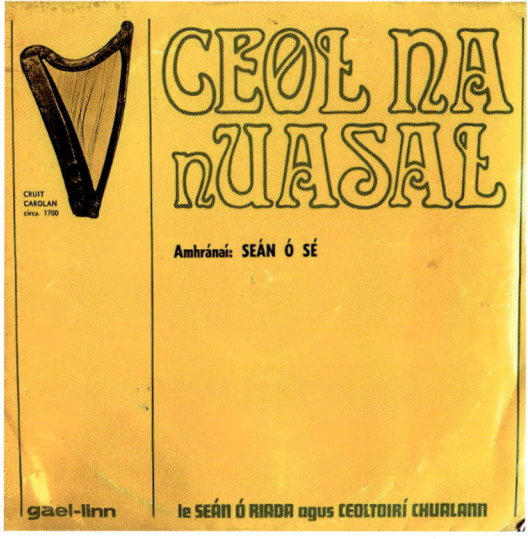

Many of the poets and harpers left Ireland with their patrons after the Battle of Kinsale and indeed by the 1792 harp festival in Belfast there were only a mere twelve or fifteen harpers left in the country. This is where Seán picked up the specimens as it were and started to play the pieces collected by Edward Bunting at this festival. Seán had to extract or decipher the melodies as Bunting and the method of staff notation at the time could not convey accurately the music as played in the Irish idiom. Nowadays it seems obvious and easy to do this as the Irish ear has grown used to and assimilated once again the rhythms and sounds of this music but in the early 1960s, this was not the case and Seán had to blaze away on his own. This LP was about the idea of this music. The Planxty once again became part of an ordinary musician's repertoire and songs disregarded and receding into the mists of time were heard once more. The word planxty itself is a little bit of a mystery. It is usually associate with the harper Toirdhealbhach Ó Cearbhalláin (Turlough O'Carolan) and there are at least two possible explanations: (1) that it comes from the Gaelic word *pleanc* which means to hit. In this case the meter is usually tertiary

Éamon de Buitléar, John Kelly, Seán Keane, Martin Fay, Michael Tubridy, Seán Potts, Paddy Moloney, Foreground: Seán Ó Riada.

or threes, and one could see a simple dance where the first of the three notes is hit with a strong slap to the floor in a kind of dance that seems would suit people of little musical or dancing ability but who had to partake in the afternoon and evening soirees of drawing-rooms of the big house who could afford to hire harpers and so on. There is also a Greek world that equates with shattering and that also makes sense. The track listing is as follows:

A1. Caitlín Triail (song as Gaeilge – Seán Ó Sé and Band).
A2 Comhsheinm Uí Chearbhalláin (instrumental arrangement of an eighteenth- century harp piece).
A3 Pléaráca na Ruarcach (instrumental arrangement of eighteenth-century harp piece by O'Carolan).
A4 Planxty Maguire (instrumental arrangement of a planxty by O'Carolan).
A5 An Chúilfhionn (song as Gaeilge by O'Carolan – Seán Ó Sé and Band).
Side B started with:

B1 Thugamar féin an Samhradh Linn (song as Gaeilge – Seán Ó Sé and Band).
B 2 Seán Ó Díghe (song as Gaeilge – Seán Ó Sé and Band).
B3 Tabhair Dom do Láimh (instrumental arrangement of eighteenth-century harp piece by Ruairí Dall Ó Catháin).
B4 Ag Taisteal na Blárnan (this poem is an Aisling in Irish by Eoghan Rua Ó Súilleabháin – Seán Ó Sé and Band).

FROM THE BEGINNING of this period Gael Linn and Ceoltóirí Chualann, Seán Ó Sé and Seán Ó Riada regularly issued EPs or short playing or mini vinyl records. They were cheap and were the main stay of the pop music industry – Top of the Charts stuff. It was unusual, at the time, for Irish matériel to be thus published. But Gael Linn were innovative and bold. The first of these EPs was *An Poc ar Buile* (GL2), composed by Cúil Aodha poet Domhnal Ó Mulláin. Seán Ó Sé had heard the poet sing it as he and some other local artists visited Coláiste Íosagáin where Seán Ó Sé was a student. Seán had near relations in Cúil Aodha and was aware of the local culture and people even though he was a boarding pupil. In 1960 Seán was a recently qualified teacher and was also performing locally around Cork and indeed, further afield. He was involved with Cabaret Gael Linn, when Gael Linn and Roibard Mac Góráin, CEO of Gael Linn introduced him to Seán Ó Riada. Ó Sé has described his first meeting with Ó Riada well in his own autobiography *An Poc ar Buile – The life and times of Seán Ó Sé* (Collins Press 2015). Suffice to say that, that very first day they recorded two songs. Shortly afterward they recorded the EP version of *An Poc ar Buile* with the band. On its release, it surprised many as being in Irish it was thought it might be a minority interest. However, it rapidly became highly successful, and the song became ubiquitous in all schools and community gatherings around the country. Seán Ó Sé was nicknamed 'The Pucker' and that name has followed him around the world for the next seventy years. More importantly, it cemented a relationship with the band members and Ó Riada family that lives to this day.

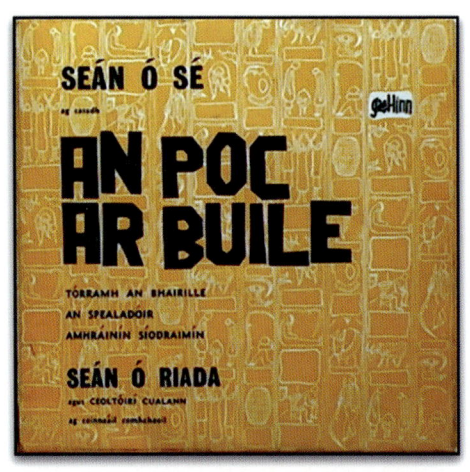

Single's usually had two pieces of music or songs. The A side was the main item and the flip side of the disk carried a throw away or filler item. It was not unusual that the B side sometimes outshone the A side. As I said, these were called singles. The EP usually had four tracks and often ran at a speed of forty-five revolutions a minute on the gramophone turntable.

This was the case with the release *An Poc ar Buile* (GL2). On side A was An Poc ar Buile along with another song Torramh an Bharaile. Side B listed An Spealadóir and Amhráinín Síodraimín. The seven-inch cover was of an orange background with light, little cartoon figurines and items etched in pale yellow. The design was by Caoimhín Ó Marcaigh.

The second EP (GL3) was *Neillí* and again contained four tracks. The title song or track was based on a short children's song from West Kerry to which Seán Ó Riada added verses as he and Seán Ó Sé drove to Dublin on their monthly foray to record the *Fleadh Cheoil an Radio* programmes. The tracks were: 1 – Neillí; 2 – Príosún Chluain Meala; 3 – An Spailpín Fánach and 4 – Táim-se im' Chodladh.

Mo Chailín Bán/Tá mo Mhadra (GL5) followed. The four tracks were 1 – Mo Chailín Bán; 2 – Tá mo Mhadra; 3 – He's not Guilty My Lord and 4 – Valley of Knockanure. It is probable that Seán Ó Riada added a few verses to this ditty, *Tá mo Mhadra* also to make it long enough for its original broadcast slot on the radio programme *Fleadh Cheoil an Radio*.

Their fourth EP (CES 004) was called Príosún Chluain Meala/Valley of Knockanure

It did make sense to release these shorter recording formats as they were used in radio airplay and promoted the band, and the two Seán's, as well as the LPs and the radio programme *Fleadh Cheoil an Radio*.

Concerts were regularly performed as well such as the Gael Linn Gaiety concert in 1966.

♪

Seán had been working with Gael Linn since the mid 1950s producing other traditional projects for them. As their staff was very active in the capital's cultural and social life at the time, Seán's influence was frequently to be felt in the many ways ideas, artists and musicians Gael Linn promoted and so on. The approaching fiftieth anniversary since the Irish revolution and the founding of the state was approaching in 1966 and many projects and concerts took place.

By the way, GL 4 was an EP of four songs by the great singer Seosamh Ó hÉanaí, which Seán Ó Riada directed. It is worth noting also that the first of the published LPs with Gael Linn and with Seán Ó Riada's music was actually pre-Ceoltóirí Chualann. It was called *Ceolta Éireann* CEF 001 LP published in 1958. It consisted of sixteen tracks. Side A had eight arrangements by Seán of traditional songs. The singer was Cork tenor Tomás Ó Súilleabháin. Seán composed and played the piano accompaniment for these traditional songs. These songs on side A were:

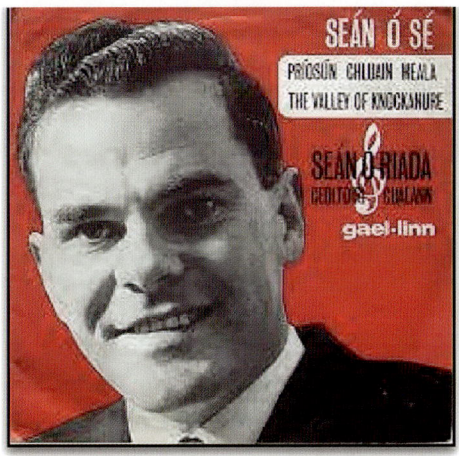

1. An Réaltan Leanbach
2. Cú-cú-ín
3. Cuaichín Ghleann Néifinn
4. Thugamar féin an Samhradh Linn
5. Seán Ó Duibhir a' Ghleanna
6. Mo Mhúirnín Bán
7. An tAmhráinín Síodraimín
8. Cnocáinín Aerach Chill Muire

They were rather formal in their approach and are pretty unique in their attitude and sound. Side B also consisted of eight tracks arranged for orchestra (in this case the Radio Éireann Light Orchestra) and were as follows:

1. Ríl (Éamonn Ó Gallchobhair)
2. Caoine Bhean Choinn Uí Laoire (Arthur Duff)
3. Séamus 'ac Murchaidh (Éamonn Ó Frighil)
4. Iníon an Phailitínigh (Seoirse Bodley)
5. Slán le Máigh (Seán Ó Riada)
6. Caoineadh na hÓige (JF Larchet)
7. Meascra Ríleanna (Fachtna Ó hAnnracháin)
8. Úr-chnoc Chéin Mhic Cainte (T.C. Ó Ceallaigh)

As with the other Gael Linn recordings, Peter Hunt was the engineer and studio involved.

Another Gael Linn release that featured Seán Ó Riada during these years was titled *1916 Mar do Cumadh an Aisling* (CEF 014) which was released in 1966 to commemorate fifty years since the 1916 Easter Rising. Amongst the texts were:

- The Testament of Freedom from Wolfe Tone to Charles Stewart Parnell
- Maidin Luain Chinchíse (Micheál Óg Ó Longáin (1766–1837)
- Cath Chéim an Fhiaidh (Máire Bhuí Ní Laoghaire 1774–1848)
- Song of the Whiteboys [or Ribbonmen] (Antoine Ó Raifteirí 1779–1835)
- Fáinne an Lae (Edward Walsh 1805–1850)
- An Drúcht Gheal Cheoigh (Fr Charles O'Neill 1887–1963/Séamas Ó Grianna 1889–1969)
- Fornocht a Chonac Thú (Pádraig Mac Piarais 1879–1916)
- An Dord Féinne (Pádraig Mac Piarais 1879–1916)
- Cáit Ní Dhuibhir (Traditional)
- Ó Bhean a'Tí cad é an bhuairt sin ort (Traditional)

- The Holy Streets of Dublin (Traditional)
- I'll sing you a song of peace and love (Traditional)
- All around my Hat by Peadar Kearney

This LP consisted of text and poetry readings with musical interludes and bridges played by Seán Ó Riada on harpsichord. The singers Nicolás Tóibín, Dolly MacMahon, Fonnuala MacLochlainn, and Tomás Ó Súilleabháin sang verses of songs related to the theme and the actors Breandán Ó Dúill, Niall Tóibín and Conor Farrington recounted the various texts and poems as introduced by Mac Réamoinn. It was scripted and presented by Seán Mac Réamoinn. Mac Réamoinn (1917–2007) was an Irish journalist and broadcaster with a deep interest in Irish culture, language and religious affairs. Fluent in Irish, English and French, he entered the Irish diplomatic service in 1944 but moved over into the national broadcaster Radio Éireann in 1947. He spent years travelling Ireland's countryside recording and collecting folklore. He was a journalist who was very much a part of the revival in Irish culture and music in the late 1950s and 1960s and a friend of Seán Ó Riada, and of Gael Linn, where he was an active participant in their projects.

Some of the recorded tracks of Seán playing the harpsichord here were later reissued posthumously on a compilation of solo keyboard playing by Seán under the title *Port na bPucaí* – a Gael Linn issue (ORIDADCD07) in 2014.

♪

THE RADIO PROGRAMMES *Fleadh Cheoil an Radio* and *Reacaireacht an Riadaigh* were broadcast from 1962–1969. But Ceoltóirí Chualann could be seen and heard in concert or at special occasions in Dublin's Mansion House, The Gaiety Theatre or at festivals such as the Glór na nGael presentation to the town of Abbeyfeale by President de Valera in 1963.

At this stage Seán was pre-occupied with his University College Cork work and was also branching out into other areas. His friendship with Gareth Browne grew during the 1960s and they both fed each other's creative curiosity and attention. For some reason I find myself interchanging Gareth and Garech. We knew Garech de Brún as Gareth Browne when I first knew him in the mid 1960s. He was like a member of family, familiar and intimate with our private household. He began to use his name as Gaeilge about then and this was Garech de Brún but within the family, we still always called him Gareth with affection. Garech was then used if we were in public. Woodtown publication had originally started out in the beginning of the 1960s with Garech's interest in the pipes. He had been taking lessons from Leo Rowsome along with the likes of Liam Óg O' Flynn, Paddy Moloney and so on. Pipers was a very small confraternity that time. Garech's first LP was Rí na bPíobairí – King of the Pipers. It was a vinyl release in 1959 on Garech's new Claddagh label. The subsequent Claddagh label releases ran something like this:

Title	Artist	Cat. No.	Year
Chieftains 1	The Chieftains	CC2	1964
Dolly	Dolly MacMahon	CC3	1967
Once I Loved (Songs from the West of Ireland)	Sarah & Rita Keane	CC4	1968
The Northern Muse	Séamus Heaney/John Montague	CCT 4	1968
The Battle of Aughrim	Richard Murphy	CCT 7	1969
Star Above the Garter	Denis agus Julia Murphy	CC5	1969
Chieftains 2	The Chieftains	CC7	1969
Deora Áille	Máire Áine Nic Dhonnachadha	CC6	1970
The Boy in the Gap	Paddy Taylor	CC8	1970
Fair Eleanor O Christ Thee Save	Thomas Kinsella	CCT 6	1971
The Drones and the Chanters (Irish Pipering) (Cass, Album)		4CC 11	1971
Chieftans 3	The Chieftains	CC10	1971
Ó Riada's Farewell	Seán Ó Riada	CC12	1972
By Sandymount Strand	Valentine Iremonger	CCT12	1972
The Liffey Banks Traditional Irish Music played by Tommy Potts		4 CC 13	1972
The Green Sailed Vessel	Robert Graves	CCT14	1972
Crow – Ted Hughes	(X2 Lp)	CCT 9-10	1973
Chieftains 4	The Chieftains	CC14	1973
Chieftains 5	The Chieftains	CC16	1975
Carolan's Receipt	Derek Bell	4CC 18	1979
The Pipering of Willy Clancy Vol. 1	Willie Clancy	CC32	1980
The Pipering of Willy Clancy Vol. 2	Willie Clancy	4CC 39	1983
Ó Riada's Farewell (cd, album)	Seán Ó Riada	83200-2	1999

AND SO ON. Obviously this list is not complete, but it gives a flavour of Garech's interests and clearly shows his belief in poetry reading on vinyl. It seems to me that Gareth's interest or influence on the label dwindled a bit during the late 1970s onwards. I did not get the same feeling of enthusiasm from him and their projects and it seemed to be more a business being run professionally by the organisation, rather than his own creative endeavours.

Woodtown was to be the publishing wing of Gareth's set up. He and Seán decided that Woodtown would be the ideal vehicle for Seán to release his classical works. To this extent there was a brief agreement under which Woodtown would publish a 'classical' work of Seán's every year and Seán would stay exclusively with Woodtown for this purpose. But then death intervened again when Seán died in October 1971.

But the first of these classical releases appeared with *Vertical Man* in 1969. In the meantime, Seán was very involved with Gareth in various other projects, as were Ceoltóirí Chualann also involved. One such project was to record the long poem by Mayo poet Richard Murphy entitled *The Battle of Aughrim*. As with all Garech's personal projects, all the arts were brought to bear on this project also. Thus, with *Vertical Man* I well remember Jeffrey Craig, an Australian photographer, being around for the summer of 1968. His photographic portraits, in black and white, were wonderful and are, by far, the best of Seán.

When working on The Battle of Aughrim, the assembling of the cast of voices to read the various characters in the poem was done with great care. Richard would make the long trip down from Inish Boffin Island or Cleggan and before he and Seán would disappear into Seomra Seán as we called Seán's work room, we would enjoy listening to Richard recount his adventures and his descriptions of various boats and sailing or his insights into our bleak historical past. Listening-in to himself and Seán discussing Anglo-Irish history and the wars, over 700 years of history and their manifestations in today's Ireland, was fascinating and evocative for the likes of me and my big ears.

Richard was born in 1927 near Shrule on the Mayo-Galway border. He was a descendant of both Charles I of England and Patrick Sarsfield. It seemed to me that, in spite of his Anglo-Irish background, and his affection for same, that he identified with Sarsfield. His long poem *The Battle of Aughrim* (1968 – Claddagh CCT 7 LP), was originally commissioned for radio by the BBC. Straddling Ireland's two very different cultures was *The Battle of Aughrim*'s central theme. The title poem is a long narrative about the decisive Protestant victory over Catholic forces in 1691. His ancestors had fought on opposite sides and Murphy declared, 'My underlying wish was to unite my divided self, as a renegade from a family of Protestant imperialists, in our divided

country in a sequence faithful to the disunity of both.' *(Irish Times* obituary, 31 Jan 2018). It was during this time or shortly after that he purchased Ard Oileán (High Island) which became such a central part of his life. We lost touch when Seán died.

The LP credits are thus:

> Read by Cyril Cusack, Cecil Day-Lewis, Ted Hughes, Niall Tóibín and Margaret Robertson; Music by Seán Ó Riada; played under his direction by Ceoltóirí Chualann; Recorded (and Broadcast) by the BBC Third Programme, August 1968; Liner notes by Richard Murphy and Ted Hughes; Produced by Douglas Cleverdon.

♫

THE READING OF the long poem was divided into sections, interspaced with musical bridges or interludes. The pieces of music or arrangements included the band playing arrangements of Mo Ghille Mear, Marbhna Luimnighe, Anach Cuan, Marcshlua Uí Néill, An raibh tú ar an gCarraig and some cadences or riffs on harpsichord by Seán including a section of Henry Purcell's Sefauch Farewell.

As I have already said, this production was foreshadowed by the Gael Linn release of the previous year called *1916 Mar do Cumadh an Aisling* (CEF 014). This kind of synchronicity arises due to the small cadre of cultural and creative people who made up the artistic pool in Ireland of the time. Various themes and ideas floated to the top and cross-pollinated various projects being assembled by the few Irish production or publishing entities around. Seán Ó Riada was the source of much creative imagination and ideas in that milieu. This arose out of his interests and constant research and understanding of the Gaelic Nation, that had nearly disappeared completely from the face of the earth by then, as greater prominence was being given to imported ideas and fashions from the New World surrounding our island.

DURING THE LATER years of the 1960s, from 1968 to 1971, Seán became very involved with many different projects, and indeed, different areas of Irish life. He was appointed to the board of a string of hotels to be placed in all the Gaeltachts along the Irish Western Seaboard. Gaeltarra Éireann were the semi-state body tasked with providing employment in these Gaeltacht areas. These were pockets of rural populations or communities that still lived their lives through the medium of the Gaelic language and all its cultural associations in music, song, craft and livelihoods, etc. Seán was also commissioned with helping and contributing to various reports. I remember, in particular, a lot of his time contributing to the Devlin report, a state commissioned report delving into the running of the state and its civil service. But Seán's main interest was the Gaelic language and the various solutions that might help save it and its communities for the future welfare of that same Irish Nation. He was an advocate for the provision of a Gaelic language radio station and supported the pirate radio station *Saor Radió Chonamara* in 1970. He switched his and the Cór Cúil Aodha's allegiance from Oireachtas na Gaeilge, held annually in Dublin, to their rival Oireachtas na nGael which was held in Ros Muc, Connemara. He began to voice a view of this indigenous culture and indeed one of the few film clips we have of him speaking was on this subject on Danish television in 1967. He became involved in social endeavours and was instrumental in bringing the first two factories to his area via Gaeltarra Éireann. His wife, my mother Ruth, had also become very socially active and had set up a Co-operative promoting crafts and culture. Seán was involved in her work. They discussed various ideas and talked plans out in our kitchen.

Seán also was in demand from various international organisations and was frequently caught up in various delegation from the USA or the Soviet Union, with friend and distant cousin, Mick O'Riordan of the Irish Communist Party. Thus he was in the throes of planning visits by Ceoltóirí Chualann, combined with Cór Chúil Aodha, to the Kentucky Derby, Moscow and the Breton Festival of Quimper, a more 'pure' cultural festival then the Lorient Festival, but both instigated by the wonderful Breton, Polig Monjarret. He began to see concerts and performance in a more commercial light I suppose. This may have been triggered by a little jealousy of the success of Paddy and The Chieftains though he never admitted to anything but affection for The Chieftains and said so in an interview when he was door-stepped in Dublin airport on his way home from London. He said: 'In as much as a father would criticise his sons, I have nothing but the greatest admiration for The Chieftains, after all they are the product of my own band Ceoltóirí Chualann. I presume the

Rehearsal RadioÉireann: Left to right: Éamon de Buitléar, John Kelly, Seán Keane, Martin Fay, Michael Tubridy, Seán Potts, Paddy Moloney and Seán Ó Riada at harpsichord in front.

interviewer, Liam Nolan, had expected to draw negative comments from Seán.

As the 1960s drew to a close and Seán found himself involved in many new different aspects to life, stemming from an increased interest in social and community life and also in his pursuance of the idea of the Gaelic Nation and his increasing range of interests. However, he still found time to organise the most famous of the Ceoltóirí Chualann concerts and releases. I refer to the Ó Riada sa Gaiety concert which was on Sunday 30 March 1969 at 8.00 p.m. When tickets were announced, a queue formed that stretched around the block and all tickets were gone within an hFour. This is in a time when no internet, mobile phones or other communication methods existed and when local radio had not yet arrived. Seán had decided to commemorate theFF northern poet, Peadar Ó Doirnín, and I would think that Tomás Ó Fiaich had some influence on Seán in this. Tomás was a great fan and promoter of Ó Doirnín and was of also of northern extraction. Seán and Tomás had a growing friendship at this stage, which had taken root some five years earlier with the translation into Gaelic of the Roman Catholic mass – that is, to the vernacular language of the people – a result of the Second Vatican Council deliberations in 1962–63. Tomás always liked to appropriate the role of singing the celebrants parts of the mass in the Seán Ó Riada Aifreann 1 available on *Ceol an Aifrinn & Aifreann 2* for the rest of his life, even after he had progressed to being bishop and later cardinal and primate of all Ireland.

Many of Ó Doirnín's poems were not songs and this resulted in Seán once again composing new melodies and floating them into the tradition. The standout melody of this concert was a poem called 'Mná na hÉireann' or 'Women of Ireland'. Seán Ó Sé, as always, was the singer and voice that Seán had in mind when composing this melody. I enclose a scan of the concert's programme on the following pages to give you an idea of how commercials or advertisements were handled in Ireland then. Again, I remind the reader that this period was pre-internet and multiple-broadcasters. Sponsorship was different in those days. Regulation was also not like now, with regard to alcohol, cigarette smoking and insurance requirements for venues. The Gaiety was the premier venue of its kind in the country in 1969. The full programme is reproduced in the miscellaneous section of this book.

♪

IT IS INTERESTING to see the line-up of the Gael Linn 1916–1966 commemorative concert and the line-up for the 1969 concert. In the space of three short years, Ceoltóirí Chualann had progressed to sell out the whole theatre, on their own, and in less than one hour. The actor Niall Tóibín was the presenter or Fear an Tí on the night and the concert started with a trumpet fanfare to welcome the attending President de Valera.

The reviews and reaction were very positive. Seán had organised the recording of the event with the help of Éamon de Buitléar. Éamon suggested his own sound engineer Pat Hayes for the job. It was around this time that Seán had dipped his toe into the commercial world around the fledgling music industry in Ireland. With his new roles as advisor to the hotel group and involvement with international interests through the Department of External Affairs or its staff. He was a very busy man but any mutterings or notions he had to disband Ceoltóirí Chualan faded and he began to see their commercial possibilities. The increasing success of the Ceoltóirí break-away band, The Chieftains, may have coloured his view also but I think it was more his company and milieu of those years from 1967 to his death, that influenced him. I have already mentioned his intention of bringing the band, augmented with his choir, Cór Cúil Aodha, to the USA, Moscow and Quimper. He had also paired up with Len Clifford who at the time was a pools collector for Gael Linn. The Gael

Seán Ó Riada, Seán Ó Sé, Niall Tóibín, Pres. Éamon de Valera, Ruth Ó Riada and Breandán Ó Buachalla.

Linn Pools is a private lottery run by a cultural charity. Its aim is the furthering and restoration of the Irish language, culture and the Gaeltacht areas. The pools started in 1953 and were highly successful. A team of ticket sellers constantly travelled the nation, going door-to-door, selling their tickets for their monthly draw and were and are well supported by the people of Ireland. The money earned from the pools or lottery was ploughed into the charity or trusts projects which included everything from schemes to subsidise income for small Gaeltacht farmers with a variety of projects such as beekeeping and growing fruit, to small cottage-craft industries, to subsidies and schemes to bring children from the English-speaking parts of the country, to spend three months living with a Gaeltacht family and attending a Gaeltacht school. This immersive method, compared to the bigger, better known Gaeltacht summer three-week courses, sprang up in the 1950s and 1960s. It was a very good way for a child to learn Irish. Gael Linn were also into publishing and had started their own record label in the 1950s.

The famous 1969 Gaiety Concert left to right: Seán Ó Riada, Peadar Mercier, Éamon de Buitléar, Seán Ó Sé (standing), Martin Fay, Seán Keane, John Kelly, Seán Potts, Michael Tubridy, Paddy Moloney.

Now Seán was setting himself up with Len being his 'manager' and promoter. The Gaiety was their initial project. Once the recording had been finished Seán then gave the tape to Gael Linn to publish under their label.

Len and Seán ran the next concert the following year in Cork City Hall. This time they used the theme of O'Carolan, whose 300th anniversary occurred in 1970. I well remember the excitement and the stress of the event. To the extent that on the evening of the concert, I had to give my black shoes to Len, as he was wearing brown shoes. Len and Seán had decided that a more formal approach in style was required and one can see from the photographs that the Gaiety concert did indeed present them in formal wear. The president's attendance may have been one of the ways they sold the idea initially to the band but by Cork the following year there was some stress on this matter of style and I remember Len buying black socks for all, and so on. Then, the last-minute discovery that he had brown shoes himself forced the late shoe swap. How he fitted his feet into my smaller shoes for the evening reminds me of nothing but discomfort for him. I don't think the concert was as successful as the Gaiety, in that the band were at home in Dublin and the logistics of coming to Cork and rehearsals in preparation were not as easily organised. The advertising was not great either. However, the biggest problem was the fact that one of the stereo legs feeding into the tape-recording machine was faulty and the concert was only recorded on one mono input or leg. The actual concert was not published or released, until the following year. By then Seán had died.

The sleeve notes for these releases were as usual, by Seán Mac Réamoinn and the cover design for the Gaiety album was by Liam Miller, while that of the Cork concert, now released as *Ó Riada*, was by Éamon's sister-in-law, Mary Lamb.

In his final year Len and Seán talked about acquiring a small hotel in Killarney where he intended to play on piano himself, on a weekly basis. They also were planning Irish music courses or summer schools. They had plans for films and so on. In fact, Len was now the 'doer' for Seán's creative impulses and I think they would have made a great team. Len sacrificed a lot in those few years and was devastated by Seán death. He had been a non-practising solicitor and after Seán's demise returned to law and ended up being a well-known judge, having been appointed to the bench under a Fine Gael government. We were all very fond of Len. He was a 'martyr for the fags' (cigarettes) and smoked Majors as if they were going out of fashion. He seemed to have relentless, constant energy and I am sure his loving family had to sacrifice much also when he was bounding along with Seán's projects.

My father died in a London hospital in October 1971. During his three-week stay there, we were hoping that he would benefit from some very new medical advances. He did not obviously. But for those three weeks, those closest to him made the troubling trip to his bedside where my mother Ruth sat of course. Len was amongst those chosen few. I was there myself for the second week. When Seán died at the end of the third week my mother turned to Len as they left the hospital and gave him Seán's briefcase which had Seán's current work materials. The brief case and been a Christmas present from Ruth to Seán the previous Christmas. Many years later and shortly after Len died, his family posted that case to me and told me how Len had used it every day to go to work during his life. His lovely warm-hearted wife, Marge, died afterwards on 3 October 2011 exactly forty years, to the day, after Seán. God rest them both.

♫

To sum up, Ceoltóirí Chualann were a band composed of the finest of traditional musicians, performing Irish traditional music, in a manner never heard before. They have been described as the interpreters of the creative stream constantly flowing from my father. As well as the music, there was laughter, fun and above all friendship.

And why did Seán found this band? These are his own words in 1961 as spoken

in a radio series called *Our Musical Heritage*. It was a radio road trip where Seán introduced and explained Irish music to the listener – its sound and art, its meaning and depth and origin and why we should hold on to it as our own native voice.

He said of the band:

> I have given a fair amount of thought to the idea of playing Irish music as a group activity. It seems to me that this is one of the important ways in which Irish music could develop. Let us postulate, therefore, an ideal type of céilí band or orchestra. The first thing it must have is variety – which, expressed through variation, is a keystone of traditional music. It must not, therefor, flog away all the time, with all the instruments going at once, like present day Ceilí Bands. Ideally, it would begin by stating the basic skeleton of the tune to be played; this would then be ornamented and varied by solo instruments, or by smaller groups of solo instruments. The more variation the better, so long as it has its roots in the tradition, and serves to extend that tradition, rather than destroy it by running counter to it.

♫

So now I leave you with the arrangements. These were annotated constantly by Michael Tubridy and Éamon de Buitléar as they acted as band secretaries. Éamon made a copy of his two volumes of arrangements which he gave me in the early 1980s. Michael Tubridy gave me a copy of his notes in 2018. I had the use of Seán's own archives of course (now in the UCC archives) and used my own memories as witness and frequent phone calls to Seán Keane. The constant aid and editing by Seán Ó Sé was the rock upon which I worked in assembling the lot. I enclose a few pictures of the notes' volumes, so that you can see what they looked like originally.

All I ask is that you always credit Seán and Ceoltóirí Chualann if you play or record them. My intention is that everyone has access to them rather than a chosen or privileged few. If you wish to publish them, please inform us through oifig@seanoriada.ie and we will ensure that proper track is kept of all such recordings and publications and the arrangements, copyrights, etc.

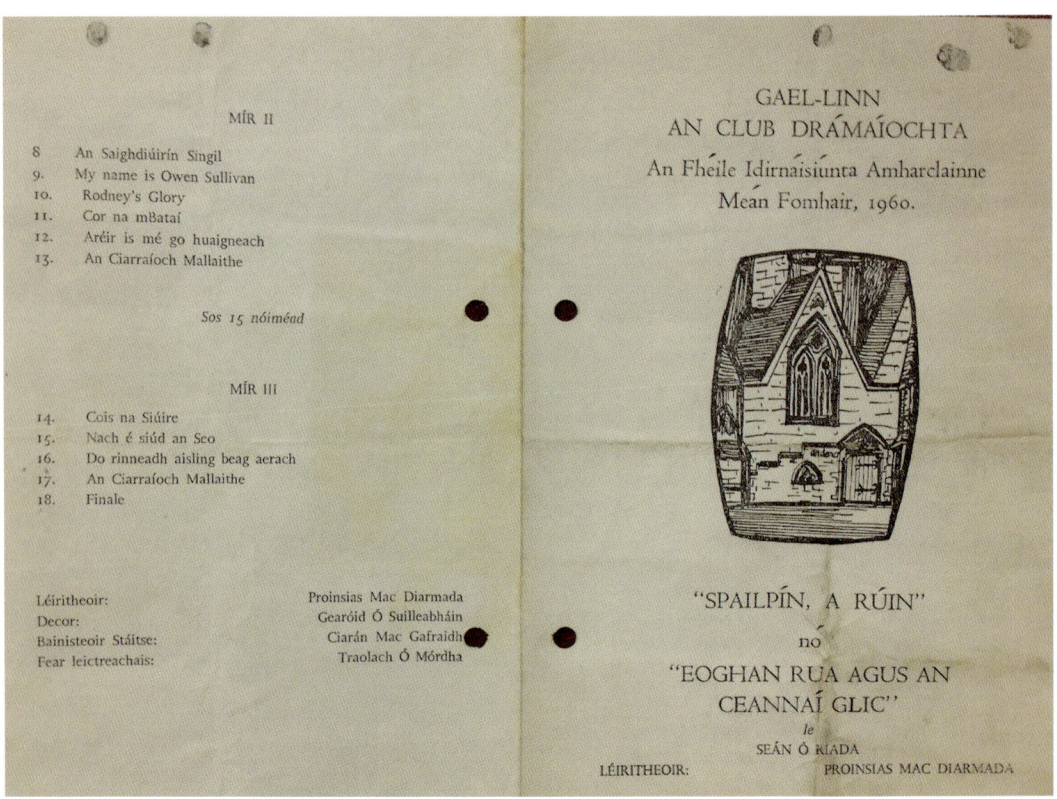

Index of the Band's List of Arrangements

Name of tune/arrangement	Page
1. Abbey Reel (Redican's)	67
2. Ace and Deuce of Pipering	67
3. A Ghrá Luí Lámh Liom	68
4. Ag Taisteal na Blárnan (Stácadh an Mhargaidh)	68
5. Ag Taisteal na Sléibhte	68
6. After Aughrim's Great Disaster	68
7. The Airy Bachelor	68
8. Airéir is mé go hUaigneach	68
9. Aithrí Chathal Bhuí (He is not Guilty My Lord)	69
10. Aililiú na Gamhna (Amhrán) (Fonn Mall)	69
11. Amhráinín Síoduimín	69
12. Anach Cuan	69
13. An Raibh tú ar an gCarraig	97
14. Anything for John Joe	70
15. Arabia	70
16. Ar an Loing Seo Pheaidí Loingsigh	70
17. Ar Éirinn ní n'eosfainn cé hí	70
18. Ar Maidin Dé Máirt	72
19. The Ashplant	71
20. An tAthair Walsh (see tatter)	71
21. Babaró	72
22. Bacach Buí na Léige	73
23. An Banbh	73
24. Bán Chnoic Éireann Ó	73
25. Banks of Sullane	73
26. Banna Strand	74
27. Bard of Armagh	74
28. Barley Grain	74
29. Barrel of Porter & Seán Buí (Sweet Biddy or Paddy Clancy)	74
30. Barry's Column	75
31. Battering Ram (Blackthorn Stick)	80
32. Bean a'Tí	75
33. Bean Dubh a' Ghleanna	75
34. Beggarman	75

35.	Beidh Aonach amáireach i gCo. an Chláir	76
36.	Beidh Sport Againn & Off She Goes	76
37.	Bill Harte's Jig (Newport Lass)	154
38.	Bín Lisín Aerach a Bhrogha (Air – Ar Éirinn ní n'eosfain cé hí)	77
39.	An Bínsín Luachra	77
40.	Bhí Bean Uasal	78
41.	Bhíosa lá i' Port Láirge	78
42.	Bhíosa lá i gCill Áirne	79
43.	Bímse i gcónaí 'Radaireacht	79
44.	Blackbird, The	80
45.	Blackthorn Stick	80
46.	Bold Thady Quill	81
47.	Bonaparte's Retreat	81
48.	Bonnie Bunch of Roses Oh	82
49.	Botháinín íseal gan Fálthas	82
50.	Boy in the Boat	82
51.	Boy in the Gap	82
52.	Boyne Hunt	83
53.	Boys of Kilmichael	83
54.	Boys of the Loch	83
55.	Brennan on the Moore	83
56.	Brian O'Lynn	84
57.	Brianach Óg, An	84
58.	Brídín Deas Uí Néill	84
59.	Bruach na Carraige Báine	84
60.	Buachaill Caol Dubh	84
61.	Buck in the Wood	85
62.	Bucks of Oranmore	85
63.	Bumper Squire Jones	85
64.	Butcher's March	124, 159, 160
65.	By the Light of the Silvery Moon (melody: Curragh of Kildare)	86
66.	Cailín Bán	86
67.	Cailín Deas Donn	87
68.	Cailín Deas Rua	87
69.	Cailín Rua, An	87
70.	Cailíní Deasa Mhuigheo	88
71.	Cailíní an Fhactory	88
72.	Cailleach an Airigid	89
73.	Cailleach a' Túirne (Maid at the Spinning Wheel)	89
74.	Cáit Ní Dhuibhir	90

75.	Caitlín Triail	90
76.	Capaillín Bán	90
77.	Caoineadh an Spailpín	90
78.	Callaghan's Reel	126, 146, 173
79.	Carolan's Concerto	91
80.	Carraig an Aoibhnis	91
81.	Carraig Aonair	92
82.	Carraig Donn	92
83.	Casadh an tSugáin	92
84.	Casaim Araon na Géanna Romhainn	92
85.	Castle Kelly	93
86.	Cath Chéim an Fhiaidh	93
87.	Cat in the Corner (The Hag with the Money)	141
88.	Cathaoir an Phíobaire	94
89.	Ceol a' Mhála	95
90.	Ceol a' Phíobaire	95
91.	Charles O'Connor	96
92.	Chase me Charlie	96
93.	Chéad Mháirt den fhomhair, An	96
94.	Cherish the Ladies	96
95.	Chief O'Neill	97
96.	Chúilfhionn, An	97
97.	Ciarraíoch Mallaithe	98
98.	Clár Bog Déil	99
99.	Na Cleaganna (an Mhóin)	99
100.	Cnocáinín Aerach Chill Mhuire	99
101.	Cois a' Ghaorthaidh	100
102.	Cois na Siúire	101
103.	Collier's Reel	101
104.	Comhcheadal a h-aon	225
105.	Connaught Heifers	101
106.	Contentment is Wealth	102
107.	Cóta Caoin Caol	102
108.	Craig's Dragoons (Sweet William Craig's Dragoons)	102
109.	Cruiscín Lán (Maidin Áluinn Gréinne)	143
110.	Cuan Bhéilínse	103
111.	Cuckoo's Nest + Leitrim Fancy	103
112.	Cup of Tea (and Ashplant)	71
113.	Diarmuid Ó Dubhda	104
114.	Dí Eidí Dí a Dí (An Puirtín)	104

No.	Title	Page
115.	Dingle Regatta	104
116.	Diver the Dancer	105
117.	Domhnal na Gréinne (Leg of a Duck/Loan of my bellows)	105
118.	Droigheán Donn, An	105
119.	Drops of Brandy	106
120.	Druimfhionn Donn Dílis	106
121.	Drowsey Maggie	106
122.	Dunmore Lassies	107
123.	Dwyer's Hornpipe	108
124.	Éamon Magháine	108
125.	Eibhlín a Riúin	108
126.	Eilí Gheal Chiúin Ní Cearbhaill	108
127.	Emigrant's Jig (Port a' Deoraí)	109
128.	Eochaill	109
129.	Ewe Reel, The	109
130.	Faill Mór	110
131.	Fanny Power	110
132.	Farewell to Connaught	110
133.	Farewell to Erin	110
134.	Feadóg an Iolair (O'Donoghue's March – of Glen Flesk)	111
135.	Fenians of Cahirsiveen (to air of My Beauty of Limerick)	111
136.	Fiach an Mhadra Ruaidh	112
137.	Flannel Jacket / Heather Breeze / Sheehan's	113
138.	Floggin' Reel	113
139.	Foggy Dew	114
140.	Fox Chase	114
141.	Foxhunters Jig + Hunting the Hare	117
142.	Frank Roche's Favourite	117
143.	Frieze Breeches	118
144.	Frost is All Over	118
145.	Fuaireasa Cuireadh Chun dul ar an bPósadh	119
146.	Fylemore, you're the Place	119
147.	Galbally Farmer (Rakes of Kildare)	120
148.	Galway Races	120
149.	Gamhnaichín, An	121
150.	Gander in the Pratie Hole	121
151.	Gaoth Aneas, An	122
152.	Gardaí an Rí	122
153.	Garden of the Daisies	122
154.	Garrett Barry's Jig	123

155.	Gather around the Fireplace + Colliers	123
156.	Gather around the Fireplace (played as a jig)	124
157.	Geaftaí Bhaile Bhuí	124
158.	George Brabazon	124
159.	Ghaoth Aniar Aneas, An	124
160.	Gile mo Chroí	125
161.	Gimlet, The Munster	152
162.	Gleann Cam	125
163.	Glen Lea	125
164.	Goirtín (Eornan), An	125
165.	Gorman's / The Hut in the Bog	126
166.	Gorman's / Callaghan's	126
167.	Habit Shirt, An	126
168.	Hewlet	127
169.	Hide and Go Seek	127
170.	High Caul Cap	127
171.	Humours of Ballyconnell	127
172.	Humours of Carrigaholt	128
173.	Humours of Ennistymon (Coppers and Brass)	128
174.	Hunting the Hare See Foxhunters	91
175.	Im' Aonar Seal	129
176.	Iníon an Fhaoit ón nGleann	129
177.	Iníon an Phailitínigh	129
178.	Irish Molly	129
179.	Irish Rag	129
180.	Irish Washerwoman	130
181.	Is Trua gan Gáirdín Úll agam	130
182.	Ivy Leaf	131
183.	Jackson's Grove Hornpipe	131
184.	Jackson's Morning Brush	131, 145
185.	Jazz	130, 132
186.	Jenny Picking Cockles/Jenny's Welcome to Charlie	132
187.	Jenny's Wedding	132
188.	Jig Set in A (For *Reacaireacht*) Chase me Charlie/Walshe's Hornpipe/Limerick Lasses	133
189.	Jig Set in A (For Fleadh Cheoil 196–'69) Peeler and the Goat/ Chase me Charlie/Walshes'	133
190.	Job of Journey Work	134
191.	Kerry Harriers	134
192.	Kerry Hornpipe	135

193.	Kid on the Mountain		136
194.	Kitty Come Down (The Gimble)		136
195.	Lady on the Island		137
196.	A Lady Stood		137
197.	Langstrom's Pony		137
198.	Laurel Bush	See scores	235
199.	Leather away the Wattle Oh		138
200.	Leg of the Duck (Dónal na Gréinne)		139
201.	Leitrim Fancy (See Cuckoo's Nest)		139
202.	The Light of the Moon (melody like The Curragh of Kildare)		139
203.	Little Beggerman, The (Rigadoon – Red-Haired Boy)		139
204.	An Lon is an Chéirseach		140
205.	Longford Collector, The		140
206.	Lord Inchiquin		141
207.	Madame Bonaparte		141
208.	Maguire's March		141
209.	Mahony's Frolics (Cat in the Corner)		141
210.	Mabel Kelly (Máible Ní Cheallaigh)		142
211.	Maid of the Sweet Brown Knowe		142
212.	Maid at the Spinning Wheel		142
213.	Madcap (Sixpenny Money)		155
214.	Maidin Úluinn Ghréinne		143
215.	Maidrín Ruadh		143
216.	Máire Bheag na Gruaige Báine (Cois na na Bríghde Thiar)		144
217.	Máiréad de Róiste		144
218.	Máire (Móirín) Ní Chuilleanáin		144
219.	Marbhna Eoghain Uí Néill		144
220.	Marbhna Luimní		144
221.	Marc Shlua Uí Néill (Marcaíocht Uí Néill)		145
222.	Mhóin, An – see Na Cleaganna		145
223.	Miller's Daughter		145
224.	Miners of Wicklow		146
225.	Miss McLeod's Reel		146
226.	Mná Dé hAoine		147
227.	Mná na hÉireann		147
228.	Mo Chailín Bán		147
229.	Mo Ghile Mear		148
230.	Moladh don Athair Séamus Máinséal		148
231.	Molloy's Jig		148
232.	Molly Bán		149

233.	Molly St George	149
234.	Mo Mhuirnín Bán	149
235.	Money from America	149
236.	Morrison's Jig	150
237.	Mo Thaighleach (Mo Thúirnín Línn)	150
238.	Mount Phoebus' Hunt	151
239.	Mug of Brown Ale (Old Man Dillon)	151
240.	Muileagán Dubh Ó	152
241.	Muircheartach MacAnna	152
242.	Munster Gimlet	152
243.	Murphy's Hornpipe	152
244.	Murphy's Reel (Mulvihill's Reel)	153
245.	My Love in the Morning	153
246.	Ná beadh buachaillín deas ag Síle	153
247.	Nách Fada an Lá	154
248.	Napper Tandy (Wearing of the Green)	154
249.	Newport Lass (Trip to Athlone)	154
250.	Ó Neillí, Neillí	154
251.	Nuair a ghabhaimhse tríd an mBaile seo (Gleann Cam)	155
252.	Old Tipperary	155
253.	Old Joe's Jig + Sixpenny Money	155
254.	O'Mahony's Frolics (The Cat in the Corner) See 111	156
255.	One Day for Recreation	156
256.	Ó Riada's Favourite	157
257.	Óró Sé do Bheatha 'bhaile (Dord Féinne)	157
258.	Oró nách é siúd an seó	158
259.	Oró Bog Liom í	159
260.	Outlaw of the Hill	159
261.	Paddy Clancy (Sweet Biddy Daly or the Barrel of Porter)	74
262.	Páirc an Fhomhair	159
263.	Peeler and the Goat	159
264.	Peigín Leitir Mhór	160
265.	Píce an tSúgaire	160
266.	A Phlúirín na mBan Donn Óg	160
267.	Piper's Chair	161
268.	Plains of Boyle	161
269.	Planxty Drury	161
270.	Planxty Irwin	162
271.	Planxty Johnson	162
272.	Planxty Maguire	162

273.	Pléaráca na Ruaircach	163
274.	Poc ar Buile, An	163
275.	Polka Set	164
276.	Port na bPucaí	164
277.	Pósadh (Fuaireasa Cuireadh chun dul ar an bposadh)	165
278.	Pretty Girls of Mayo	166
279.	Priest and his Boots	166
280.	Príosún Chluain Meala	166
281.	Pup Came Home from Claodach	167
282.	Ráca Breagh mo Chínn	167
283.	Races of Cahirsiveen	167
284.	Raedh Chnoc Mná Duibhe	168
285.	Raghadsa ar an Aonach	169
286.	Raghadsa is mo Cheataí	169
287.	Raibh tú ar an gCarraig?	169
288.	Jig - 3 drummers	169
289.	Ráiteachas na Tairingreacht	170
290.	Raithineach a Bhean Bheag	170
291.	Rakes of Clonmel	170
292.	Reddigan's	171
293.	Reddigan's (Abbey Reel)	171
294.	Red-haired Boy (Reel)	171
295.	Réice Luimnighe	172
296.	Repeal of the Union	172
297.	Rights of Man	173
298.	Ril Mhór Bhaile an Chaladh	173
299.	Rocky Road to Dublin	174
300.	Rógaire Dubh	174
301.	Rogha Beethoven	174
302.	Rogha an Riadaigh	175
303.	Róisín Dubh	175
304.	Rolling in the Rye Grass	176
305.	Rolling on the Rye Grass (Ballet)	177
306.	Rolling Wave	177
307.	Ruadhraí Ó Mórdha (Máirseáil Rí Laoise)	177
308.	Saighdiúirín Singil	178
309.	Salamanca	178
310.	Sceilpín Draighneach	178
311.	Seachrán Carn tSaoghail	178
312.	Seán a' Bhríste Leathair	179

313.	Seán Buí – see Barrell of Porter	74
314.	Seán Ó Dighe	179
315.	Seán Ó Duibhir/Éistíg Liomsa Sealad – See Aughrim's Great Disaster	68
316.	Seán Ó Duibhir a' Ghleanna	179
317.	'Sé Fáth mo Bhuartha	180
318.	Seoladh na Gamhna sa bhfásach	180
319.	Shaskeen Reel	180
320.	Shíle Ní Ghadhra, A	180
321.	Ships are Sailing	181
322.	Ship in Full Sail	181
323.	Sí Beag, Sí Mór	182
324.	Sí Bhean Locha Léin	183
325.	Since Boney is Down	183
326.	Since Mary she went to Bonane	183
327.	Sioda 'tá id' Bhfalleit, An	183
328.	Sláinte Bhreá Hewlett	183
329.	Slán agus Beannacht le Buairibh an tSaoil	184
330.	Sliabh na mBan	184
331.	Slide	184
332.	Spailpín a Rúin	185
333.	Spailpín Fánach	185
334.	An Spealadóir	186
335.	Speic Seoigheach	187
336.	Spéir Bhean Mhilis, An	188
337.	Sporting Paddy	188
338.	Stácadh an Mhargaigh (Ag Taisteal na Blárnan)	188
339.	Stad Airiú Rógaire	189
340.	Staicín Eornan	189
341.	Star of Munster	190
342.	Steampacket	190
343.	Strawberry Blossom	193
344.	Súiste Geal Beag Bán (air of Casadh an tSugáin)	193
345.	Súiste Buí, An (Yellow Flail)	194
346.	Sunshine Hornpipe	194
347.	Swallow's Tail – Sligo Maid	194
348.	Sweet Bonie will I ne'er see you more	195
349.	Sweet William Craig's Dragoons	195
350.	Tabhair dom do Lámh	195
351.	Tá Gaeghil Bhocht Cráite	195

352.	Tailliúr Aerach – see Ding Dong	196
353.	Táim Breoite go Leor	196
354.	Táimse ar an mBaile Seo	197
355.	Táimse in Arrears	197
356.	Táimse Im' Chodhladh	197
357.	Tá 'na Lá	198
358.	Tá mo Mhadra, Níl mo Mhadra	200
359.	Tap Room	200
360.	Tarraing go ciúin, go ciúin	201
361.	Tatter Jack Walsh – see an tAthair Walsh	201
362.	Teetotaller	202
363.	Tell her I am	202
364.	There was a Lady	203
365.	Three little Drummers	203
366.	Three Sea Captains	203
367.	Thugamar féin an Samhradh Linn	203
368.	Tiarna Mhuigheo	204
369.	Tiocfaigh an Samhradh	204
370.	Tommy Cohen's Reel	204
371.	Tons of Bright Gold	205
372.	Torramh an Bharraile	205
373.	Toss the Feathers	206
374.	TrímRachaigh Subhail	206
375.	Trip to Athlone – see Newport Lass	154
376.	Trip to Durrow / Up against the Buachalán's	206
377.	Tripping to the well	207
378.	An t-Úll	207
379.	Union of Macroom	207
380.	Valley of Knockanure	208
381.	Wearing of the Green – see Napper Tandy	208
382.	Wexford Hornpipe	208
383.	Whinney Fields of Leitrim	209
384.	The White Cockade (An Coileachóg Bán)	209
385.	Wife of the Bold Tenant Farmer	209
386.	William Tell	210
387.	Willie Dear	210
388.	Wind that Shakes the Barley	210
389.	Woman of the House	211

The Arrangements

♪

Seán called each part of the tune A or B or C and so on. He would then distribute the order and combination of instruments during the playing of the arrangement so that the whole duration was always changing colour and tone in rather the same way that one orchestrates in European terms. But he would arrange a solo section interspersed with the combinations of instruments as well as a tutti or Whole Band (WB).

One must remember that the musicians are reading their notes as playing hence repeating the AA BB Whole band twice rather than writing down AA BB Whole Band x 2 or such.

The arrangement would appear something like:
Name of tune
XXXXXX

A A BB	Whole Band
AA	Fiddles
BB	Whistles and flute
AA	Pipes and Box drones and bodhrán
BB	Whistles Flutes and Fiddles
AA BB	Whole Band
AA BB	Whole Band

'A' means the first part or half of a two-part tune. 'B' is the second half of the tune. If there is a third part to the tune it is called 'C' and so on.

The name of the tune provides the melody used. Sometimes you may see where I have inserted a bar or two of the start of the melody so as to indicate which version of the melody was used. Chanter means the chanter of the pipes without its drones whilst pipes indicate full set. Drones indicates drones on their own. Drones were played by other instruments also and the drone 'note' is indicated.

'Chorus' (usually a one-part melody) is the word indicating the full melody of the song and 'Curfá' is what they used to indicate a song refrain. 'Bodh' is sometimes used to indicate Bodhrán and 'Harps' is used as shorthand for harpsichord.

This same structure was applied to the arrangement of songs also.

On occasion I have listed a note or series of notes, say in a drone such as say A E'. The ' on the E here means the E' is in the second octave. Likewise, an A with A, indicates an A sounding an octave below middle C.

Sharps and flats are indicated from time to time as hashtag and b

There is a page of counter melodies in the miscellaneous section. They are from Michael Tubridy's notes and he was the most able player of contra melodies.

On occasion, especially in the listing of Box chords, one may see say a D with it underlined <u>D</u> – and this indicates a stressed chord or note. For example, one might find an A followed by a D. The D is the start of the line but the A is note sang or played before the first line. Something like: There was a young man from … or I once was a man from … compared to say the line Once I was a waterman.

Underline means a stressed beat or note and it would have an extra emphasis when played.

I have used the spelling of titles as I found them. Some tunes have several names.

The Abbey Reel

AB	Flute
AB	Box
AB	Whistle, Chanter
AB	Whole Band
AB	Fiddles
AB	Whole Band
AB	Flute & 2 Whistles
ABAB	Whole Band

Ace and Deuce

Version # 1

A	Harps (Harpsicord)
A	Fiddle, Flute, Whistle
B	Harps
B	Fiddle, Flute, Whistle
AB	Chanter
AA	Whole Band
BB	Whole Band

Version # 2

Intro on Fiddles or on Harps

A	Canter + Fiddle Chords (Martin)
A	Whistle, Flute, Accordion Chords (Harps instead of Accordion)
B	Chanter, Fiddle Chords
B	Whistle, Flute, Accordion Chords (Harps instead of Accordion)
AABB	Whole Band
AA	Fiddles
BB	3 Whistles, Fiddle Chords (Martin)
A	Harps
A	Fiddle, Flute, Whistle
B	Harps
B	Fiddle, Flute, Whistle
AA	Whole Band
BB	Whole Band

End on full chord G Maj. (B on Flute, G on Whistle D' on Chanter)

A Ghrá Luí Laimh Liom
AAB	Flute, Harps	
	AAB	3 Fiddles, Harps
	AAB	Whole Band

Ag Taisteal na Sléibhte
Verse 1	Seán Ó Sé	Harps
An tAthair Jack Welsh		Whole Band
Verse 2	Seán Ó Sé	Harps
An tAthair Jack Welsh		Whole Band
Verse 3	Seán Ó Sé	Whole Band

After Aughrim's Great Disaster (Éistíg Liomsa Sealad) (BBC3 – 8 minutes)
Intro	Bodhrán	(roll – Seán Potts)
	A	Chanter
	B	Whistle, Flute, Chant
	A	Whole Band, Bodhrán (strike at each beat)
	B	Whole Band, Martin at Oct. Thrills on Whistle

Ag Taisteal na Blárnan
Intro	Harps	(Last line)
Verse 1	Seán Ó Sé	Harps
Verse 2	Seán Ó Sé	Whole Band

The Airy Batchelor
Intro		Harps
Verse 1	Seán Ó Sé	Harps, Bodhrán – repeat last line
Verse 2	Seán Ó Sé	3 Whistles – repeat last line
Verse 3	Seán Ó Sé	3 Whistles – repeat last line
Verse 4	Seán Ó Sé	3 Whistles, Box – repeat last line
Verse 5	Seán Ó Sé	3 Whistles, Box – repeat last line
Verse 6	Seán Ó Sé	Fiddles. 3 Whistles, Box – repeat last line
Verse 7	Seán Ó Sé	Whole Band – repeat last line

Airéir is mé go hUaigneach
Version # 1
Intro		Harps
Verse 1	Seán Ó Sé	Harps
Verse 2	Seán Ó Sé	Whole Band

Version # 2 (instrumental)
AABB	Fiddles, Harpsichord
AA	Fiddles, Whistles, Flute, Harpsichord

| | BB | Whole Band |

Aithrighe Chathail Buí
- Verse 1 Seán Ó Sé — Harps
- Verse 2 Seán Ó Sé — Harps, Fiddle (Octave Contra – Martin), Pipes
- Verse 3 Seán Ó Sé — Whole Band (Last Line Soft)

Aililiú na Gamhna
- Intro — Harps
-   Seán Ó Sé — Harps
- Chorus — Whole Band
-   Seán Ó Sé — Chanter
- Chorus — Whole Band
-   Seán Ó Sé — Viola
- Chorus — Fiddles, Viola
-   Seán Ó Sé — Box
- Chorus — Flute, Whistle (omit whistle during Aililiu words), Box (no pause)
- Chorus — Whole Band (whole band singing and hold last note)

Amhráinín Siodruimín Siosúram Sóigh

Version # 1
- Verse 1 Seán Ó Síocháin Whole Band
- 3 Sea Captains AB Harps
- Verse 2 Seán Ó Síocháin Whole Band
- Patsy Geary's (jig) AA 3 Fiddles
- Verse 3 Seán Ó Síocháin Whole Band
- Verse 3 Whistles
- Verse 4 Seán Ó Síocháin Whole Band Last phrase repeated twice

Version # 2
- Verse 1 Seán Ó Sé Whole Band
- Verse 2 Seán Ó Sé Whole Band
- 3 Sea Captains AA Chanter, Bodhran
- Verse 3 Seán Ó Sé Whole Band
- Verse 4 Seán Ó Sé Whole Band Last line of verse repeat x 4

Anach Cuan (D min)
- Intro — Harps (Farraige)
- Notes on Whistle & Box (D min chord) Flutter tongue on flute (B)

Verse 1	AB	Viola or Fiddle (Martin)
Intro		Repeated
Verse 2	AB	Viola, Flute, Whistle, Harps
Intro		Repeated
Verse 3	A	Chanter & Harps
Verse 3	B	Whole Band
Intro Repeat		

Anything for John Joe (medley)

Anything for John Joe	ABAB	Whole Band
Tripping to the Well	AABB	Fiddles
Tripping to the Well	AABB	Whole Band
Ma, Ma, Will You Buy	AB	Harps (or Chanter)
Ma, Ma, Will You Buy	AB	Whole Band
Girl I left behind me	AABB	Flute, Whistles
Girl I left behind me	AABB	Whole Band
Kiss behind the Door	AABB	Box, Fiddle
Kiss behind the Door	AABB	Whole Band
Kiss behind the Door	AABB	Whole Band

Arabia

	ABA	Whole Band 

Ar an Loing Seo Pheaidí Loingsigh

Intro		Harps
Verse 1	Seán Ó Sé	Harps
Verse 2	Seán Ó Sé	Harps, Chanter
Verse 3	Seán Ó Sé	Harps, Whole Band
Verse 4	Seán Ó Sé	Harps, Whole Band

Ar Éirinn Ní n'eosfainn cé hí

Version # 1

Verse 1	Seán Ó Síocháin	Acc. Bass
Verse 2	Seán Ó Síocháin	Whole Band

Version # 2

Verse 1	Seán Ó Síocháin	Harps
Verse 2	Seán Ó Síocháin	Flute, Whistle, 2 fiddles, Acc. Bass
Verse 3	Seán Ó Síocháin	Whole Band

Version # 3

	Verse 1 Seán Ó Síocháin	Fiddle, Box
	Verse 2 Seán Ó Síocháin	Flute, Whistle
	Verse 3 Seán Ó Síocháin	Flute, Whistle, Chanter
	Verse 4 Seán O Síocháin	Whole Band
	Box chords:	G C G G A D
		G C G G C G
		G G F♮ C, E G A D
		G C G G C G

The Ashplant

	ABAB	Whole Band
Reel of Bogey	AB	Fiddle (John)
	AB	Whole Band
Dunmore Lassies	AB	Flute
	AB	Whole Band
	AB	Fiddle (Martin)
	AB	Whole Band
	AB	Whistle
	AB	Whole Band
	AB	Fiddle (Seán)
	AB	Whole Band
Cup of Tea	AB	Chanter (Harps)
	AB	Whole Band

An tAthair Jack Walsh

	A	Pipes
	A	Box
	B	Pipes
	B	Box
	AA	Whole Band
	BB	Whole Band
	A	Fiddle
	A	Box
	B	Fiddle
	B	Box
	AB	Drones & Chanter
	AABB	Whole Band – Jig Time
	AABB	Whole Band
	AABB	Whole Band

Ar Maidin Dé Máirt
    Intro   Harps
    Verse 1   Seán Ó Sé   Harps
    Verse 2   Seán Ó Sé   Flute, Whistle
    Verse 3   Seán Ó Sé   Whole Band

Babaró
Version # 1
    Intro   Harps
    Verse 1   Seán Ó Sé   Harps
    Verse 2   Seán Ó Sé   Harps
    Verse 3   Seán Ó Sé   Harps
    Verse 4   Seán Ó Sé   Harps
Cúnla   AABB   Whole Band
    Verse 5   Seán Ó Sé   Whole Band

Version # 2
    Intro   Harps
    Verse 1   Seán Ó Sé   Harps
Cúnla/Frieze Britches   AABB   Whole Band
    Verse 2   Seán Ó Sé   Harps
Cúnla/Frieze Britches   AABB   Whole Band
    Verse 3   Seán Ó Sé   Harps
Cúnla/Frieze Britches   AABB   Whole Band
    Verse 4   Seán Ó Sé   Whole Band
Cúnla/Frieze Britches   AABB   Whole Band
    Verse 5   Seán Ó Sé   Harps
    Verse 5   Seán Ó Sé   Whole Band
    Note: Éamon has Cúnla, Mick has Frieze Britches)

Bacach Buí na Léige
    Intro   Harps
    Verse 1   Seán Ó Sé   Harps
    Chorus   Whole Band
    Verse 2   Seán Ó Sé   Harps
    Chorus   Whole Band
    Verse 3   Seán Ó Sé   Harps
    Chorus   Whole Band
    Verse 4   Seán Ó Sé   Harps
    Chorus   Whole Band
    Verse 5   Seán Ó Sé   Harps
    Chorus   Whole Band and repeat

Box Chords:	C C C C
	F F G G
	C C C C
	F F G --
	C G C C
	F D G G
	C C F D
	G G C --

An Banbh

Verse 1	Seán Ó Sé	Harps
Curfá	Seán O Sé	Harps
Curfá		Whole Band
Verse 2	Seán Ó Sé	Harps
Curfá	Seán Ó Sé	Harps
Curfá		Whole Band
Verse 3	Seán Ó Sé	Harps
Curfá	Seán Ó Sé	Harps
Curfá		Whole Band
Verse 4	Seán Ó Sé	Harps
Curfá	Seán O Sé	Harps
Curfá	Seán O Sé	Whole Band
	Box Chords:	D A A D A D
		D A A D A D
Curfá		A D A A A D. D

Bán Chnoic Éireann Ó

Verse 1		Seán Ó Sé	Fiddles, Whole Band coming in at last 'Bán Chnoic Éireann Ó'
Verse 2	A	Seán Ó Sé	Harps
	B		Harps, Chanter, Whole Band in on last 'Bán Chnoic Éireann Ó'
Verse 3		Seán Ó Sé	Whole Band

Banks of Sullane

Version # 1

Intro		Harps
Verse 1	Seán Ó Sé	Harps
Verse 2	Seán Ó Sé	Harps, Box E Drone
Verse 3	Seán Ó Sé	Harps, Fiddles, No Box
Verse 4	Seán Ó Sé	Whole Band, Box with coupler

Version # 2
  Verse 1   Seán Ó Sé   Harps, Box E Drone
  Verse 2   Seán Ó Sé   Flute, Whistle, Box E Drone
  Verse 3   Seán Ó Sé   Whole Band – no Box
  Verse 4   Seán Ó Sé   Whole Band, Box with coupler

Banna Strand
  Intro   Harps
  Verse 1   Seán Ó Sé   Harps
  Verse 2   Seán Ó Sé   Harps, Box Chords
  Verse 3   Seán Ó Sé   Harps, Box Chords, Fiddles
  Verse 4   Seán Ó Sé   Harps, Box Chords, Fiddles, Whistle, Flute
  Verse 5   Seán Ó Sé   Harps, Box Chords, Whole Band
             Box Chords: C G C G
                                D G C D (full chord)
                                D G C G
                                C G C G

Bard of Armagh
  Verse 1   Seán Ó Sé   Harps
  Verse 2   Seán Ó Sé   Whistle
  Verse 3   Seán Ó Sé   Whistle, Fiddle (Low Octave)
  Verse 4   Seán Ó Sé   3 Fiddles
  Verse 5   Seán Ó Sé   Whole Band

Barley Grain
  Verse 1   Seán Ó Sé   Harps
  Verse 2   Seán Ó Sé   Harps, Whistle
  Verse 3   Seán Ó Sé   Harps, Whistle, Flute
  Verse 4   Seán Ó Sé   Harps, Whistle, Flute, Pipes
  Verse 5   Seán Ó Sé   Harps, Whistle, Flute, Pipes, Box
  Verse 6   Seán Ó Sé   Harps, Whistle, Flute, Pipes, Box, Fiddle
  Verse 7   Seán Ó Sé   Whole Band
  Verse 7   Seán Ó Sé   Whole Band
           Each extra instrument comes in at chorus

Barrel of Porter & Seán Buí
Barrel   AABB   Box (Sonny)
Barrel   A   Fiddle
Barrel   A   Chanter
Barrel   B   Fiddle
Barrel   B   Chanter

Barrel	AABB	Whole Band
Seán Buí	AABB	Whistle, Flute, Chanter
Seán Buí	AABB	Whole Band
Barrel	AABB	Fiddles & Boxes
Barrel	AABB	Whole Band

(Barrel of Porter aka Biddy Daly/Paddy Clancy)

Barry's Column

	Verse 1	Seán Ó Sé	Harps, Drum
Follow me up to Carlow	AB		Whole Band
	Verse 2	Seán Ó Sé	Harps
Return from Fingal	A		Whole Band
	Verse 3	Seán Ó Sé	Harps
Follow me Up to Carlow	AB		Whole Band
	Verse 4	Seán Ó Sé	Harps
Rosc Catha	AB		Whole Band
	Verse 5	Seán Ó Sé	Harps
		Seán Ó Sé	Harps, Chanter in on 2nd half
Barry's Col (2nd half)		Seán O Sé	Whole Band
Barry's Col (2nd half)		Seán O Sé	Whole Band

Bean a' Tí

	AABB	Flute, Bodhrán
	AABB	Fiddle, Bodhrán
	AABB	Pipes, Bodhrán
	AABB	Whistle Flute, Bodhrán
	AABB	Whole Band
	AABB	Whole Band
Box Chords:		A A D D
		A A D D
		A A D G
		A A A G
		A A D A D

Bean Dubh a' Ghleanna (Instrumental)

Verse		Fiddle (Martin)
Verse		Whole Band
As Hornpipe	AABB	Flute, Whistle
	AABB	Harps
	AABB	Chanter
	AABB	Whole Band

Beggarman

A	Fiddle
A	Whole Band
B	Fiddle
B	Whole Band
AABB	Whole Band
AABB	Harps
A	Chanter
A	Flute Whistle
B	Chanter
B	Flute, Whistle
AABB	Whole Band

Beidh Aonach Amáireach

Intro		Harps
Verse 1	Seán Ó Sé	Harps
Verse & chorus		Whole Band
Verse 2	Seán Ó Sé	Harps
Verse & chorus		Whole Band
Verse 3	Seán Ó Sé	Harps & Whole Band

Pause on last line

Beidh Spórt Againn & Off She Goes

Intro		Whole Band (Long F & Long E)
	AB	Whole Band
	A	Whole Band
	B	Flute
	A	Whole Band
	B	Box (Éamon)
	A	Whole Band
	B	2 Fiddles
	A	Whole Band (Slowly)
	B	Chanter
	A	Whole Band
Jig	AABB	Fiddle (J. Kelly)
	BA	2 Whistles
		Chanter – Run of notes ending on F
		Whole Band plays long note on F & E
	AB	Whole Band
	ABA	Whole Band getting much faster with pause before last 4 bars

Bínn Lisín Aerach a Bhrogha

Intro		Harps
Verse 1	Seán Ó Sé	Harps
Verse 2	Seán Ó Sé	Harps, Whistle, Flute, Fiddles
Verse 3	Seán Ó Sé	Whole Band, Box Chords

Box Chords:: G C G G A D
   G C G G C G
   G G F♮ C, E G A D
   G C G G C G

An Bínsín Luachra

Version # 1

Intro		Harps
Verse 1 – 1st Half	Seán Ó Sé	Harps
2nd half	Seán Ó Sé	Drones, Fiddle
Verse 2 – 1st Half	Seán Ó Sé	Harps, Drones
2nd half	Seán O Sé	Box Chords
Verse 3 – 1st Half	Seán Ó Sé	Harps, Drones
2nd half	Seán O Sé	Whole Band & Box Chords

Box Chords: (Ceartú beag déanta ag POR)
   D   A   D   G, A (First half of verse)
   D   A   D   A   (lines 5 & 6)
   D   G   A, D   G,A (line 7)
   D,A   D,A   A   G,D (line 8)
   G (as finishing note)

Version # 2

Intro		Harps
Verse 1	Seán Ó Sé	Harps
Verse 2	Seán Ó Sé	Harps
Verse 3	Seán Ó Sé	Harps

Instrumental version Bínsín Luachra/Job of Journey Work

Drone by Whole Band		Fiddles F# (D string) and A (G string)
		Viola D+A
		Box D Chord, Flute Bottom D, Whistles
		Bottoim A
1st chorus		Tune on Harps with Whole Band Drone
Job of Journey Work	B	Harps, WB drone, 2nd half twice with Box drones
Job of Journey Work	AB	Chanter, WB drones
Job of Journey Work	BB	Harps, WB drones
	AB	Whole Band, and Box drone

	AABB		Whistle, Flute, Chanter with Whole Band joining in at Bar 9
			Slow for last few notes

Bhí Bean Uasal (Carrickfergus)
Version # 1

Intro			Harps
	AB	Seán Ó Sé	Harps
	AB	Seán Ó Sé	Harps, Fiddle
	AB	Seán Ó Sé	Harps, Flute, Whistle, Fiddle
	AB	Seán Ó Sé	Whole Band
		(If only 3 Verses required, leave out 2nd AB)	

Version # 2 (Instrumental)

AB		Fiddle in D
AB		Fiddle, Flute, Whistle, Chanter in G
AB		Whole Band in G

(Vocal version of same)

AB	Seán Ó Sé	Harps, Fiddle in D
AB	Seán Ó Sé	Harps, Fiddle, Flute, Whistle in G
AB	Seán Ó Sé	Whole Band in G

Box Chords: Emin A D Emin A D
D Emin A D Emin A D
D G A D Emin A
D Emin A D Emin A A D

Bhíosa Lá i' bPort Láirge
Version # 1

	A	Seán Ó Sé	(Harps) (optional – a question of tuning)
	A		Whole Band
	BB		Whole Band
	A	Seán Ó Sé	(Harps)
	A		Whole Band
	BB		Whole Band
Ma, Ma will you …			(sung by whole band)
Mary Duggan	A		3 Whistles
Mary Duggan	A		Whole Band
Mary Duggan	B		3 Whistles
Mary Duggan	B		Whole Band
Bhíosa Lá	A	Seán Ó Sé	(Harps)
	A		Whole Band

	BB		Whole Band
	A	Seán Ó Sé	(Harps)
	A		Whole Band
	BB		Whole Band

Version # 2 (in C)

Verse 1	A		Whole Band
	A	Seán Ó Sé	Box, Fiddle, Whistle, Flute
	B		Whole Band
	B	Seán Ó Sé	Whole Band
Verse 2	A		Whole Band
	A	Seán Ó Sé	Box, Fiddle, Whistle, Flute
	B		Whole Band
	B	Seán Ó Sé	Whole Band
Verse 3	A		Whole Band
	A	Seán Ó Sé	Box, Fiddle, Whistle, Flute
	B		Whole Band
	B	Seán Ó Sé	Whole Band

Bhíosa lá i gCill Áirne

Verse 1	Seán Ó Sé	Harps – last line repeat
Verse 2	Seán Ó Sé	Harps – last line repeat
Verse 3	Seán Ó Sé	Harps – last line repeat
Verse 4	Seán Ó Sé	Harps – last line repeat
Verse 5	Seán Ó Sé	Harps, 3 whistles impov. – last line repeat
Verse 6	Seán Ó Sé	Harps, 3 whistles improv. – Whole Band in on last line
Verse 7	Seán Ó Sé	Whole Band
Verse 8	Seán Ó Sé	Whole Band – rall on last line

Box Chords: G G G C D
G C G D G

Bímse i gConaí 'Radaireacht

Intro		Harps
Verse 1 (A)	Seán Ó Sé	Harps
Chorus (B)	Seán Ó Sé	Whole Band – singing
AB		Whole Band
Verse 2	Seán Ó Sé	Harps
Chorus	Seán Ó Sé	Whole Band – singing
AB		Whole Band
Verse 3	Seán Ó Sé	Harps

Chorus		Seán Ó Sé	Whole Band – singing
	AB		Whole Band
Verse 4		Seán Ó Sé	Harps
Chorus		Seán Ó Sé	Whole Band – singing
	AB		Whole Band
		AB	Whole Band – Slow down in last verse/AB

The Blackbird
Version # 1

	AABB	Harps (Speeding up towards end of 2nd B)
	AA	Pipes
	BB	Fiddles (octaves)
	A	Flute, Whistle
	A	Flute, Whistle, Chant
	B	Flute, Whistle,
	B	Flute, Whistle, Chant
	AAABB	Whole Band
	B	Harps slowing down

Version # 2

	AABB	Harps (Air)
	AA	Pipes
	B	Fiddles (octaves)
	AAB	Flute, Whistle, Pipes
	AAB	Whole Band – Harps ending

Blackthorn Stick

	AABB	3 Whistles (in harmony)
	A	Fiddle (John) Fiddle Chords D & G (Martin)
	A	Fiddle (John) Fiddle Chords (Martin)
	B	Fiddle (John) Fiddle Chords (Martin)
	B	Fiddle (John) Fiddle Chords (Martin)
	AA	Pipes
	BB	Box

Battering Ram

	AA	Flute
	BB	Flute, Whistle
	CC	Flute, Whistle, Chanter

Blackthorn Stick

	AA	2 Fiddles

| | | | BB | 2 Fiddles, Box Chord |
| | | | AABB | Whole Band |

Bold Thady Quill (in G)

	Intro			Thrill in D
	Verse 1	Seán Ó Sé		Harps
Oró Bog Liom í		ABA		Whole Band
	Verse 2	Seán Ó Sé		Harps
Oró Bog Liom í		ABA		Whole Band
	Verse 3	Seán Ó Sé		Whole Band

Bonaparte's Retreat

Version # 1

		AABB	Fiddle (John)
		AAB	Whistle
		A	2 Whistles
		A	Harps
		B	2 Whistles
		B	Harps
		AABB	Whole Band

Version # 2

	Intro		Harps
		AABB	Fiddle (John Kelly)
		AABB	Whole Band
		A	Whistle, Chanter, Fiddle Plucked
		A	Whistle, Chant, Fiddle played), Counter-melody Fiddle (S O R)
		B	Whistle, Chanter, Fiddle Plucked
		B	Whistle, Chanter, Fiddle (played)
		A	2 Whistles
		A	Harps
		B	2 Whistles
		B	Harps
		AABB	Whole Band

Version # 3

		A	Harps
		A	Pipes
		B	Harps
		B	Pipes
		AB	Whole Band
		A	3 Fiddles

	A	3 Whistles
	B	3 Fiddles
	B	3 Whistles
	AAB	Whole Band

Bonnie Bunch of Roses Oh

Verse 1 1st half	Seán Ó Sé	Solo
Verse 1 2nd half	Seán Ó Sé	Harps
Verse 2	Seán Ó Sé	Fiddles, Box (chord D drone)
Verse 3	Seán Ó Sé	Whole Band & Pipes drones

An Botháinín íseal gan Fálthas (8:15) Bealtaine – 1 May/ Reel Green Fields of America

	Air	Harps treble with Pipes drones
Bealtaine		Flute, Whistle, Chanter, Fiddles/Viola with Bass D drone on box
	Air	Flute, Whistle, Chanter, Drones Fiddles/Viola A+D Boxes Bass D
Bealtaine		Fiddles, Viola and Harps (drone effect)
	Air	Whole Band with Viola and Harps drone effect
Bealtaine		Flute, Harps
Green Fields		Fiddle (John)
Green Fields		Whole Band

Boy in the Boat

	AA	Whistle, Bodhrán (hand)
	BB	Whistle, Bodhrán
	AABB	Whole Band, Bodhrán (hard stick)
Road to Lisdoon	AB	Box
Boy in the Boat	AA	Whistle, Flute Bodhrán (hand)
	BB	Pipes, Flute Bodhrán (hand)
	AABB	Whole Band
	AABB	Whole Band

Boy in the Gap

ABB	Harps
ABB	Whole Band
ABB	2 Fiddles
ABB	Whole Band
ABB	Pipes, Flute, Whistle, Box Drones
ABB	Whole Band

| | | ABB | Whole Band |

Boyne Hunt

		AB	Whistle, Flute (Pipes, Fiddle/yap)
		AB	Whistle, Flute, Chanter
		AB	Whole Band (Pipes, Fiddle/yap)
			Fiddle Arr. (Yapping)
		AB	Flute
			Fiddle Arr. (Yapping)

Boys of Kilmichael

Intro	(Last Line)	Harps
Verse 1	Seán Ó Sé	Harps
Chorus	Seán Ó Sé	Whole Band – singing and playing
Verse 2	Seán Ó Sé	Harps
Chorus	Seán Ó Sé	Whole Band – singing and playing
Verse 3	Seán Ó Sé	Harps/ chanter
Chorus	Seán Ó Sé	Whole Band – singing and playing
Verse 4	Seán Ó Sé	Harps, Chant, Flute, Whistle
Chorus	Seán Ó Sé	Whole Band – singing and playing
Chorus	Seán Ó Sé	Whole Band – singing and playing

Chorus: So here's to the boys of Kilmichael
Those brave lads so gallant and true
Who fought 'neath the bold Tommy Barry
An conquered the red White and blue

Boys of the Loch

		AABB	Whole Band
		AABB	Whole Band
		AABB	2 Whistles, Flute
		AA	Fiddle
		BB	Box
		AABB	Whole Band

Brennan on the Moore

Verse 1	Seán Ó Sé	Harps
Verse 2	Seán Ó Sé	Harps, Box chords
Verse 3	Seán Ó Sé	Harps, Box, Whistle, Flute
Verse 4	Seán Ó Sé	Harps, Box, Whistle, Flute, Chanter
Verse 5	Seán Ó Sé	Whole Band
	Box Chords:	D G A D
		D A D
		D C A (single) GA (full)

| | Curfá: | D D A-D G-D G-D |

Brian O'Lynn

	AABB	Whole Band
	AABB	Box (Sonny)
	AABB	Whole Band
	AABB	Flute, Whistle, Chanter
	AABB	Whole Band
	AABB	Fiddle (Gildas' version)
	AABB	Band

An Brianach Óg
Intro		Seán Ó Sé	Harps
	Verse 1	Seán Ó Sé	Harps
	Verse 2	Seán Ó Sé	Harps
	Verse 3	Seán Ó Sé	Whole Band

Brídín Deas Uí Néill
	Verse 1	Seán Ó Sé	Harps
	Verse 2	Seán Ó Sé	Harps
	Verse 3	Seán Ó Sé	Harps, Flute, Fiddle (Martin)
	Verse 4	Seán Ó Sé	Harps, Whole Band

Bruach na Carraige Báine (1:50)

| | Verse 1 | Seán Ó Sé | Base drone A on Box, Bodhrán, Bones. |

| Contentment is Wealth | AA | | Fiddles & Whistles, Bodhrán, Bones |
| | Verse 2 | Seán Ó Sé | Base note on Box, Bodhrán, Bones |

Sister jig			
	AA		Fiddles & Whistles, Box drone A, Bodhrán, Bones
	Verse 3	Seán Ó Sé	Whole Band
	Verse 4	Seán Ó Sé	Whole Band

An Buachaill Caol Dubh
Version # 1
	Verse 1	Seán Ó Sé	Harps
	Verse 2	Seán Ó Sé	Harps
	Verse 3	Seán Ó Sé	Harps

Version # 2

	AB	Fiddle
	A	Fiddle, Pipes
	B	Whole Band

Version # 3

	AB	Fiddle
	AB	Whole Band

Bucks of Oranmore

	ABCD	Pipes
	ABCD	Whole Band
	ABCD	Whistle, Flute – taking alternate phrases
	E	Fiddle
		Improvisation Harpsichord
	A	Whole Band
	BC	Chanter
	D	Whole Band

The Buck in the Wood

	AABB	Whole Band
	AABB	Flute, Whistles, Fiddles with alternating chords
	AABB	Chanter, Box
	AABB	Harps
	AABB	Whole Band

Bumper Squire Jones

Version # 1

	AABB	Harps, Chanter
	AABB	Flute, Whistle, Box
	AABB	3 Whistles
	AABB	Fiddles
	AABB	Whole Band

Version # 2

	AABB	Harps
	AABB	Harps, Pipes
	AABB	Flute, Whistle, Box
	AABB	3 Fiddles
	AABB	Whole Band

Version # 3 (in Seán Ó Riada's own hand in Éamon de Buitléar's notes)

As a song	Intro	Harps

AABB		Whole Band
A	Seán Ó Sé	Harps
B	Seán Ó Sé	Whistles & Harps
AABB		Whole Band
A	Seán Ó Sé	Fiddle & Harps
B	Seán Ó Sé	Pipes & Harps
AB		Whole Band
A		Whole Band
A	Seán Ó Sé	Harps
B	Seán Ó Sé	Whole Band
B		Whole Band

By the Bright Silvery Light of the Moon

Verse 1	Seán Ó Sé	Harps
Chorus	Seán Ó Sé	Whole Band
Verse 2	Seán Ó Sé	Harps
Chorus	Seán Ó Sé	Whole Band
Verse 3	Seán Ó Sé	Harps
Chorus	Seán Ó Sé	Whole Band

Cailín Bán (Limerick is Beautiful) (3:40)

Version # 1

Verse 1	Seán Ó Sé	Harps,
Verse 2	Seán Ó Sé	Harps, Box Chords
Verse 3	Seán Ó Sé	Harps, Box Chords, 2 Fiddles, Flute
Verse 4	Seán Ó Sé	Whole Band last 2 bars softly

Version # 2

Verse 1	Seán Ó Sé	Harps
Verse 2	Seán Ó Sé	Harps, Box Chords
Verse 3	Seán Ó Sé	Harps, Box Chords, Fiddles
Verse 4	Seán Ó Sé	Whole Band
	Box Chords:	G D G C G C G
		C D Emin C G A D
		C D Emin C G A D
		G D G C (fade) G C< G

Cailín Deas Donn

Version # 1

Verse 1	Seán Ó Sé	Harps
Chorus	Seán Ó Sé	Box Bones, Bodhrán, Harps
Verse 2	Seán Ó Sé	Harps

Chorus	Seán Ó Sé	Box Bones, Bodhrán, Flute, Whistle, Fiddle, Harps
Verse 3	Seán Ó Sé	Harps
Chorus	Seán Ó Sé	Box Bones, Bodhrán, Flute, Whistle, Fiddle, Harps
Verse 4	Seán Ó Sé	Harps
Chorus	Seán Ó Sé	Whole Band
Chorus	Seán Ó Sé	Whole Band
Chorus	Seán Ó Sé	Whole Band
Chorus	Seán Ó Sé	Whole Band

Version # 2

Intro		Harps
Verse 1	Seán Ó Sé	Harps & 3 whistles
Chorus	Seán Ó Sé	Whole Band
Verse 2	Seán Ó Sé	Harps & 3 whistles
Chorus	Seán Ó Sé	Whole Band
Verse 3	Seán Ó Sé	Harps & 3 whistles
Chorus	Seán Ó Sé	Whole Band
Verse 4	Seán Ó Sé	Harps & 3 whistles
Chorus	Seán Ó Sé	Whole Band

Cailín Deas Rua (Red-Haired Man's Wife)

Version # 1

Verse 1	Seán Ó Sé	Harps, Box Chords
Verse 2	Seán Ó Sé	Harps, Fiddles
Verse 3	Seán Ó Sé	Harps, Chanter
Verse 4	Seán Ó Sé	Whole Band
	Box Chords:	A A D G A D
		A D C D A D
		A D A D A D
		A D G D A D

Version # 2 (Instrumental)

Verse 1		Chanter
Verse 2		Harps, Chanter
Verse 3		Whole Band
Verse 4		Whole Band & Box Chords

An Cailín Rua

Version # 1

AB	Whistle, Flute, Pipes Drones
AB	Whistle Flute Chanter

AB	Whistle, Flute, Chanter, Fiddles
AB	Whistle, Flute, Chanter, Fiddles, Acc. and box chords

Slow last line (Flute and hold F#)

Version # 2

Verse 1	Seán Ó Sé	Harps, Box Chords
Verse 2	Seán Ó Sé	Harps, Box Chords, Fiddles
Verse 3	Seán Ó Sé	Harps, Box Chords, Fiddles, Chanter
Verse 4	Seán Ó Sé	Whole Band
Verse 5	Seán Ó Sé	Whole Band

Box Chords: G C G CD
G C G DG
G C G CD
G C G DG

Last note on last verse is very short

Cailíní Deasa Mhuigheo

AB	Pipes
AB	Fiddle
AB	Flute
AB	Box
AB	Harps Base & Whistle
AB	Harps Base & Whistle, Flute
AB	Harps Base & Whistle, Flute, Fiddles
AB	Harps Base & Whistle, Flute, Fiddles, Pipes
AB	Whole Band
AB	Whole Band

Cailíní an Fhactory

Verse 1	Flute, 2 whistles
Chorus	Flute, 2 whistles, Harps
Verse 2	Whole Band
Chorus	Whole Band

(Chorus = second half or turning of the melody)

Box Chords: G C D Emin C D Emin C
D G CA Emin C D G D G
G C D Emin C D Emin C
D G CD Emin C D Emin D G

Cailleach an Airgid
Version # 1

	A Darach Ó Catháin	
	AABB	Whole Band
	A	Chanter
	A	Whole Band
	B	Box
	B	Whole Band
	AB Darach Ó Catháin	Flute, Bodhrán
	A	Fiddle, Bodhrán
	A	Whistle, Chanter, Bones
	B	Flute, Bodhrán
	B	Whistle, Chanter, Bones
	AA	Boxes
	BB	Boxes, Fiddles
	AB Darach Ó Catháin	Flute, Bodhrán
	AABB	Whole Band
	AB Darach Ó Catháin	Flute, Bodhrán
	Chorus	Whole Band Singing

Version # 2

	AABB	Flute
	AABB	Fiddles
	AABB	Box
	AABB	Whistles, Flute
	AABB	Whole Band
Leg of the Duck		Chanter
Leg of the Duck		Whole Band
Cailleach an Airgid	AABB	Whole Band
	AABB	Whole Band

Cailleach a' Túirne/Maid at the Spinning Wheel

	AABBCCDD	Whole Band
	AA	Fiddles
	BB	Pipes
	CC	Fiddles
	DD	Pipes

	AA	Flute, Whistle
	BB	Box
	CCDD	Whole Band

An Caipilín Bán

	Seán Ó Sé	Accordion (chords) (in G)
	Seán Ó Sé	Whistle, Flute Accordion (in G)
Verse 3	Seán Ó Sé	Whistle, Flute, 2 fiddles Box chords (in D)
Verse 4	Seán O Sé	Whole Band in D Box Chords

Box Chords:

G Chords:	G C G C G
	G D G C D
	G D G Emin CD
	G C G C G
D Chords:	D G D G D
	D A D G A
	D A D G A
	D G D G D

Cáit Ní Dhuibhir

	Seán Ó Sé	Harps
	Seán Ó Sé	Harps, Fiddles, Whistles
Verse 3	Seán Ó Sé	Whole Band

Caitlín Triall

Intro		Harps (Last line of verse)
	Seán Ó Sé	Harps
Intro		Harps
	Seán Ó Sé	Harps, 2 Whistles, Flute
Intro		Harps
Verse 3	Seán Ó Sé	Whole Band

Caoineadh an Spailpín (4:10)

Intro		Box Chords
	AB	Whistle (Paddy), Box Chords
	AB	Whistles, Flute and Box Chords, end with Box Chords
Version # 2	AABA	Chanter, Box Chords

AA	Chanter, flute, Box chords
BA	Whole Band, Box Chords

Version # 3

Intro		Box
	A	Whistle, Box Chords (for Reacaireacht)
	B	Whistle, Flute, Box Chords
	AB	Whole Band, Box chords. Ending on Box

Box Chords: A A G A A G A A G G A
G G G A A G A G A A G A G A

Carolan's Concerto

Version # 1

A	Harps
A	Chanter
B	Harps
B	Chanter
AB	Whole Band
A	Fiddle
B	3 Whistles
AABB	Whole Band

Version # 2

A	Harps
A	Harps, Chanter
B	Harps
B	Harps, Chanter
AABB	Whole Band

Version # 3

A	Harps
A	Whole Band
B	Harps, Chanter
B	Whole Band
A	Harps, 3 Whistles
B	Whole Band

Carraig an Aoibhnis

AAB	Harps

AAB		Harps, Fiddles
AAB		Whole Band

Carraig Aonair

Verse 1	Seán Ó Sé	Harps
Verse 1	Seán Ó Sé	Harps
Verse 3	Seán Ó Sé	Whole Band
Verse 4	Seán Ó Sé	Whole Band

or traditional version Seán Ó Sé and Harps

Carraig Donn

Version # 1

AABA	in D	Fiddle (Martin) in D
AABA	in G	Chanter, Whistle, Flute, Box chords
AAB	in G	Whole Band
A	in G	Chanter, Fiddle (harm. Martin) Box chords

Version # 2

Seán Ó Sé	Harps,
Seán Ó Sé	Fiddle (low Octave), Flute, Whistle, Box Chords
Seán Ó Sé	Whole Band

Box Chords: G C D G
G C D G
DG Emin A* D
(Alternative: DG D G D)
G C D G

* single i.e., lower of the 2 bass buttons in A

Casadh an tSugáin

Box Chords: <u>G</u> D G C G D G C <u>G</u>
C <u>G</u> C G D G C
<u>D</u> G D-G C-G

Casaim Araon na Géanna Romhainn

Verse 1	Seán Ó Sé	Harps
Verse 2	Seán Ó Sé	Flute, Fiddle, Whistle, Chanter
Verse 3	Seán Ó Sé	Whole Band

Castle Kelly

Version # 1

Intro	B	Slowly on chanter and pause
	ABB	Whole Band (Up to tempo)
	ABB	Whole Band
	ABB	Box, Fiddles
	ABB	2 Whistles, Flute
	ABB	Whole Band
	ABB	Whole Band

Version # 2 (Gaiety)

Intro		Harps
	AABB	Whole Band

Version # 3 (Gaiety)

A	Fiddles
BB	Fiddles, Box
A	Flute, Whistle, Chanter, Box
B	Whole Band

Version # 4 (Gaiety)

Intro		Whistle, Fiddles in 5ths
	A	Fiddles
	A	Fiddles, Pipes (faster)
	BB	Whole Band

Cath Chéim an Fhiaidh

Version # 1 (Ó Éamon)

A	Pipes
A	Pipes, Box Chords
B	Whole Band
A	Pipes, Box Chords
A	Pipes, Box Chords, Whistle, Flute
B	Whole Band
A	Whole Band

Box Chords: D A D A D G D A D A A
              D A D A D G D G, A D G D
              D G A-D A D G A D A D
              D A D A D G D G A D G D

Version # 2 (Ó Mick)

	AA	Fiddle Whistles
	BA	Fiddles, Whistles, Bodhrán
	AA	Fiddles, Chant, Flute, Box Chords
	BA	Whole Band, Box Chords

Version # 3 (Ó Mick)

	AA	Chanter, Box
	BA	Chant, Whistle, Fiddle, Flute Box
	AA	Chant, Whistle, Fiddle, Flute
	BA	Whole Band, Box Chords last three lines

Version # 4 (Ó Mick)

Verse 1	Seán Ó Sé	Box Chords
Verse 2	Seán Ó Sé	Whole Band

Version # 5 (Ó Mick)

Verse 1	Seán Ó Sé	Harps
Verse 2	Seán Ó Sé	Harps, Box Chords
2nd Half		Whole Band
Verse 3	Seán Ó Sé	Harps, Box Chords
2nd Half		Whole Band

Version # 6 (Ó Mick)

	A	Chanter
	A	Chanter, Whistle, Flute, Box Chords
	B	Whole Band, Harps
	A	Whole Band, Harps, Box Chords

Version # 7 (Mick) (for Reacaireacht)

	A	Chanter
	A	Chanter, Box Chords
	B	Whole Band
	AAB	Whole Band

Version # 8 (Mick)

All verses	Seán Ó Sé	Harps

Cathaoir an Phíobaire (See arrangement end of book)

	A	Harps
	A	Whole Band

B	Harps
B	Whole Band
A	Pipes
A	Whole Band
AABB	Whistles
AABB	Whole Band
AABB	Whole Band

Box Chords: # 1

G D G-C D
G D G-D G
G-C D G E C D D
G-C D D G-D GG

2

G D G-C D G D G-A D-G
G D G A-D G-C D G-D D-G

Ceol a' Mhála

AB	Pipes
AB	Pipes
AB	Pipes, Harps
AB	Whole Band
AB	Pipes, Harps
AB	Whistles (3)
AB	Harps, Pipes
AB	Whole Band

Harps: 13 notes/beats to high G. End Whole Band G

Ceol a' Phíobaire (also Pósfaidh mé an t-Iascaire)

	Verse 1 & Chorus	Seán Ó Sé	Harps
	Verse 1 & Chorus		Whole Band
	Verse 2 & Chorus	Seán Ó Sé	Harps
Polka		AABB	Whole Band
	Verse 3 & Chorus	Seán Ó Sé	Harps
Polka		AB	Whole Band
	Verse 4 & Chorus	Seán Ó Sé	Whole Band (singing and playing)

Charles O'Connor

A	1st 4 bars	Whole Band, 2nd 4 bars Harps
A	1st 4 bars,	Whole Band, 2nd 4 bars Harps
B		Pipes
B		Whole Band
A		Harps
A		1st 4 bars, Fiddles, 2nd 4 bars Flute, Whistle
B		Pipes
B		Whole Band
A	1st 4 bars	Flute, whistle, Pipes, 2nd 4 bars Fiddles
A	1st 4 bar	Flute, whistle, Pipes, 2nd 4 bars Fiddles
B		Harp
B		Whole Band

Chase Me Charlie

		Harps
	Seán Ó Sé	Harps

An Chéad Mháirt den fhomhair (Na Gamhna Geala)

Verse 1	Seán Ó Sé	Harps
Verse 2	Seán Ó Sé	Box Chords
Verse 3	Seán Ó Sé	Box Chords, Fiddle (Martin)
Verse 4	Seán Ó Sé	Box Chords, 3 Fiddles, Flute
Verse 5	Seán Ó Sé	Box Chords, Whole Band

Box Chords: D G A G D
D ADG A G D
D ADG D G* A
D G A G D
* or Emin   Lead with A

Cherish the Ladies (Jackson's thought) Jig 5 parts

Cherish the Ladies Jig	AABB	Whole Band	
Rodgers Jig	AABB	Whole Band	
Ivy Leaf (reel)	AABB	Whole Band	
Bank of Ireland (Reel)	AABB	Whole Band	

Up against the Búchallán's AABB   Whole Band

Chief O'Neill
Version # 1

	AABB	Fiddles
	AABB	Pipes, Box Drone D chord
	AABB	Whole Band
	AA	Fiddles
	BB	Whole Band

Version # 2

	A	Whistle, Flute,
	ABB	Whistle, Flute, Fiddles A, DA Drone, Bodhrán
	AABB	2 Fiddles, Bodhrán Pipe-Drone (on prev. Line 4B)
	AABB	Chanter, Box Drone Chord D, Harps drone D
	AABB	Whole Band Box chord D
	AABB	Harps
	AA	Harps, Fiddle (John Kelly) Whistle, Flute, chant
	BB	Whole Band, Box Chord. Whole Band hold last note

Version # 3
Intro   Harps

	AABB	Whistle, Flute, Fiddle Drone
	AABB	2 Fiddles, Fiddle Drone
	AABB	Chanter, Box Drones
	AABB	Harps
	AABB	Whole Band

An Chúilfhionn

Version # 1

Verse 1 Seán Ó Sé	Harps
Verse 2 Seán Ó Sé	Harps, Chanter
Verse 3 Seán Ó Sé	Box chords, Whole Band (joining in softly and strengthening. Chanter drops out for last 2 lines of 3rd Verse

Box Chords: D D D D
    D D E G A
    D D A D

D D E A D

Version # 2

AAB	Harps
AA	Harps, Whistle
B	Harps, 2 fiddles in octaves
AA	Harps, Chanter, Flute
B	Whole Band
AA	Harps
B	Whole Band first half with Harps finishing last half of B

Version # 3

Verse 1	Harps
Verse 2	Harps, Flute, Whistles, Fiddles
Verse 3	Chanter
Verse 4	Whole Band

Ciarraíoch Mallaithe

Version # 1

Verse 1 Seán Ó Sé	Box Chords
Verse 2 Seán Ó Sé	Harps, with Box Chords on Óró
Verse 3 Seán Ó Sé	Whole Band, Box chords – end CC-G

Version # 2

A	Acc.
AB	Whole Band
A	Fiddles, Box chords
A	Whole Band, Box Chords
B	Flute, Whistle, Box Chords
Last Phrase (Óró)	Whole Band

Version # 3

AAB	Chanter with Whole Band in on last Óró
AAB	Whole Band

Version # 4

AA	Chanter Solo
B	Chanter Solo, Bass notes box
AAB	Whole Band, Bass notes Box

Box Chords: G D G C D-D G G-- C G

```
                              G D G C G-D G G-- C G
                              G C G C G D G
                              G C G C G D G
                              G-- C G
```

An Clár Bog Déil (5:00)

Intro		Harps
Verse 1	Seán Ó Sé	Harps (in D)
Verse 2	Seán Ó Sé	Harps(D), Whistle, Flute, Viola
Verse 3	Seán Ó Sé	Whole Band and Harps in G

Box Chords: G C G C G D G C G C D G
DG C G C D Emin G C G C G

Na Cleaganna (an mhóin)

	Verse 1	Seán Ó Sé	Box Chords
	Verse		Whole Band
	Verse 2	Seán Ó Sé	Box Chords
Jackson's	AA		Whole Band
	Verse 3	Seán Ó Sé	Box Chords
Jackson's	BB		Whole Band
	Verse 4	Seán Ó Sé	Box Chords
	Verse		Whole Band
	Verse 5	Seán Ó Sé	Box Chords
	Verse		Whole Band

Box Chords: A A D D
A A D D
A A D G
A A A G
A A D AD

Cnocáinín Aerach Chill Mhuire / Cill Mhuire

Version # 1

Verse 1	Seán Ó Síocháin	Box Chords
Verse 2	Seán Ó Síocháin	Whistle, Flute, Fiddle (pizz)
Verse 3	Seán Ó Síocháin	Flute, Pipes, Box Chords
Verse 4	Seán Ó Síocháin	Whole Band Spoken Word

Chorus	Whole Band and singing

Sin horó é horó a Bhauchailín Bhreá
Sin horó é horó e, sin chugham do láimh
Tá jug ar an mbórd agus ba choir é bheith Lán
Go n-ólfaimís sláinte Chill Mhuire

Box Chords: G C D G D̲ G D G
G C D G D̲ G D G
Curfá: G C-D E* A* D* A*   (* = minor chord)
G C-D G D̲ G D-G

Version # 2

	AABA	Words Spoken Box
	AABA	Whistle, Flute, Box Chords
	AABA	Chanter, Flute, Box Chords
	AABA	Whole Band, Box Chords
	AA	Whole Band, Box Chords
	BA	Whole Band, Box Chords, Whole Band singing
	AABA	Whole Band, Box Chords

(AABA here are A = first 2 lines of melody B = the Chorus – lines 5 and 6 of the melody)

Version # 3

Verse 1	Seán Ó Síocháin	Harps, Box Chords
Verse 2	Seán Ó Síocháin	Harps, Chanter, Box Chords
Verse 3	Seán Ó Síocháin	Harps, Chanter, Fiddles, Box Chords
Verse 4	Seán Ó Síocháin	Whole Band

Cois a' Ghaorthaigh

Version # 1

Verse 1	Seán Ó Sé	Harps
Verse 2	Seán Ó Sé	Harps, Fiddle on 3rd Line (Martin) + Pipes on 4th line
Verse 3	Seán Ó Sé	Whole Band

Version # 2 (Instrumental)

Verse 1	Harps in D
Verse 2	Whole Band in D

Version # 3

Verse 1	Seán Ó Sé	Harps
Verse 2	Seán Ó Sé	Harps, Drones

	Verse 3	Seán Ó Sé	Whole Band
Cois na Siúire			
	Verse 1	Seán Ó Sé	Harps
	Verse 2	Seán Ó Sé	Harps + Fiddle on 3rd Line (Martin) + Pipes on 4th line
	Verse 3	Seán Ó Sé	Whole Band
Collier's Reel			
Version # 1			
		AABB	Box (Sonny)
		AABB	Whole Band
		AABB	Fiddle, Pipes Drone
		AABB	Whole Band
		AABB	Chanter
		AABB	Whole Band
Tom Billy's		AABB	Flute
Colliers		AABB	Whole Band
Farewell to Eirinn		AABB	Whistle
Colliers		AABB	Whole Band
Version #2			
		AABB	Harps
		AABB	Harps, Whistle
		AABB	Harp Whistle, Flute
		AABB	Harps, Whistle, Flute Fiddles
		AABB	Harps, Whistle, Flute, Fiddles, Chanter
		AABB	Harps, Whistle, Flute, Fiddles, Chanter, Box
		AABB	Whole Band
		AABB	Whole Band
Connaught Heifers			
Version # 1 (Alleliú # 3)			
		AB	Whole Band
		AB	Whole Band
		AB	2 Fiddles (John & Seán)
		AB	Pipes

	AB	3 fiddles, Flute, Whistle
	AB	Whole Band
	AB	Whole Band
	AB	Whole Band

Version # 2 (Alleliú # 3)

	AB	Harps
	AB	Whole Band
	AB	Chanter
	AB	Whistle, Flute
	AB	Whole Band
	AB	Fiddles
	AB	Chanter, Flute
	AB	Whole Band
	AB	Whole Band

Cóta Caoin Caol

Verse	Harps, Fiddle
Verse	Harps, 3 Fiddles, Flute
Verse	Whole Band

Contentment is Wealth/13 June/Dear Old Skibbereen (7:20)

Skibbereen	Verse		Pipes
	Verse		Whole Band (last note end long drawn out)
Contentment		AB	Whistle
		AB	2 Fiddles, Viola
13 June jig		AB	Whole Band
		AB	Whole Band
Contentment		AB	Whole Band
		AB	Harps
		AB	Whole Band
Skibbereen (First line)			Harps
Skibbereen (last line)			Whole Band

Craig's Dragoons

Intro		Harps
Verse 1	Seán Ó Sé	Harps
Sash		Whole Band

Verse 2	Seán Ó Sé	Harps
Rule Britannia		Whole Band
Verse 3	Seán Ó Sé	Harps
Sash		Whole Band
Verse 4	Seán Ó Sé	Harps
Sash		Whole Band
Verse 5	Seán Ó Sé	Harps

Cuan Bhéilínse

Version # 1

Sea Sounds		Bodhrán & Bones (alternate trills as sea waves)
	A	Chanter
	A	Chanter, Box, Whistle
	BA	Whole Band
	AA	Chanter, Whistle (rubbing sound of Bodhrán)
	BA	Whole Band, Bodhrán & Bones

Version # 2

Intro		Piano
	Seán Ó Sé	Piano, Pipes (join in second half last line) Box Chords, 2 Whistle, Flute
	Seán Ó Sé	Piano, Pipes (join in second half last line), Chords
Verse 3	Seán Ó Sé	Piano, Pipes (join in second half last line), Chords

Version # 3 (Alleliú Prog. 4)

Intro		Piano
	Seán Ó Sé	Piano, Pipes (join in second half last line) **Chord**: Box, G. 2 Whistles, E'+B, Flute G
	Seán Ó Sé	Whole Band **Chord**: Box, G. 2 Whistles, E'+B, Flute G

Cuckoo's Nest + Leitrim Fancy

Cuckoos's Nest	AABB	Harps (played as slow air in G)
	Pause	

	AA	Flute (normal tempo)
	BB	Flute, Whistle
	CC	Flute, Whistle, Chanter
	AA	Fiddles
	BB	Boxes
	CC	Fiddles
Leitrim Fancy	AABB	Whole Band in D
Cuckoo's Nest	AABB	Whole Band in D
	Pause	
	AABB	Harps (played as slow air in G)

Diarmuid Ó Dubhda

Verse	Whole Band
Verse	Whole Band
Verse	Harps
Verse	Harps, Chanter
Verse	Harps, Chanter, 3 fiddles
Verse	Whole Band
Verse	Whole Band

Dí -i-dí á dí (An Puirtín)

Intro		Harps
Verse 1	Seán Ó Sé	Harps, Box Chords
Bridge/interlude		Harps
Verse 2	Seán Ó Sé	Harps, Pipes, Box Chords
Bridge/interlude		Harps
Verse 3	Seán Ó Sé	Whistle, Flute, Fiddles Box Chords
Verse 4	Seán Ó Sé	Whole Band
Verse 5	Seán Ó Sé	Whole Band (in A)

Last Line/Chorus x 5, where possible band members singing also as they play)

Box Chords: G C D G
G C D G
C G DG C DAD
G C D G

Dingle Regatta
Intro   Bodhrán

	A	1 voice lilting (Paddy), Bodhrán
	A	Whole Band Lilting Bodhrán
	B	Whole Band Lilting, Flute
	B	Whole Band Lilting, Flute, Box Sonny) Bodhrán
	CC	Whole Band Playing
	AABB	Fiddles – octaves, Bodhrán
	CC	Whole Band
	A	Whistle (Seán Potts), Bodhrán
	A	3 Whistles, Bodhrán
	B	Whistle (Seán Potts), Bodhrán
	B	3 Whistles, Bodhrán
	CC	Whole Band
Box Chords:		D A D G A D D A D B min A D
		D A D G A D D A D G A D

Diver the Dancer (Slip Jig)

	AB	Whistle
	AB	Whistle, Flute
	AB	Whistle, Flute, Fiddles
	AB	Whistle, Flute, Fiddles Boxes
	AB	Whistle, Flute, Fiddles, Boxes, Chanter
	ABAB	Whole Band
		end on a long note

Domhnal na Gréinne

Leg of the Duck	AABB	Whole Band
Loan of my Bellows	AABB	Seán Potts, Whole Band
Leg of the Duck	AABB	Whole Band

An Droighneán Donn

Version # 1

Verse		Harps, Fiddle Low reg. (Martin)
Verse		Harps, Flute, Whistle, Chanter
Verse		Harps
Verse		Whole Band

Version # 2
- Verse — Harps
- Verse — Harps, Flute, Whistle
- Verse — Whole Band

Drops of Brandy (3:25)

	Intro	Harps (Jangle Box imitation)
	AABB	Flute
	AABB	Flute, Whistle (Octave)
	AABB	Flute, Whistle, Chanter in 3rds
	AABB	Boxes, Harps
	AABB	Fiddles (Octaves), Whistles (one in 3rds)
	AABB	Harps
	AABB	Whole Band
	AABB	Whole Band
	AABB	Whole Band
		End on G Maj. (Flute on D)

A Druimfhionn Donn Dílis

    Seán Ó Sé   Harpsichord all verses

Drowsie Maggie

Version # 1

	AB	Fiddle (John K.)
	AB	Fiddles, 3 whistles (single Notes E, B E')
	AB	Whole Band, Harps
	AB	3 Whistles Box Emin drone on Box Base
	AB	Whole Band, Box E drone on Box base
	AB	Whole Band, Box E drone on Base
	AB	Whole Band, Box E drone on Base
		end on long last note

Version # 2

	AB	Whole Band
	Figure	Whole Band
	AB	Pipes and Figure
	AB	Pipes, flute Figure
	AB	Pipes, Flute, Whistle Figure
	AB	Pipes Flute, Whistle, Fiddles Figure

Figure	Whole Band
AB	Whole Band
AB	Whole Band

Figure: E - -D | E - - D | E -- D | E - - D

Dunmore Lassies
Version # 1

AABB	Flute
AABB	Whistle & Flute
AABB	Whole Band

Liffey Banks

AABB	Whistle & Flute
AABB	Chanter
AABB	Whole Band
AABB	Whole Band

Version #2
12 bars Intro from

	Flute, Fiddle, Bodhrán & Bones
AABB	Flute & Bodhrán
AA	Tune is Whistle, Fast contra-melody in second whistle, Slow contra-melody Flute
AA	with fast contra-melody – no slow contra-melody
A	Tune on Whistle & Flute, slow contra-melody on 2nd whistle, fast contra-melody on Fiddle, single bass notes on Box
A	But slow contra-melody only
B	Tune – Fiddle & Box + single Box Bass note (drone)
B	With contra-melody on Chanter, Bones rhythm
B	Tune Whistle, Flute, Box (no coupler) New contra-melody – Chanter, Bass notes Viola
Repeat	
C	Tune – Chanter New fast contra-melody in 5ths on Whistle, Flute, Viola on Bass notes

	Repeat	
C		Tune Fiddles, Box+Coupler, Box Bass notes
	Repeat	
A		As before
B		As before
C		As before segue into D
D		As written, The repeat in the 2nd half is fully written out. The last five bars after the double bar to be played slowly, Crescendo

Dwyer's Hornpipe

AABB	Whole Band in D
AABB	Whole Band in D
AABB	Fiddle in G
AABB	Harps in G
AABB	Whole Band in D
AABB	Whole Band in D

Éamon Magháine

Verse 1	Seán Ó Sé	Harps
Verse 2	Seán Ó Sé	Harps, Fiddle (Martin)
Verse 3	Seán Ó Sé	Harps, 3 Fiddles
Verse 4	Seán Ó Sé	Whole Band

Eibhlín a Rúin (G)

Verse 1	Seán Ó Sé	Harps
Verse 2	Seán Ó Sé	Harps, Chanter, Flute
Verse 3	Seán Ó Sé	Harps, Chanter, Flute, Fiddles (Octave)
Verse 4	Seán Ó Sé	Whole Band

Eilí Gheal Chiúin

Drone – Box & Fiddles: John open A&E, Martin-E&A, Seán D'&B, Box D

AB	Whistle (Drone – Box & Fiddles Chord D)
AB	Whistle, Flute (Box & Fiddles Chord D)
AB	Piano/Harps & Whistle/Flute
AB	Whole Band, Box Chord

End Whole Band on Drone Chord, Whistle A Flute F#, Chanter E

Emigrant's Jig (Port a Deoraí) (4:20)

Intro		Bones (4 bars)
	AB	Bones, Whistle
	AB	Bones, Whistle, Flute,
	AB	Bones, Whistle, Flute, Fiddles,
	AB	Bones, Whistle, Flute, Fiddles, Boxes
	AB	Bones, Whistle, Flute, Fiddles, Boxes, Chanter
	AB	Bones, Whistle, Flute, Fiddles, Boxes, Chanter, Bodhrán
	AB	Bones, Whistle, Flute, Fiddles, Boxes, Bodhrán E' AB Bones, Whistle, Flute, Fiddles, Bodhrán E' on Chanter, Boxes,
	AB	Bones, Whistle, Flute, Bodhrán E' on Chant, Boxes, Fiddles
	AB	Bones, Whistle, Bodhrán E' on Chanter, Boxes, Fiddles, Flute
	A	Bones, Whistle
	B	Whole Band – end on E/E'

Eochaill

Verse	Harps
Verse	Harps, Flute, Whistle
Verse	Harps, Fiddle
Verse	Harps, Chanter
Verse	Whole Band
Verse	Whole Band

The Ewe Reel

	AABB	Whole Band (+ Bodhrán)
	AABB	Whole Band
	AABB	Whistle, Flute
	AA	Chanter
	BB	3 Fiddles, Whistle
	AABB	Whole Band
	AABB	Whole Band

Faill Mór

Verse 1	Seán Ó Sé	Bodhrán, Chords (Box)

Faill Mór — Whole Band

Verse 2	Seán Ó Sé	Bodhrán, Chords (Box)

Maidrín Rua — Whole Band

Verse 3	Seán Ó Sé	Bodhrán, Chords (Box)

Sligo Maid — Whole Band

Verse 4	Seán Ó Sé	Bodhrán, Chords (Box)

Boys won't leave the Girls alone — Whole Band

Verse 5	Seán Ó Sé	Bodhrán, Chords (Box)

Chords: AAAE AADE AAAA DDDE
Chorus: AAAE AACA
End: EEEA

Fanny Power

Intro			Harps
Verse 1	AB	Seán Ó Sé	Harps
	A		Box, Fiddle
	B		2 Whistles/Flute
Verse 2	AB	Seán Ó Sé	Harps
	B		2 Whistles. Flute
Verse 3	AB	Seán Ó Sé	Whole Band

Farewell to Connaught (2:20)

AABB	Whole Band
A	Bones, Paddy Lilting
A	Whole Band
B	Bones, Paddy Lilting
B	Whole Band
A	Chanter, Whistle
A	Chanter, Whistle, Bodhrán
BB	Whole Band
AB	Fiddle (John Kelly's version)
AABB	Whole Band

Farewell to Erin

AABB	Whole Band

AABB	Whistle
AABB	Whole Band
AABB	Fiddle (John)
AABB	Whole Band
AABB	Flute, Fiddle (Seán)
AABB	Whole Band
AABB	Chanter
AABB	Whole Band
	Finish on E

Feadóg an Iolair (Fead an Iolair)

Version # 1

ABC	Harp
ABC	Harps, Chanter
ABC	Harps, Chanter, Whistle, Flute
ABC	Harps, Chanter, Whistle, Flute, Fiddles
ABC	Whole Band, Bodhrán
ABC	Whole Band, Bodhrán

Version # 2

ABC	Pipes
ABC	Whole Band
ABC	Harps
ABC	Whole Band
ABC	3 Fiddles
ABC	Whole Band
ABC	Whole Band

Fenians of Cahersiveen

Verse 1	Seán Ó Sé	Harps
Oró Bog Liom í AA		Whole Band
Verse 2	Seán Ó Sé	Harps, 2 Whistles, Flute
Oró Bog Liom í AA		Whole Band
Verse 3	Seán Ó Sé	Harps, 2 Whistles, Flute
Oró Bog Liom í AA		Whole Band
Verse 4	Seán Ó Sé	Whole Band

Fiach an Mhadra Ruaidh

Version # 1

	Verse 1	Seán Ó Sé	Harps, Drones
	Chorus		Whole Band
	Verse 2	Seán Ó Sé	Harps, Drones
	Chorus		Whole Band
	Verse 3	Seán Ó Sé	Harps, Drones
	Chorus		Whole Band
	Verse 4	Seán Ó Sé	Harps, Drones (D)
	Chorus		Whole Band (D)
	Verse 5	Seán Ó Sé	Harps, Drones (D)
	Chorus		Whole Band (D)
	Chorus x 4		Whole Band (D)

X = AAGFEDECA
Y = AAGFEDEFD

Version # 2

Chord: Box (D maj.) Fiddle (A maj.)

		Figure XY	Whistles
		Figure XY	Whistles
Maidrín Rua			Fiddle, Box (D/G Bass)
		Repeat	
Maidrín Rua			Pipes, Flute, Whistle
	Chorus		Whole Band
		Repeat	
Fiach an Mhadra Ruaidh			Fiddles, Flute, Pipes, Whistle, Box
		Figure X	Whistles, Flute, Pipes
Merry Harriers	AB		Flute
	A		Flute, Fiddle
	B		Flute, 2 Fiddles, Whistle
	AB		Whole Band
		Figure XY	Whole Band
		Figure XY	Whole Band
		Scales	Whole Band, Box Chord D
		A Trill	Whole Band
Fiach an Mhadra Ruaidh	AA		Chanter, Fiddle, chords (Box D, Fiddle G)

AA		Flute, Whistle, Chanter, Fiddle, Chords Box A, B
AA		Flute, Whistle, Chanter, Chords Box A, B
Horn Effect		Pipes, Whistle, Flute
end on Bark		Pipes
Mount Phoebus A		Whole Band
Verse 1	Seán Ó Sé	Harps, Fiddles in at 2nd half
Mount Phoebus B		Whole Band
Verse 2	Seán Ó Sé	Harps
Mount Phoebus AB		Whole Band
Verse 3	Seán Ó Sé	Harps
Mount Phoebus A		Whole Band
Verse 4	Seán Ó Sé	Harps
Maidrín Rua		Whole Band
Maidrín Rua		Whole Band
Maidrín Rua		Whole Band
	Stop – Ronnie Tally Ho!	
Maidrín Rua		Whole Band

Flannel Jacket / Heather Breeze / Sheehan's

Flannel Jacket	AABB	Whole Band
	AABB	Whole Band
	AABB	Whole Band
Heather Breeze	AABB	Fiddles
Flannel Jacket	AABB	Whole Band
Sheehan's	AA	Flute
Sheehan's	BB	Flute, Whistle, Chant
Flannel Jacket	AABB	Whole Band

Floggin' Reel (2:55)

Version #1

ABC	Whole Band
ABC	Concertina (John)
ABC	Flute
ABC	Flute, Whistle
ABC	Pipes
ABC	Whole Band

	ABC	Whole Band
		End short A
Version # 2		
	ABC	Whole Band
	A	Flute
	B	Whistle
	C	Pipes
	A	Pipes
	BC	Boxes
	ABC	Fiddle
	ABC	2 Whistles, Flute
	ABC	Whole Band

Foggy Dew

Verse 1		Seán Ó Sé	Harps
Verse 2		Seán Ó Sé	Harps, Chanter
Verse 3		Seán Ó Sé	Whole Band

Fox Chase

X = AAGFEDECA
Y = AAGFEDEFD

Intro		X + Y + Chords (Drone Chord D)
		X + Y + Chords
		Fiddle + Chord
Chorus		Whole Band
Chorus		Whole Band
Chorus		Whole Band
Chorus		Whole Band
	X+Y+ X+Y + Chords	Fiddle Flute, Chanter + Chords
Chorus x 4		Whole Band
	X+Y + X+Y + Chords	
		Box + Chords
Chorus x 4		Whole Band
	X + Chords	
Merry Harriers	AB	Flute (slowly)
	A	Flute, Fiddle
	B	Flute, 2 Fiddles, Whistle
	AB	Whole Band – Abrupt Stop
	X + Y + X + Y	

D Scale x 5		Fiddle, Pipes, Flute, Whistle. Finish with Trill on A
Maidrín Rua	AA	Pipes + Pipp
	AA	Flute and Whistle + Pipp
	AA	Flute, Whistle, Chanter and Chords
'Horn'	(ADF')	Pipes Whistle, Flute
'Bark'		Pipes
Mount Phoebus Hunt	AA	Flute, Whistle
	BB	Flute, Whistle, Chanter
	AABB	Whole Band
	AA	2 Fiddles
	BB	Whistle, Flute
	AB	Whole Band
	8 Bars	Bodhrán and Bones altering rhythm into Jig Time
Langstrom's Pony	A	Chanter (1st phrase)
	A	2 Fiddles (2nd Phrase answering)
	A	Chanter (3rd Phrase)
	A	2 Fiddles (4th Phrase)
	A	Whole Band
	B	Chanter (1st phrase)
	B	2 Fiddles (2nd Phrase answering)
	B	Chanter (3rd Phrase)
	B	2 Fiddles (4th Phrase)
	B	Whole Band
	AABB	3 Whistles + Box Chord
	CCDD	Box – Whistles Chord (C, C, C, B C, C, C)
	A	Fiddle + Box Chord
	A	Whole Band + Box Chord
	B	Fiddle + Box Chord
	B	Whole Band + Box Chord
	CCDD	Whole Band + Whistles Chord
	8 Bars	Bodhrán and Bones altering rhythm into Reel Time
Boyne Hunt	AB	Whistle Flute and Chanter with 'Yips'

	AB	Whistle Flute, Chanter + Fiddle with 'Yaps'
	AB	Whole Band + Chanter Yips and Fiddle Yaps
	AB	Flute
	Solo Fiddle	Fiddle (Martin)
Boyne Hunt	AB	Flute
	Solo Fiddle	Fiddle (John)
Boyne Hunt	AB	Whistle, Flute
Maidrín Rua		Pipes solo
	Box Solo	Box (Sonny solo in Bb)
Boyne Hunt	AB	3 Whistles (C Whistles) in F
	AB	Fiddles, Boxes
Maidrín Rua in A		Whole Band chanter and flute
	Figure x 8 times + D Scales	Fiddle
	Scales	Fiddles, Flute, etc.
	Horn Motif (ADF')	Fiddle, Flute, Whistle
	Horn Motif	Whole Band x 3
	Long note G	Whole Band
Lament		Harps
		Harps, Pipes + Box Chords
		Pipes, Fiddles + Box Chords
		Whole Band
Foxhunter's Jig	AB	Whole Band (in D)
	AB	Fiddles
	AB	Whole Band
	AB	Chanter
	AB	Whole Band
	AB	Chanter, + Figure on Whistle, Flute
	AB	Fiddles + Figure on Chanter, Whistle, Flute
	AB	Boxes, Fiddles + Figure on Chanter, Whistle, Flute
	AB	Chanter in G
	AB	Whistle, Flute, in G, Chanter (in 3rds)

	AB	Whole Band in G
	AB	3 Whistles in G
	AB	Whole Band in D + Whistles with jig
	AB	Whole Band in D + Whistles with jig
	AB	Whole Band in D + Whistles with jig
	X+Y+ X+Y	
		Finish Chord of D (F on Flute)

Foxhunter's Jig (+Hunting the Hare)

Foxhunter's	AABB	Whole Band
	AABB	Whole Band
	AABB	Pipes, Flute, Whistle, Box Drone D
	AABB	Pipes, Flute, Whistle, Box Drone D
Hunting the Hare	AABB	Pipes, Flute, Whistle, Box Drone D
	AABB	Whole Band
	AABB	Whole Band
	AABB	Whole Band
Foxhunter's (in G)	AABB	Pipes, Flute, Whistle,
Hunting the Hare D	AABB	Pipes, Flute, Whistle, while Fiddles, Box, Foxhunters jig in D
	AABB	Pipes, Flute, Whistle, while Fiddles, Box – jig in D
Foxhunters		
	AABB	Pipes, Flute, Whistle, while Fiddles Foxhunters jig in D
		Tutti end long Chord D Major

Frank Roche's Favourite

Intro		Harps
	AB	Whole Band
	AB	Harps
	AB	3 Whistles
	AB	Fiddles
	AB	Chanter
	AB	Fiddle (John), Box
	ABA	Whole Band

Frieze Breeches

A	Chanter
A	Whole Band
B	Chanter
B	Whole Band
C	Chanter
C	Whole Band
D	Chanter
D	Whole Band
E	Chanter
E	Whole Band
A	Box
A	Fiddles
B	Flute, Whistles
B	2 Fiddles
CC	Boxes
DD	2 Fiddles
EE	Boxes
A	3 Whistles
A	Whole Band
BB	Boxes
C	3 Whistles
C	Whole Band
DD	2 Fiddles
EE	Whole Band

Frost is All Over

AABB	Pipes Drones, Whistle, Flute
AABB	Whole Band
AA	Whole Band Singing
BB	Whole Band
A	Fiddles
A	Pipes
B	Fiddles
B	Pipes
AABB	Whole Band

> *What would I do if I married a soldier*
> *What would I do only carry his gun*
> *What would I do if the kettle boiled over*
> *What would I do only fill it again.*
> *The Praties are dug and the frost is all over*
> *Molly O Hara curl your wig*
> *The cows are in milk and the geese are in clover*
> *Now is the time to fatten the pig.*

Fuaireasa Cuireadh chun dul ar an bPósadh

	AB	Whole Band
Song		
Hocksty		Whole Band
Song		
Hocksty		Whole Band
		Hocksty, Hickety, Hickety um
		Hocksty Hodee, Mickey um

Fylemore, You're the Place

	Verse 1	Seán Ó Sé	Box Chords
	Chorus		Whole Band singing & playing
		ABA	Whole Band
	Verse 2	Seán Ó Sé	Box Chords
	Chorus		Whole Band singing & playing
Maidirín Rua (Scoil Bharr d'Ínse tune)			
		ABAB	Whole Band in A
Fylemore			
	Verse 3	Seán Ó Sé	Box Chords
	Chorus		Whole Band singing & playing
Sligo Maid		AABB	Whole Band
	Verse 4	Seán Ó Sé	Box Chords
	Chorus		Whole Band singing & playing
I'll Tell me Ma (Ronnie singing)			
		AB	Whole Band playing Ronnie Singing
	Verse 5	Seán Ó Sé	Box Chords
	Chorus		Whole Band singing & playing
	Verse 6	Seán Ó Sé	Box Chords/Whole Band playing
	Chorus		Whole Band singing & playing

Box Chords: A A A E   A A D E

                              A A A A D D D E
                              A A A E
                              A A E A

Galbally Farmer (Rakes of Kildare)
Intro   Fiddle
Line 1   Fiddle
Line 2   2 Fiddles
Line 3   2 Fiddles, Flute
Line 4   Fiddles, Flute, Whistles
              AA   Chanter played as slow air
              B1   Whistle, Flute
              B2   Chanter
              B1   Whistle, Flute
              B2   Chanter
              AABB   Whistle, Flute, Chanter (improv.)
                                         count 4 beats
Jig   AABB   Whole Band (in Amin)
              AABB   Box (Sonny)
              AABB   Fiddle (John)
              AABB   Whole Band (D)
                                         Chords (D chord)
              Box Chords: D A GEGC A C in D maj.

Galway Races (D)
       Verse 1   Seán Ó Sé   Whole Band
Traveller (G)   AA   Whole Band
       Verse 2   Seán Ó Sé   Whole Band
Traveller   BB   Whole Band
       Verse 3   Seán Ó Sé   Whole Band
Boys of Fair Hill (D)   Whole Band
       Verse 4   Seán Ó Sé   Whole Band
Galway races   Ronnie Commentary (Stall Woman) Whole Band
       Verse 5   Seán Ó Sé   Whole Band
Galway races   Ronnie Commentary (Bookie)   Whole Band
       Verse 6   Seán Ó Sé   Whole Band
Traveller   AA Ronnie Commentary (Describing Horses) Whole Band

	Verse 7	Seán Ó Sé	Whole Band
Traveller	BB	Ronnie	(Increasing tempo as Ronnie gives race commentary) Whole Band
	Verse 8	Seán Ó Sé	Whole Band ending slowly

An Gamhnaichín

Verse 1	Seán Ó Sé	Box Drone G
Verse 2	Seán Ó Sé	Harps, Box Drone G
Verse 3	Seán Ó Sé	Harps, 2 Fiddles (Octaves) Box Drone G
Verse 4	Seán Ó Sé	Harps, 2 Fiddles (Octaves) Flute, Box Drone
Verse 5	Seán Ó Sé	Harps, 2 Fiddles, Flute, Chanter Box Drone
Verse 6	Seán Ó Sé	Whole Band

Stop for last few words ('Ní fíor pioc ó Sheán)

Box Chords: G C G C G
G C G C
G C D Emin
C D Emin C D-G

Gander in the Pratie Hole

Version # 1

AABB	2 Fiddles (Fiddle plucked)
AABB	Whole Band
AABB	Whistle, Flute
A	2 Whistles, Flute
A	2 Accordions
B	2 Whistles, Flute or AABB
B	2 Accordions
AABB	Whole Band
AABB	Whole Band (omitted – Aileliu prog.)

Version # 2

AABB	Flute
AABB	Whole Band
A	Fiddles
A	Box
B	Fiddles
B	Box
AABB	Whole Band

AABB	Whistle, Flute, Chanter
AABB	Whole Band
AA	John Kelly, Martin plucking
BB	Sonny, Éamon with Paddy plucking
AABB	Whole Band

An Gaoth Aneas

Intro Chord		Box Chord G - - -
		Whistle B - - -
(Flutter Tongue)		Flute D - - -
(Flutter Tongue)		
	AB	Flute, Box Chords
	AB	Harps, 2 Fiddles, & Martin (Octaves)
		Box Chords
	AB	Harps, Chanter, Whistle, Box Chords
	A	Harps
	B	Whole Band, Box Chords

Box Chords: G G C D, G D G G
　　　　　　　G G C D, G D G G,
　　　　　　　G C G D, Emin G D (f#a) D (d f#a)
　　　　　　　G C G D, Emin C, D C G

Gardaí an Rí

	Intro		Harps
	Verse 1	Seán Ó Sé	Whole Band, Bodhrán
Frank Roche's	A		Whole Band, Bodhrán
	Verse 2	Seán Ó Sé	Whole Band, Bodhrán
Frank Roche's	BA		Whole Band, Bodhrán
	Verse 3	Seán Ó Sé	Whole Band, Bodhrán
	– Repeat Chorus		

Garden of Daisies

Version # 1

Intro drone		Box Chord D, Whistles A, F#, D
A		Fiddles & intro Drone
A		Whole Band
B		Fiddle & Drone

	B	Whole Band
	Pause	
	Drone	Box Chord D, Fiddle D chord
	A	3 Whistles, Drone
	A	Whole Band
	B	3 Whistles, Drone
	B	Whole Band Box Chord D last 8 bars)
Version # 2		
	AABB	Harps
	AABB	Harps, 3 Whistles
	AABB	Harps, Whistles, 2 Fiddles
	AB	Whole Band
	A	Pipes
	A	Flute
	BB	2 Whistles, Flute
	A (second A)	Harps, D Chord Whistles A&F, Flute D

Garrett Barry's Favourite/Sergeant's Jig

GB	AABB	Pipes
GB	AABB	Whole Band
SE	AABB	Box (Sergeant Early)
GB	AABB	Fiddle, Whistle
GB	AA	Flute
GB	BB	Chanter
GB	AABB	Whole Band
GB	AA	Harps
GB	BB	Pipes

Gather around the Fireplace (+Colliers) (Reels)

Fireplace	AB	Whole Band
Colliers	AB	Fiddle
Fireplace	AB	Whole Band
Colliers	AB	Flute
Fireplace	AB	Whole Band
Colliers	AB	Pipes
Fireplace	AB	Whole Band

Colliers	AB	Harps
Fireplace	ABAB	Whole Band

Gather around the Fireplace/Money from America/Butcher's March (jigs)

Gather ...	ABAB	Whole Band
Money ...	ABAB	Whole Band
Butcher's ...	ABAB	Whole Band
Gather ...	AB	Whole Band
Money ...	AB	Whole Band
Butcher's ...	AB	Whole Band

Geaftaí Bhaile Bhuí

Verse 1	Seán Ó Sé	Harps
Verse 2	Seán Ó Sé	Harps, Fiddles + Flute, Whistle (in on B)
Verse 3	Seán O Sé	Whole Band

George Brabazon

AABB	Harps
AABB	3 Whistles
AABB	3 Fiddles
AABB	Whistle, Flute, Chanter
AABB	Harps, Fiddles, Chanter
AABB	Whole Band
AABB	Whole Band

End on G chord: D on flute, B on chanter, G' Whistle

An Ghaoth Aniar Aneas

Version # 1

AABB	Fiddle
AABB	Fiddle, Flute
AABB	Fiddle, Flute, Whistle
AABB	Box
AABB	Whole Band
AABB	Chanter, Fiddle (Martin), Whistle
AABB	Fiddle, Flute, Box
AABB	Whole Band

Version # 2

A	Harps
A	Harps 3 Fiddles
B	Harps
B	Harps, 3 Fiddles (Martin Octaves)
AABB	Accordion
AABB	Whistles, Flute Fiddles (Martin Octaves)
AABB	Chanter, 2 Fiddles (John, Seán)
AABB	Whole Band

Gile mo Chroí

Version # 1 Gaiety

Chorus	Harps
Chorus	Whole Band – no chords

Version # 2 Gaiety

	Whole Band after Box Chord intro D
Box Chords:	D G A D
	A D

Gleann Cam

Intro		Harps
Verse 1	Seán Ó Sé	Harps
Verse 2	Seán Ó Sé	Harps, Chanter
Verse 3	Seán Ó Sé	Whole Band
Verse 4	Seán Ó Sé	Harps
Verse 5	Seán Ó Sé	Harps, Chanter
Verse 6	Seán Ó Sé	Whole Band

GlenLea

Intro		Harps
Verse 1	Seán Ó Sé	Harps
Verse 2	Seán Ó Sé	Whole Band
Verse 3	Seán Ó Sé	Fiddles (1st half of Verse)
		Whole Band (2nd half of Verse)

An Goirtín Eornan

Version # 1

Verse 1	Seán Ó Sé	Harps

Verse 2	Seán Ó Sé	Harps, 3 Fiddles
Verse 3	Seán Ó Sé	Whole Band

Version # 2 (for Reacaireacht)

Verse 1	Seán Ó Sé	Harps
Verse 2	Seán Ó Sé	Harps, Pipes
Verse 3	Seán Ó Sé	Whole Band

Version # 3

Verse 1	Seán Ó Sé	Harps
Verse 2	Seán Ó Sé	Harps
Verse 3	Seán Ó Sé	Harps
Verse 4	Seán Ó Sé	Harps

Gorman's / The Hut in the Bog

Version # 1

Gorman's	AB	Flute
	AABB	Whole Band
	AABB	Whole Band
Hut in the Bog	ABC	Box, Fiddle
	ABC	Whole Band
Gorman's	AA	Harps
	BB	Harps, Whistle, Chanter
	AABB	Whole Band

Version # 2

Gorman's/Callaghan's

Gorman's	AB	Flute	
	AABB	Whole Band	
Callaghan's	AB	Flute	
	ABAB	Whole Band	
	AB	Flute	
Gorman's	AABB	Whole Band	

An Habit Shirt (4/1/1969) (G)

Verse 1		Seán Ó Sé	Harps
High Reel	A		Harps, Chanter finish with held G
Verse 2		Seán Ó Sé	Harps, Chanter
High Reel	A		Harps, Chanter, Fiddles – finish with held G

	Verse 3	Seán Ó Sé	Harps, Chant, Fiddles
High Reel	A		Harps, Chant, Fiddles, Box – finish with held G
	Verse 4	Seán Ó Sé	Harps, Chant, Fiddles, Box
High Reel	A		Whole Band – finish with held G
	Verse 5	Seán Ó Sé	Whole Band

Hewlet

AB		Whole Band
A		Harps, Pipes
B		4 Bars Harps, 4 Bars Fiddles
	Last part B	Whole Band
A		Flute, Whistle
B		Flute, Whistle, Pipes (4 bars) Fiddles (4 Bars)
	Last part B	Flute, Whistle, Fiddles
AB		Whole Band

Hide an Go Seek

Verse 1	Seán Ó Sé	Harps
Verse 2	Seán Ó Sé	Harps, Flute, Whistles
Verse 3	Seán Ó Sé	Harps, Flute, Whistles, Fiddles
Verse 4	Seán Ó Sé	Harps, Flute, Whistles, Fiddles, Box
Verse 5	Seán Ó Sé	Whole Band

High Caul Cap

AABB	Chanter
AABB	Whole Band
AABB	Whistles, Flute, Fiddle (Octaves)
AABB	3 Fiddles
AABB	Harpsichord
AABB	Whole Band

Humours of Ballyconnell

Version # 1

ABC	Whole Band
ABC	Concertina

	ABC	Flute
	ABC	Whistle, Flute
	ABC	Pipes
	ABC	Whole Band
	ABC	Whole Band
Version # 2		
	ABC	Flute, Bodhrán
	ABC	Flute, Whistle, Bodhrán
	ABC	Fiddles
	ABC	Chanter
	ABC	Whole Band
ABC		Whole Band

Humours of Carrigaholt (John Kelly's Reel) / Judy Delaney

Humours	AB	Flute
	AB	Flute
	AB	Fiddle (John K)
	AB	Fiddle
Judy Delaney	AB	Flute
	AB	Flute
		Fiddle (John K)
	AB	Fiddle
Humours	AB	Flute
	AB	Flute
	AB	Fiddle (John K)
	AB	Fiddle

Humours of Ennistymon (3:50)

A	Whistle, Flute
A	Whole Band
B	Fiddles
B	Whole Band
C	Chanter, Box
C	Whole Band
AABBCC	Whole Band
AABBCC	3 Whistles (F, A and D)
A	Fiddles

A	Boxes
B	Fiddles
B	Boxes
C	Fiddles
C	Boxes
AABBCC	Whole Band

Otherwise called Coppers & Brass by Sonny and Felix Doran (3rd part attributed to M. Coleman)

Im' Aonar Seal

Verse 1	Seán Ó Sé	Harps
Verse 2	Seán Ó Sé	Harps, Fiddle, Flute
Verse 3	Seán Ó Sé	Whole Band

Iníon an Fhaoit ón nGleann

Verse 1	Seán Ó Sé	Harps
Verse 2	Seán Ó Sé	Harps, Pipes
Verse 3	Seán Ó Sé	Harps, Flute, Fiddles
Verse 4	Seán Ó Sé	Whole Band

Iníon an Phailitínigh

Intro (Garden of Daisies) A		Harps (Set Dance rhythm)
Verse 1 AAB	Seán Ó Sé	Harps (Garden of Daisies)
link (3 thrums)		Harps
Verse 2 AAB	Seán Ó Sé	Harps, 3 Whistles (up to tempo)
Verse 3 AAB	Seán Ó Sé	Whole Band

Irish Molly

AABB	Pipes
AABB	Whole Band
AABB	Box
AABB	Whole Band
AABB	Flute
AABB	Whole Band
AABB	Whole Band

Irish Rag, The Rose Tree in full bloom, The Leg of the Duck

| Irish Rag | AABB | Whole Band |
| Irish Rag | AABB | Whole Band |

Rose Tree	AABB	Whole Band
Rose Tree	AABB	Whole Band
Leg of the Duck	AABB	Whole Band
Leg of the Duck	AABB	Whole Band
Irish Rag	AABB	Whole Band
Rose Tree	AABB	Whole Band
Leg of the Duck	AABB	Whole Band
Irish Rag	AABB	Whole Band
Rose Tree	AABB	Whole Band
Leg of the Duck	AABB	Whole Band

Irish Washerwoman (8:10)

(A demonstration on relationship with various versions and their sound and evolution)
(Intro speech – S. Ó R. On relationship with Bach)

Bach Version	AABB	Harpsichord
Explanatory speech – S.Ó R.		
Céilí version	AABB	Whole Band
Explanatory speech – S. Ó R.		
Fr Mathew Hall version	AABB	Fiddle (Martin Fay)
Explanatory speech – S. Ó R.		
Reel version	AABB	Pipes
	AABB	Whole Band
'Alleliu tá an Poc an Buille'		Ronnie singing
Funeral March Version in Emin.	AB	3 Whistles
Explanatory speech – S. Ó R.		
Jazz version	AABB	Whistles, Fiddle, Flute
		Finish on chord F
Explanatory speech – S. Ó R.		
Irish W.W. Played in Jig time	AABB	Whole Band
	AABB	Whole Band

Is Trua gan Gáirdín Úll agam

Verse 1	Seán Ó Sé	Harps
Chorus	Seán Ó Sé	Whole Band
Polca 1	AB	Whole Band
Verse 2	Seán Ó Sé	Whole Band

Chorus	Seán Ó Sé	Whole Band	
Polca 2	AB	Whole Band	
Verse 3	Seán Ó Sé	Harps	
Chorus	Seán Ó Sé	Whole Band	
Polca 1	AB	Whole Band	
Verse 4	Seán Ó Sé	Whole Band	
Chorus	Seán Ó Sé	Whole Band	
Polca 2	AB	Whole Band	
Verse 5	Seán Ó Sé	Whole Band	
Chorus	Seán Ó Sé	Whole Band	
Chorus	Seán Ó Sé	Whole Band	

(As near as I can decipher it POR)

Ivy Leaf

B	Fiddle
AB	3 Fiddles
AB	3 Fiddles, Flute
AB	3 Fiddles, Flute, Whistle
AB	3 Fiddles, Flute, Whistle, Chanter
ABAB	Whole Band
A	Harps (8 Bars)
ABAB	Whole Band

Jackson's Grove Hornpipe

AABBCCDDEE	Pipes
AABB	Whole Band
AA	Flute, Whistle
BB	Fiddles
AABB	Harps
AABBCCDDEE	Whole Band

Jackson's Morning Brush

Intro	Pipes (cock-crow 3 times)
AA	Whistle, Flute
BB	Whistle, Flute, Chanter
AABB	Whole Band
AA	3 Whistles

CC	Fiddle
BB	3 Whistles
DD	Fiddle
AA	3 Whistles
CC	Box
BB	3 Whistles
DD	Box
AABB	Whole Band

Jazz

AABB	Whole Band
AABB	Whole Band

Jenny Picking Cockles

AABB	Flute
AABB	Whole Band
AABB	Whistle
AABB	Whole Band

Jenny's welcome to Charlie AABB — 2 Fiddles

AABB	Whole Band
AABB	Chanter
AABB	Whole Band

Jenny's Wedding (4:35)

AABB	Whole Band
AABB	Box (Sonny)

Whole Band play 1st note in each Bar

AABB	Box (Sonny)

Whole Band play same notes twice as fast

AABB	Box (Sonny)

Whole Band play same notes twice as fast again

Series twice	Whole Band
repeated series twice	Chanter
Breakdown of series x 4 times	Whole Band DDFD, etc.
Piece on fiddle	Martin
AACA CCEC EEGE A	Whole Band
ditto	Whistles in 3rds
DDFD AACA CCEC	Whole Band

	DDFD AACA CCEC	Whole Band ending in trill
	AB	Fiddle (John Kelly)
	AABB	Whole Band
Series:	DACE DCFB	
	DACE DCFB	
	D'ED'CD' C A D'	
	D'ED'CD' C A D'	

Jig Set in A (For Reacaireacht)
(3 tunes – Chase me Charlie – Walshe's Hornpipe – Limerick Lasses)

Chase me Charlie	AA	Fiddle (Seán)
	AA	3 Fiddles
Walshe's	AB	Fiddle (Seán)
	AB	3 Fiddles
Limerick Lasses	AB	Fiddle (Seán)
	AB	3 Fiddles
Chase me Charlie	AA	Fiddle (Seán)
	AA	Whole Band
Walshe's	B	Fiddle (Seán)
	AB	Whole Band
Limerick Lasses	AB	Fiddle (Seán)
	AB	Whole Band
Chase me Charlie	AA	Whole Band

Jig Set in A (For Fleadh Cheoil 1968–1969)

Peeler and the Goat	AB	Harps, Fiddles, Drones – G&D – strings
Chase me Charlie	AA	Fiddle (Seán)
	AA	3 Fiddles
Walshe's	AB	Fiddle (Seán)
	AB	3 Fiddles
Peeler and the Goat	AB	Harps, Fiddles, Drones – G&D – strings
Chase me Charlie	AA	Fiddle (Seán)
	AA	Whole Band
Walshe's	AB	Fiddle (Seán)
	AB	Whole Band

Peeler and the Goat	AB	Harps, Fiddles, Drones – G&D – strings

Job of Journey Work
Version # 1

	AABB	Harps
	AA	Fiddles
	B	Flute
	B	Flute, Whistle
	A	Pipes
	A	Whole Band
	B	Pipes
	B	Whole Band

Version # 2

Intro		Harps
	A	Chanter
	A	Whole Band
	B	Chanter
	B	Whole Band
	AA	Fiddle
	B	Flute
	B	Flute, Whistle
	A	Chanter
	A	Whole Band
	B	Chanter
	B	Whole Band
Ending		Harps

Version # 3 (4.20)
As Version # 2 without Harps intro and ending

Kerry Harriers/The Golden Folk

	AB	Flute
	AB	Flute, Whistle
	AB	Flute, Whistle, Fiddle
	AB	3 Fiddles
	AB	Chanter

	ABAB	Chanter, Box
The Golden Folk	ABABABAB	Canter, Box
	pause	
Kerry Harriers	AB	Whole Band

Kerry Hornpipe (3:15)
Version # 1

	A	Fiddle
	A	2 Fiddles, Viola
	BB	Whistles, Flute, Fiddles
	AABB	Whole Band
	AA	Boxes
	BB	3 Whistle
	AA	Whistles, Flute, Fiddles
	B	2 Fiddles, Viola
	B	Fiddle

Version # 2 (8 Minutes)

	A		Fiddle
	A		2 Fiddles
	B		2 Fiddles, 2 Whistles, Flute
	B		2 Fiddles, 2 Whistles, Flute, Boxes
	AA		Whole Band
	B		2 Fiddles, 2 Whistles, Flute
	B (1st half)		2 Fiddles
	B (2nd half)		1 Fiddle
Bhíosa Lá i bPort Láirge (G)	8 bars		Bodhrán
	A		Whole Band (G)
	A	Darach	Box, Whistle, Flute, Fiddle
	B		Whole Band (G)
	B	Darach	Box, Whistle, Flute, Fiddle
	A		Whole Band (G)
	A	Darach	Box, Whistle, Flute, Fiddle
	B		Whole Band (G)
	B	Darach	Box, Whistle, Flute, Fiddle
	A		Whole Band (G)
	A	Darach	Box, Whistle, Flute, Fiddle

	B		Whole Band (G)
	B	Darach	Box, Whistle, Flute, Fiddle
Irish Jaunting Car			
	A		Whole Band
	A		Whistles, Flute
	B		Whole Band
	B		Whistles, Flute
	A		Box
	A		Whole Band
	B		Pipes
	B		Whole Band
Bhíosa Lá i bPort Láirge (G)	8 bars		Bodhrán
	A		Whole Band (G)
	A	Darach	Box, Whistle, Flute, Fiddle
	B		Whole Band (G)
	B	Darach	Box, Whistle, Flute, Fiddle
	A		Whole Band (G)
	A	Darach	Box, Whistle, Flute, Fiddle
	B		Whole Band (G)
	B	Darach	Box, Whistle, Flute, Fiddle

Kid on the Mountain

ABCDE		Whole Band
ABCDE		Fiddle
ABCDE		Flute, Whistle, Pipes
ABCDE		Whole Band

Kitty come down (The Gimble)

AB	Chanter
AB	Fiddle (John)
AB	Whole Band
AB	Harps
AB	Whistle, Flute
AB	Whole Band ending on long G

F# always except in solos

Lady on the Island
Version # 1

AB	Fiddle (Seán Keane)
AB	Whole Band
AB	3 Fiddles
AB	Whole Band
Wind that shakes the Barley AB	John Kelly
AB	John Kelly
AB	Flute, Whistle, Pipes
Lady on the Island AB	Whole Band
AB	Whole Band

A Lady Stood (in her father's garden)

Intro		Harps
Verse 1	Seán Ó Sé	Harps
Verse 2	Seán Ó Sé	Harps, Box Chords
Verse 3	Seán Ó Sé	Harps, Box Chords, Flute, Whistle, Fiddles
Verse 4	Seán Ó Sé	Whole Band

Langstrom's Pony
Version # 1

AABBCCDD	Fiddle
AABBCCDD	Whole Band
AA	Flute
BB	Flute, Whistles
CC	Flute, Whistles, Fiddles
DD	Flute, Whistles, Fiddles Pipes
AABBCCDD	Whole Band

Version # 2

A	Chanter 1/2, Fiddle 1/2
A	Whole Band
B	Chanter 1/2, Fiddle 1/2
B	Whole Band
AABB	3 Whistles, Box (Drone A maj.)
CCDD	Sonny, Whistles, Box Drones
A	Fiddle, Box Drone

	A	Whole Band, Box Drone
	B	Fiddle, Box Drone
	B	Whole Band, Box Drone
	CCDD	Whole Band, Whistles, Box Drone
Version # 3		
	A	Fiddle
	A	Whole Band
	B	Fiddle
	B	Whole Band
	C	Fiddle
	C	Whole Band
	D	Fiddle
	D	Whole Band
	AA	Flute
	BB	Flute, Whistles
	CC	Flute, Whistles, Fiddles
	DD	Flute, Whistles, Fiddles, Pipes
	AABBCCDD	Whole Band

Leather away the Wattle O

Intro	ABCD	Whistle and Flute	
Anything for John Joe	AB	Whole Band	
Verse 1	A	Seán Ó Síocháin	
	A	Whole Band	
	B	Seán Ó Síocháin	
	B	Whole Band	
Anything	AB	Whole Band	
Verse 2	A	Seán Ó Síocháin	
	A	Whole Band	
	B	Seán Ó Síocháin	
	B	Whole Band	
Anything	AB	Whole Band	
Verse 3	A	Seán Ó Síocháin	
	A	Whole Band	
	B	Seán Ó Síocháin	
	B	Whole Band	
Anything	AB	Whole Band	
Verse 4	A	Seán Ó Síocháin	

		A		Whole Band
		B	Seán Ó Síocháin	
		B		Whole Band
	Verse	ABB		Whole Band

Leg of the Duck

Leg of the Duck	AABB	Whole Band
	AABB	Whistle
	AABB	Whole Band
Mist on the Meadow	AABB	Flute
	AABB	Whole Band
	AABB	Chanter
	AABB	Whole Band
	AABB	Harps
	with band playing last line	

Leitrim Fancy

Version # 1	AABB	Harps
	AABB	Harps, Chanter
	AABB	Harps, Fiddles
	AABB	Harps, Flute, Whistle
	AABB	Whole Band

The Light of the Moon (melody like The Curragh of Kildare)

Verse 1	Seán Ó Sé	Harps
Verse 2	Seán Ó Sé	Harps, Fiddle 8 Octaves (Martin)
Verse 3	Seán Ó Sé	Harps, 3 Fiddles
Verse 4	Seán Ó Sé	Harps, 3 Fiddles, 3 Whistles, Box

The Little Beggarman (4:06) (alias 'Riggadoon' or 'Red-Haired Boy')

Version # 1

	AABB	Whistle Flute (in G)
	AABB	Chanter (A)
	AA	Fiddles in Octaves (D)
	BB	Fiddle and Pizz, Fiddle
	AA	Accordion Éamon (G)
	BB	Accordion Sonny (A)
	AABB	Whole Band (D)
	AABB	Whole Band (G)
	End on note of B, G	

Version # 2 (Alleliu # 5)

A	Fiddles
A	Whole Band
B	Fiddle
B	Whole Band
AABB	Whole Band
AABB	Harps
A	Chanter
A	Flute, Whistle
B	Chanter
B	Flute, Whistle
AABB	Whole Band

An Lon is an Chéirseach

Intro		Harps
Verse 1	Seán Ó Sé	Harps
Verse 2	Seán Ó Sé	Harps, Flute, Whistle, Fiddle
Verse 3	Seán Ó Sé	Whole Band

The Longford Collector

Version # 1

AA	Fiddle
BB	Box, Fiddle
AA	3 Whistles
BB	3 Whistles
AA	Pipes, Fiddles (chords E, B, G,)
BB	Flute, Whistle, Fiddles (chords E, B, G,)
AABB	Whole Band
AABB	Whole Band ending with long G

Version # 2

AABB	Whole Band
AABB	Fiddles
AABB	Flute, Whistle, Bodhrán
AABB	Pipes
AABB	Whole Band
AABB	Whole Band ending with long G

Lord Inchiquin

A	Harps
A	Whole Band
B	Harps
B	Whole Band
A	Chanter
A	Whole Band
B	Chanter
B	Whole Band
AABB	Whole Band
A	Fiddles
A	Whistle, Flute, Chanter
BB	Whole Band

Madame Bonaparte (set dance – for Ailiiú (tv series) 6:30

A	Pipes, Fiddle Chord
A	Whistle, Flute, Box Chord
B	Pipes, Fiddle Chord
B	Whistle, Flute, Box Chord
AABB	Whole Band
AA	2 Fiddles
BB	3 Whistles
A	Harps
A	Fiddle, Flute, Whistle
B	Harps
B	Fiddle, Flute, Whistle
AABB	Whole Band

Maguire's March

AAB	Harps
AAB	3 Fiddles
AAB	Chanter
AAB	3 Whistles
AAB	Whole Band

Mahony's Frolics (3:30) (Also Cat in the Corner)

AABB	Harps & Fiddle
AABB	Harps & Fiddle, Flute
AABB	Harps & Fiddle, Flute, Whistle

AABB		Harps & Fiddle, Flute, Whistle, Chanter
AABB		Whole Band
AABB		Whole Band + Box Chords End on long Note

Máible Ní Cheallaigh

A		Harps
B		Harps, 3 Fiddles
A	Seán Ó Sé	Harps, 3 Fiddles
B		Whole Band
A	Seán Ó Sé	Harps, Flute, 2 Whistles
B		Whole Band

Maid of the Sweet Brown Knowe

Intro		Harps
Verse 1	Seán Ó Sé	Harps, 3 Fiddles (Octaves)
Verse 2	Seán Ó Sé	Harps, 3 Fiddles (Octaves)
Verse 3	Seán Ó Sé	Harps, 3 Fiddles (Octaves), Flute, 2 Whistles
Verse 4	Seán Ó Sé	Harps, 3 Fiddles (Octaves), Flute, 2 Whistles
Verse 5	Seán Ó Sé	Whole Band
Verse 6	Seán Ó Sé	Whole Band

Repeat last Verse without any break

Maid at the Spinning Wheel

AA BB CC DD	Whole Band
AA	Fiddles
BB	Chanter
CC	Fiddles
DD	Chanter
AA	Flute & Whistle
BB	Box
CCDD	Whole Band

Maidin Áluinn Ghréinne (Crúiscín Lán)

Verse 1	Seán Ó Sé	Harps
Verse 2	Seán Ó Sé	Harps, Fiddle
Verse 3	Seán Ó Sé	Harps, Fiddle, 2 Whistles, Flute in harmony
Verse 4	Seán Ó Sé	Whistle, Flute, Pipes, Box Chords
Verse 5	Seán Ó Sé	Whole Band, Box Chords

Box Chords: G D G Emin C D
C D Emin D G
C D Emin G C D
C D Emin G C A, D
G C G C G

Maidrín Ruadh

Version # 1

Intro, Mount Phoebus' Hunt	A	Whole Band
Maidrín Rua Verse 1	Seán O Sé	Solo

Fiddles in on second half of Verse

Mount Phoebus	B	Whole Band
Maidrín Rua Verse 1	Seán O Sé	Harps.
Chorus		Whole Band
Mount Phoebus	AB	Whole Band
Maidrín Rua Verse 3	Seán O Sé	Harps
Maidrín Rua	ABAB	Whole Band
Maidrín Rua Verse 4	Seán O Sé	Whole Band
Maidrín Rua	ABAB	Whole Band
		Ronnie 'Tally Ho'

Version #2 (Alleliú)

Intro, Boyne Hunt (G)	A		Whole Band
Maidrín Rua	Verse 1	Seán O Sé	Harps.
	Chorus	Seán Ó Sé	Whole Band
	Verse 2	Seán Ó Sé	Harps
	Chorus	Seán Ó Sé	Whole Band
Boyne Hunt		AA	Whole Band
Maidrín Rua	Verse 3	Seán O Sé	Harps
	Chorus	Seán Ó Sé	Whole Band
	Chorus	Seán Ó Sé	Whole Band
	Verse 4	Seán O Sé	Whole Band, Ronnie shouts 'TallyHo'

	Chorus	Seán Ó Sé	Whole Band
	Chorus	Seán Ó Sé	Whole Band

Verse 3 and 4 progressively longer

Máire Bheag na Gruaige Báine (Cois na na Bríghde Thiar)

	Verse 1	Seán Ó Sé	Harps
	Verse 2	Seán Ó Sé	Harps, 2 Whistles, Flute in G
	Verse 3	Seán Ó Sé	Whole Band in G

Máire (Mairead) de Róiste

	Verse 1	Seán Ó Sé	Harps
	Verse 2	Seán Ó Sé	Harps, Fiddles
	Verse 3	Seán Ó Sé	Whole Band

Máire Ní Chuilleanáin (A Maj.) Version of Bhíosa Lá 'bPort Láirge)

	Verse 1	Seán Ó Sé	Harps
	Verse 2	Seán Ó Sé	Harps, Bodhrán
	Verse 3	Seán Ó Sé	Harps, Fiddles, Bodhrán
	Verse 4	Seán Ó Sé	Whole Band

Marbhna Eoghain Uí Néill

	An Bhéarsa		Harps, Whistle
	An Bhéarsa		Harps
			Harps, 2 Whistles, Fiddles in on 2nd half
	An Bhéarsa		Whole Band

Marbhna Luimní

Version # 1

		AAB	Whistle, Fiddle (Chords G D,)
		AA	Harps
		B	Harps, Chanter
		AAB	Whole Band (Bass coupler on Box)

Version # 2 (LP Battle of Aughrim)

			Roll on Bones
			2 claps on Bodhrán
			Drones (D)
		A	Chanter, Fiddle Octave (Martin), Drones
		A	Chanter, Fiddle Octave, 2 Fiddles, Flute, Drones
		B	Harps, Drones
		AABB	Whole Band

Version # 3

			Drones (D)

A	Chanter, Fiddle Octave (Martin), Drones
A	Chanter, Fiddle Octave, 2 Fiddles, Flute, Drones
B	Harps, Drones
AABB	Whole Band

Marc Shlua Uí Néill
Version # 1

	AABB	Flute, Bodhrán
	AABB	Flute, Bodhrán, 2 Whistles
	AABB 3	Fiddles
	AABB	3 Fiddles, Box
Polka March	AB	Pipes
	AB	Pipes, Flute, Whistle
Marc Shlua	ABB	Whole Band
	AABB	Whole Band
	AABB	Whole Band

Version #2 (Máirseáil Uí Néill) (LP Battle of Aughrim)

AABB	Flute, Bodhrán
AABB	Whistle, Flute, Bodhrán
AABB	Whistle, Flute, Bodhrán, Chanter
AABB	Whole Band
	End in fade out

An Mhóin (Cleaganna)

Verse 1	Seán Ó Sé	Box (Slow)
Verse		Whole Band (in Tempo)
Verse 2	Seán Ó Sé	Box Chords
Jackson's Morning Brush AA		Whole Band
Verse 3	Seán Ó Sé	Box Chords
Jackson's Morning Brush BB		Whole Band
Verse 4	Seán Ó Sé	Box Chords
		Whole Band (in Tempo)
Verse 5	Seán Ó Sé	Box Chords
Verse 5	Seán Ó Sé	Whole Band
		Whole Band (in Tempo)

Box Chords: A A D D AADD AADG AAAG AADD

Miller's Daughter & Boy in the Gap (reel)

A	Fiddle (Martin Fay)
A	Whole Band
B	Whistle, Flute

	B	Whole Band
	AB	Whole Band
	AB	Whistle Flute, Fiddle DG & AE
	AB	Chanter, Box Chords G
	A	Box
	B	Fiddles (1 with chords DG & AE)
Boy in the Gap	AABB	Whole Band
Miller's Daughter	ABAB	Whole Band

Miners of Wicklow Jig/Reel

	AABB	Flute
	AABB	Flute, Pipes
	AABB	3 Fiddles
	AABB	Whole Band
	AABB	Whistle, Flute, Pipes
	AABB	Whole Band
	AABB	Whole Band

Miss McLeod's & Callaghan's

Intro	Figure – doh re mi fah ssoh f ah mi re (Motif in Tonic Solfa)	
	Figure (a)	Fiddle (Martin)
	Figure (b)	2 Fiddles (Martin, John)
	Figure (c)	2 Fiddles, Box
	Figure (d)	2 Fiddles, Box, Flute
	Figure (e)	2 Fiddles, Box, Flute, Whistle
Miss McLeod's	AABB	Pipes with figs a, b, c, d for 32 bars
	Figure (e)	2 Fiddles, Box, Flute, Whistle
	AABB	Box with (e) in background
	Figure (e)	2 Fiddles, Box, Flute, Whistle
	AABB	Fiddle with (e) in background
	Figure (e)	2 Fiddles, Box, Flute, Whistle
	AABB	Flute with (e) in background
	Figure (e)	2 Fiddles, Box, Flute, Whistle
	AABB	Whole Band
		Accordions alternate chords of G
	AABB	Fiddle, Flute
	AABB	Whistle, Chanter, (b) in the background

		AABB	Accordions
Callaghan's		AB	Flute
		AB	Flute, Fiddle
		AB	Flute, Fiddle, Whistles
Miss McLeod's	AABB		Whole Band and accordion chords

Mná Dé hAoine

Intro Verse and Chorus		Whole Band
Verse 1 Seán Ó Sé		Harps
Polka 1	A	Box Solo (Éamon) polka
	A	Whole Band
	B	Box
	B	Whole Band
Verse 2 Seán Ó Sé		An Bhéarsa
Polka 2	AABB	Whole Band
Verse 3 Seán Ó Sé		Harps
Bonnet trimmed in blue	A	Pipes
	A	Whole Band
	B	Pipes
	B	Whole Band
Verse 4 Seán Ó Sé		Harps
repeat Verse 4 Seán Ó Sé		Whole Band

Mná na hÉireann

Intro (last line)	Harps
Seán Ó Sé	Harps
Seán Ó Sé	Flute, Whistle, Fiddle
Seán Ó Sé	Flute, Whistle, Fiddles, Viola
Seán Ó Sé	Whole Band

Mo Chailín Bán

Verse 1 Seán Ó Sé	Harps
Verse 2 Seán Ó Sé	Box Chords
Verse 3 Seán Ó Sé	Box Chords, Flute, Fiddle
Verse 4 Seán Ó Sé	Whole Band

Box Chords: G D G C G C G

```
                        C D Emin C G A C
                        C D Emin C G A C
                        G D G C G C G
```

Mo Ghille Mear

Verse 1	Seán Ó Sé	Harps
Chorus	Seán Ó Sé	Harps, Whole Band
Verse 2	Seán Ó Sé	Harps
Chorus	Seán Ó Sé	Harps, Whole Band
Spanish Lady	B	Whole Band
Verse 3	Seán Ó Sé	Harps
Chorus	Seán Ó Sé	Harps, Whole Band
Repeat Chorus		Hold Last D

```
           Box Chords:   A A A A E A D E
                         A E A D A A E A
```

Moladh don Athair Máinséal

Version # 1

Verse 1	Seán Ó Sé	Harps
Verse 2	Seán Ó Sé	Harps, Flute, Fiddles
Verse 3	Seán Ó Sé	Whole Band

Version # 2

Verse 1	Seán Ó Sé	Harps
Verse 2	Seán Ó Sé	Harps
(Joining in on second half of Verse)		Harps, Flute, Fiddles
Verse 3	Seán Ó Sé	Harps, Flute, Fiddles
(Joining in on second half of Verse)		Whole Band

Molloy's Jig & Contentment is Wealth

Molloy's Jig	AA	Whistle
	BB	Whistle, Chanter
	AA	Whistle, Chanter, Flute
	BB	Whistle, Chanter, Flute, Fiddles
	AABB	Whole Band
Cont. is wealth	AABB	Chanter
Molloy's Jig	AABB	Whole Band

Molly Bán (in A)

Verse 1	Seán Ó Sé	Harps
Verse 2	Seán Ó Sé	Harps, Fiddles
Verse 3	Seán Ó Sé	Harps, Fiddles, Flute
Verse 4	Seán Ó Sé	Harps, Fiddles, Flute, Whistle, Box
Verse 5	Seán Ó Sé	Whole Band

Molly St George

AAB	Harpsichord
AAB	Fiddles
AAB	Whole Band

Mo Mhuirnín Bán (D)

Version # 1

A	Whistle
B	Whistle, Box Chords
AB	Whole Band, Box Chords
A	2 Whistles (Harmony)
B	Whole Band (Chanter in on last line)
AA	Whole Band

Version # 2 (Opening theme Playboy)

AB	Whistle
A – 1	Whistle, Flute, Fiddles Drone D
A – 2	Whistle, Flute, Fiddles Drone D, Box D
B	Whistle, Flute, Fiddle, Chanter, Box Chords
A–1	Whistle, Box Chords

Box Chords: G D G G D G
E D G D G G, D, G

Money from America (4:00)

Intro

2 beats	Bodhrán
6 Beats	Silence
	Laugh from Ronnie
AABBCC	Whole Band
A	Fiddle
A	2 Fiddles

B	Fiddle
B	2 Fiddles
CC	Chanter, Remainder of Whole Band Lilting
AABBCC	Whole Band
Intro x 3 times	Bodhrán and laugh
8 Bars	Bodhrán, Bones
AABBCC	3 Whistles
AABBCC	Whole Band
	End with Laugh

(G F-E DCB A-F G-B A-F G-A B-A A-G) (melody outline) ?

Morrison's Jig (D min)

Intro		Fiddle Pizz
	A	3 Whistles Fiddle Pizz
	A	3 Whistles Fiddle Pizz, Bodhrán
	BB	3 Whistles, Box Drones EG, Fiddle Pizz, Bodhrán
	AABB	Box, Bodhrán
	AABB	3 Whistles & Box Drones, Bodhrán
	AABB	Fiddles, Bodhrán, Fiddle Pizz, Whistle Drones GB, Box EG, bones

Mo Thuirnín Línn (D)

Verse 1 Line 1&2	Seán Ó Sé	Chanter
Line 3&4	Seán Ó Sé	Chanter, Whole Band
Chorus Line 5&6	Seán Ó Sé	Flute, Fiddle
Line 7&8	Seán Ó Sé	Whole Band
Verse 2 Line 1&2	Seán Ó Sé	Chanter
Line 3&4	Seán Ó Sé	Chanter, Whole Band
Line 5&6	Seán Ó Sé	Flute, Fiddle
Line 7&8	Seán Ó Sé	Whole Band
Verse 3 Line 1&2	Seán Ó Sé	Chanter
Line 3&4	Seán Ó Sé	Chanter, Whole Band
Line 5&6	Seán Ó Sé	Flute, Fiddle
Line 7&8	Seán Ó Sé	Whole Band
Chorus	Seán Ó Sé	Whole Band
Chorus	Seán Ó Sé	Whole Band

Mount Phoebus' Hunt

Version # 1

AA	Flute
BB	Flute, Whistle
AA	Chanter
BB	2 Fiddles
AA	Fiddle, 2nd Fiddle Chords, Harps
BB	Harps
AABB	Whole Band
A	2 Fiddles (Octaves)
A	Chanter
B	Harps
B	Flute, Whistle
AABB	Whole Band

Version # 2

	3 Whistles, Box Chord G
	Harps
	2 Fiddles (in Octaves)

Version # 3

AA	Flute, Whistle
BB	Flute, Whistle, Chanter
AABB	Whole Band
AA	2 Fiddles
BB	Whistle, Flute
AB	Whole Band

Langstroms' Pony 8 Bars   Bodhrán, Bones

Version # 4 (Alleliu)

Intro	Harps
A	Chanter
A	Whole Band
B	Chanter
B	Whole Band
A	Harps
A	Flute, Whistle
B	Fiddles
B	Harps
AA	Fiddles, Flute, Whistles
BB	Chanter, Box
AABB	Whole Band

Mug of Brown Ale (Old Man Dillon)

AABB	Whole Band
AABB	Whistle, Flute, Chanter (Harmony)
AA	Fiddles
BB	Boxes
AABB	3 Whistles
AABB	Whole Band

Muileagán Dubh Ó

(Key D)	Verse 1	Seán Ó Sé	Harps
(Key G)	Verse 2	Seán Ó Sé	Harps, Whistle, flute, Fiddles, Octaves
(Key G)	Verse 3	Seán Ó Sé	Whole Band

Muirceartach MacAnna (5:00)

A	2 Whistles, Flute
A	Whole Band
B	2 Whistles, Flute
B	Whole Band
A	Chanter
A	Harps
B	Chanter
B	Harps
A	Flute, Whistles
A	3 Fiddles
B	3 Whistles
B	Harps
AABB	Whole Band

The Munster Gimlet

AB	Pipes
AB	Fiddle (John Kelly)
AB	Whole Band
AB	Harps
AB	Flute, Whistle
AB	Whole Band, finish long note

These notes were inserted in the arrangement – They may be Box Chords i.e; Line 1 x 3 line 2 x1 (Part A of tune) line 3 followed by line 4 by line 3 by line 4 (part B of tune) – but I am not sure nor were any of the remaining band members).

> Line 1 A – D – G – A – D
> Line 2 A – D – CD – A – D
> Line 3 A – DA – D – A – D
> Line 4 A – D G – D – A – D

Murphy's Hornpipe (or Mulvihills)

A	Fiddle (John)
A	Fiddles in Octaves
BB	Whistles
AABB	Whole Band
AA	Box
BB	Whistles
AA	Whistles, Fiddles in Octaves
B	2 Fiddles in Octaves
B	1 Fiddle (John)

Murphy's Reel

AABB	Fiddle (John Kelly)
AABB	Flute, Whistle
AABB	Whole Band
A	Chanter
A	Box (Sonny) or Fiddles
B	Chanter
B	Box (Sonny) or Fiddles
AABB	Whole Band
AA	Flute, Whistle
B	Fiddle, Flute
B	2 Fiddles and end with chord

My Love in the Morning

AA	Flute, Fiddle
BB	Flute, Chanter, Whistle
AABB	Whole Band
AA	Boxes, Bones
BB	Whole Band
AA	Whistle, Chanter
BB	2 Fiddles
AABB	Whole Band

Ná beadh buachaillín deas ag Síle

Verse 1	Seán Ó Sé	Harps
Verse 2	Seán Ó Sé	Harps, Flute, Fiddle
Verse 3	Seán Ó Sé	Harps, Whistles, Flute, 3 Fiddles

Verse 4	Seán Ó Sé	Whole Band

Nách Fada an Lá (Dorian Mode)

Verse 1	Seán Ó Sé	Harps
Verse 2	Seán Ó Sé	Harps, Bodhrán
Verse 3	Seán Ó Sé	Harps, Bodhrán, 2 whistles, Flute
Verse 4	Seán Ó Sé	Harps, Bodhrán, 2 whistles, Flute, Fiddles
Verse 5	Seán Ó Sé	Harps, Bodhrán, 2 whistles, Flute, Fiddles, Box
Verse 6	Seán Ó Sé	Whole Band

Napper Tandy/Wearing of the Green

Verse 1	Seán Ó Sé	Box Chords
Verse 2	Seán Ó Sé	Box Chords, Harps
Verse 3	Seán Ó Sé	Box Chords, Harps, Whistle, Flute, Pipes
Verse 4	Seán Ó Sé	Whole Band

Box Chords:: G G G E G DC C D C D
EMin G C D –G

Neillí, Neillí

Intro	Bodhrán
Chorus Seán Ó Sé	Bodhrán Box Chords, Bones, Whole Band
Chorus Seán Ó Sé	Whole Band – all singing and playing
Verse Seán Ó Sé	Whole Band, Bodhrán Box Chords, Bones,

5 Verses all ditto above with 2 choruses at end
Finishing with long high yelp Yaheeee (Ronnie)

Box Chords:
Chorus: D A D A D
D A D A D
Verse: A A D A A A D A D

Chorus   Ó Neillí, Neillí, Ó Neillí Neillí an fuacht
Ó Neillí, Neillí, Ó Neillí an ghaoth anair aneas aduaigh

Newport Lass / Trip to Athlone (6:45)

Newport Lass	AABB	Whole Band
Jig (Hag with the money)	AABB	Whistle
	AABB	Whole Band
Bill Harts jig	AABB	Flute

	AABB	Whole Band
Trip to Athlone	AABB	Chanter
Trip to Athlone	AABB	Whole Band
Newport Lass	AABB	Whole Band

Second Version as above but each instrument picking own jig followed by Whole Band in the following order: Flute – Fiddle – Chanter – Fiddle – Whistle – Fiddle – Box. Arrangement started and ended with AABB Newport Lass

Nuair a Ghabhaimse tríd an mBaile seo (Gleann Cam)

Version # 1

Intro		Harps
Verse 1	Seán Ó Sé	Harps
Verse 2	Seán Ó Sé	Harps, Pipes
Verse 3	Seán Ó Sé	Whole Band

Version # 2

Verse 1		Harps
Verse 2		Whole Band
	AABB	Harps – Jig
	AABB	Whole Band – Jig
	AABB	Flute, Whistle, Chanter – Jig
	AABB	Whole Band – Jig

Old Tipperary & Leitrim Jig – Killoran

	AABB	Fiddle
	AABB	Fiddle, Flute
	AABB	Fiddle, Flute, Whistles
	AABB	2 Fiddles
Leitrim Jig	AABB	Box
	AABB	Pipes Whistle, Fiddle Plucked
	AABB	Whole Band
	AABB	Fiddle, 2nd Fiddle in counterpoint harmony, Box (Sonny)
	AABB	Whole Band (Box Chord of G – Eamon)
	AABB	Fiddles in Harmony

Old Joe's Jig & Sixpenny Money (madcap) (4:30)

Old Joe's Jig	AABB	Chanter
	AABB	Whole Band

	AABB	Flute & Whistle
	AABB	3 Whistles (harmony)
	AABB	Whole Band
Sixpenny Money	AABB	Chanter
	AABB	Whole Band
Old Joe's Jig	AABB	Whole Band
	AABB	Whole Band

O'Mahony's Frolics
Version # 1
(Gaiety)   AA   Whole Band (without Box)
                        BB   Whole Band with Box Chords

Version #2
(Gaiety)   A   Fiddle, Harps
                        A   Whistles
                        B   Fiddles, Flute, Whistle
                        B   Whole Band
                                Harps Solo

Version # 3
                        AABB   Fiddle, Harps
                        AABB   Fiddle, Harps, Flute
                        AABB   Whistle, Harps, Flute
                        AABB   Pipes
                        AABB   Whole Band
                        AABB   Whole Band

Box Chords: D–C (i.e. continue D C D C ...)
GAD (at end)
Box Chords: D C D G A D

One Day for Recreation
   Intro   Bodhrán and D Chord Box
   Verse 1   Seán Ó Sé   Box Chords
                                                      Whole Band
   Verse 2   Seán Ó Sé   Box Chords
   Girl I left behind me AB   Whole Band
   Verse 3   Seán Ó Sé   Box Chords
   Maggie in the Woods AB   Whole Band

Verse 4	Seán Ó Sé	Box Chords
Verse 5	Seán Ó Sé	Whole Band, Box Chords
Final chorus	Seán Ó Sé	Whole Band, Box Chords

Box Chords: G G G D G G G D
G D G D D D G D

Ó Riada's Favourite

AABB	Whole Band
AABB	Flute
AABB	Whole Band
AABB	Fiddle (John K)
AABB	Whole Band
AABB	Chanter
AABB	Whole Band
AABB	Fiddle (Martin)
AABB	Whole Band
AABB	Whistle
AABB	Whole Band
AABB	Fiddle (Seán K)
AABB	Whole Band
AABB	Box
AABB	Whole Band

Box Chords: G D G – G D G D D
G D G G G C D G
G G C C A D D G D G G

Oró Sé do Bheatha 'Bhaile & Gráinne Mhaol

Version # 1

Chorus (Óró)		Whole Band
Chorus		Whole Band
Verse 1	Seán O Sé	Harps
Chorus		Whole Band
Chorus		Whole Band
Verse 2	Seán O Sé	2 Whistles & Flute
Chorus		Whole Band
Chorus		Whole Band
Verse 3	Seán O Sé	3 Fiddles
Chorus		Whole Band

Chorus		Whole Band
Verse 2	Seán O Sé	Chanter & Box
Chorus		Whole Band
Chorus		Whole Band
Chorus		Whole Band

Version #2

Verse 1	Seán O Sé	Harps
Chorus		Whole Band (Singing)
Verse 2	Seán O Sé	Whole Band (Playing)
Chorus		Whole Band (Singing)
Verse 3	Seán O Sé	Whole Band (Playing)
Chorus		Whole Band (Singing and Playing)

Óró Nach é siúd an Seó

Version # 1

Intro		Fiddle
	A	Fiddle
	AB	Spoken Word
	B	Chanter
	AB	Focail ráite [Spoken Word]
	AB	Focail ráite [Spoken Word]
	Rhythm	Bodhrán
	AB	Chanter, Whistle, Fiddle drone
	Rhythm	Bodhrán
	AB	Whistle, Fiddle, Drones on Pipes
Singing of line 'Óró nách é siúd an seó'		Whole Band

Version # 2

Intro		Harps
Verse 1	Seán O Sé	Harps
Whelan's Jig	AABB	Whole Band
Verse 2	Seán O Sé	Harps
Whelan's Jig	AABB	Whole Band
Verse 3	Seán O Sé	Harps
Whelan's Jig	AABB	Whole Band
Verse 4	Seán O Sé	Harps, Whole Band
		Whole Band in on singing 'Oró nách é …

Oró Bog Liom í

Intro		Harps
Chorus	Seán Ó Sé	Whole Band, Box Chords
Verse 1	Seán Ó Sé	Harps
Chorus	Seán Ó Sé	Whole Band, Box Chords
Verse 2	Seán Ó Sé	Harps
Chorus	Seán Ó Sé	Whole Band, Box Chords
Verse 3	Seán Ó Sé	Harps
Chorus	Seán Ó Sé	Whole Band, Box Chords
Verse 4	Seán Ó Sé	Harps
Chorus	Seán Ó Sé	Whole Band, Box Chords
Verse 5	Seán Ó Sé	Whole Band, Box Chords
Chorus	Seán Ó Sé	Whole Band, Box Chords

Box Chords: G D G D G D D G
G D G D G D D G

Outlaw of the Hill

Intro		Harps
Verse 1	Seán Ó Sé	Harps
Verse 2	Seán Ó Sé	Harps, Flute, Whistle, Pipes
Verse 3	Seán Ó Sé	Harps, Flute, Pipes, Whistle, Fiddles
Verse 4	Seán Ó Sé	Whole Band
Verse 5	Seán Ó Sé	Whole Band

Páirc an Fhomhair

	ABAB	Whole Band
	AB	Flute
	AB	Fiddle
	AB	Chanter
	ABAB	Whole Band

Peeler and the Goat

Intro		Harps (or Bodhrán)
Verse 1	Seán Ó Sé	Harps (or Bodhrán)
Butcher's March	BB	Whole Band 
Verse 2	Seán Ó Sé	Harps
Butcher's March	BB	Whole Band

Verse 3	Seán Ó Sé	Harps
Butcher's March	BB	Whole Band
Verse 4	Seán Ó Sé	Harps, Fiddles
Butcher's March	BB	Whole Band
Verse 5	Seán Ó Sé	Harps, Fiddles
Butcher's March	BB	Whole Band
Verse 6	Seán Ó Sé	Whole Band

Peigín Leitir Mhóir

Intro (last Line)		Harps
Chorus	Darach Ó Catháin	Harps, Fiddle Pizz, Whistles
Verse 1	Darach Ó Catháin	Harps, Fiddle Pizz, Whistles
Chorus	Darach Ó Catháin	Harps, Fiddle Pizz, Whistles
Verse 2	Darach Ó Catháin	Harps, Fiddle Pizz, Whistles
Chorus	Darach Ó Catháin	Harps, Fiddle Pizz, Whistles
Verse 3	Darach Ó Catháin	Harps, Fiddle Pizz, Whistles
Chorus	Darach Ó Catháin	Harps, Fiddle Pizz, Whistles
Verse 4	Darach Ó Catháin	Harps, Fiddle Pizz, Whistles
Chorus	Darach Ó Catháin	Harps, Fiddle Pizz, Whistles

A Phlúirín na mBan Donn Óg

Intro		Harps
Verse 1	Seán Ó Sé	Harps
Verse 2	Seán Ó Sé	2 Whistles Flute (improvisation))
Verse 3	Seán Ó Sé	2 Whistles, Chanter, Flute, Fiddle Pizz
Verse 4	Seán Ó Sé	Whole Band

Píce an tSúgaire

Intro		Harps
Verse 1	Seán Ó Sé	Harps (in D)
Leg of the Duck AA		Whole Band
Verse 2	Seán Ó Sé	Harps
Leg of the Duck BB		Whole Band
Verse 3	Seán Ó Sé	Harps
Leg of the Duck AA		Whole Band
Verse 4	Seán Ó Sé	Whole Band
Leg of the Duck BB		Whole Band

	Verse 5 Seán Ó Sé	Whole Band
Leg of the Duck AA		Whole Band
	Verse 6 Seán Ó Sé	Whole Band (last verse in English)
Píce an tSúgaire verse x 2		Whole Band

Piper's Chair

A	Harps
A	Whole Band
B	Harps
B	Whole Band
A	Chanter and Box Drone
A	Whole Band
B	Chanter, Box Drone
AABB	3 Whistles
AABB	Whole Band

Plains of Boyle

AABB	Flute
A	Harps
A	Whole Band
B	Harps
B	Whole Band
A	Whistle, Fiddle
A	Whole Band
B	3 Whistles
B	Whole Band
A	Pipes
A	Pipes, Harps
B	Fiddles
B	Whole Band
AABB	Whole Band

Planxty Drury (Beardless Boy)

AB	Harps
AB	Harps, Chanter
A B	Flute Whistle, Box
AB	3 Fiddles

AB	Whole Band

Planxty Irwin

AB	Harps
AB	Harps, Chanter
AB	Whole Band
AB	Harps, Whistles, Flute, Viola
AB	Harps, Chanter, Harps, Fiddles, Viola
AB	Whole Band
AB	Whole Band

Planxty Johnson

A	Harps
A	Whole Band, Bodhrán
B	Harps
AAB	Whole Band, Bodhrán (abrupt stop for 1 bar end of line B 5)
AA	Whistle, Flute, Chanter
B	3 Fiddles (Martin Octave)
AAB	Whole Band, Bodhrán (Cut short at end of line 5 section B)

Planxty Maguire

Version # 1

AA	Harps
B	Harps, Chanter
AAB	Harps, 3 Fiddles (Martin Octave)
(Extra – only 4 Alleliú prog. AAB	Whole Band)
AAB	3 Whistles
AAB	Whole Band, Bodhrán

Version # 2

A	Harps
A	Whole Band
B	Chanter
A	3 Fiddles

	A	Chanter
	B	3 Fiddles
	A	3 Whistles
	A	3 Fiddles
	B	Harps
	AAB	Whole Band

Version # 3

	AA	Harps
	B	Harps, Chanter
	AA	Harps, 3 Fiddles (Martin Octave)
	B	Harps, 3 Whistles
	A	Harps, 3 Fiddles, 3 Whistles
	A	Whole Band
	B	Whole Band

Pléaráca an Ruarcach

Version # 1

	Intro	Harps (Last line of song)
	Verse 1 Seán Ó Sé	Harps
	Intro	Harps
	Verse 2 Seán O Sé	Harps, 3 Whistles
	Intro	Harps
	Verse 3 Seán Ó Sé	Whole Band
Finish with intro – Bar 1 Harps, Bar 2		Whole Band

An Poc ar Buile

	Verse 1 Seán Ó Sé	Box Chords
	Chorus Seán Ó Sé	Whole Band
	Verse 2 Seán Ó Sé	Box Chords
	Chorus Seán Ó Sé	Whole Band
	Verse 3 Seán Ó Sé	Box Chords
	Chorus Seán Ó Sé	Whole Band
	Verse 4 Seán Ó Sé	Chanter (counter-melody), Box Chords
	Chorus Seán Ó Sé	Whole Band
	Verse 5 Seán Ó Sé	Chanter (contra-melody), Box Chords
	Chorus Seán Ó Sé	Whole Band

Box Chords:
Verse   D A D D A
Chorus: D D D / D A A D

Polka Set

Version # 1

Sonny's	AB	Chanter
	AB	Whole Band
John's	AB	Box
	AB	Whole Band
Maggie	AB	Fiddles (Martin), Whistle
	AB	Whole Band
Cúil Aodha	AB	Harps
	AB	Whole Band
Denis'	AB	2 Fiddles (John & Seán), Flute
	AB	Whole Band

Version # 2

Gaiety

3 Fiddles, Box
3 Fiddles, Box, Flute
Pips on Pipes

Box Chords: G G D D
G G D D
G G D D
D D G G
G G D D
D D G D
G G D D
D D G G

Port na bPucaí

Version # 1

Intro	Box Chords Emin – A Maj.
Verse 1	Harps
Verse 2	Whole Band
Verse 3	Harps
	Whole Band in on second half

End with Box Chords; Emin – A Maj.   x 2

Version # 2
    Intro   Box Chords Emin – A Maj.
    Verse 1   Harps
    Verse 2   Whole Band
    Verse 3 Lines 1–4   Harps
                Lines 5–6   Harps, Fiddle, Whistle, Flute, Chanter
                Line 7–8   Whole Band

Version # 3
                A   Harps
                A   Harps, Pipes
                B   Whole Band
                AA   Whole Band
                B   Whole Band
                AAB   Whole Band
                End Box Chords Emin – A Maj.

Pósadh (Fuaireasa Cuireadh chun dul ar an bpósadh)

Pósadh Verse 1		Seán Ó Sé	Harps
Chorus		Seán Ó Sé	Harps
Hag with the Money	AA		Whole Band
Pósadh Verse 2		Seán Ó Sé	Harps
Chorus		Seán Ó Sé	Harps
Hag with the Money	BB		Whole Band
Pósadh Verse 3		Seán Ó Sé	Harps
Chorus		Seán Ó Sé	Whole Band
Pósadh Verse 4		Seán Ó Sé	Harps
Chorus		Seán Ó Sé	Whole Band
Pósadh Verse 5		Seán Ó Sé	Harps
Chorus		Seán Ó Sé	Whole Band
	Box Chords:	D D A D G A	
		D D D G DDAD	
		D G A	
		D G A	
		D G D A	

Pretty Girls of Mayo

	D G A D
AB	Chanter
AB	Fiddle
AB	Flute
AB	Box (May leave out)
AB	Whistle, Harps
AB	Whistle, Flute, Harps
AB	Whistle, Flute, Fiddles, Harps
AB	Whistle, Flute, Fiddles, Chanter, Harps
AB	Whole Band
AB	Whole Band
AB	Whole Band

Priest in his Boots (fuaireasa cuireadh) & Maid at the Spinning Wheel

Priest in Boots	AB		Whole Band
Fuaireasa cuireadh	AB	Seán Ó Síocháin	
Priest in Boots	AB		Whole Band
Fuaireasa cuireadh	AB	Seán Ó Síocháin	
Priest in Boots	AB		Whole Band
Fuaireasa cuireadh	AB	Seán Ó Síocháin	
Maid at Spinning	AABBCC		Whole Band
Maid at Spinning	DD		Chanter
Fuaireasa cuireadh	AB	Seán Ó Síocháin	
Priest in Boots	AB		Whole Band

Whole Band sings chorus lines:
Hoxty, Hickity, Mickity, Hum
Hoxty Hodie, Mickity, Hum

Príosún Chluain Meala

Version # 1

Verse 1	Seán Ó Sé	Harps
Verse 2	Seán Ó Sé	Harps, Fiddles
Verse 3	Seán Ó Sé	Harps, Fiddles, Flute, Whistle
Verse 4	Seán Ó Sé	Whole Band, Box Chords

			Box Chords:	G C D G D G C D Emin D G
				G C D Emin C D G D G
				C G <u>D</u> G

Version # 2
- Verse 1 — Seán Ó Sé — Box Chords
- Verse 2 — Seán Ó Sé — Box Chords
- Verse 3 — Seán Ó Sé — Box Chords, Fiddles, Flute, Whistle
- Verse 4 — Seán Ó Sé — Whole Band, Box Chords

		Box Chords:	G C D G D G C D Emin D G
			G C D Emin C D G D G
			C G <u>D</u> G

Pup Came Home from Claodach
- Verse 1 — Seán Ó Sé — Harps
- Verse 2 — Seán Ó Sé — Harps, Pipe drones, Fiddle (Martin)
- Verse 3 — Seán Ó Sé — Whistle, Flute, Drones, Fiddle Drones
- Verse 4 — Seán Ó Sé — Whole Band and Box Drones
- Verse 5 — Seán Ó Sé — Whole Band

small pause between each Verse

Ráca Breagh Mo Chínn
- Intro (1st line of Verse) — Harps
- Verse 1 — Seán Ó Sé — Harps
- Verse 2 — Seán Ó Sé — Harps, Box Chords
- Verse 3 — Seán Ó Sé — Harps, Fiddle, Viola, Box Chords
- Verse 4 — Seán Ó Sé — Whole Band, Box Chords
- Verse 5 — Seán Ó Sé — Whole Band, Box Chords

(F# in first line, all others F natural)

		Box Chords:	GD GC D CG
			G GD D G CD
			G G G CCD
			G D G C D (Bass) C G

Races of Cahirsiveen (air of Bold Thady Quill)
- Intro — Harps
- Verse 1 — Seán Ó Sé — Harps
- Oró Bog — AA — Whole Band

Verse 2	Seán Ó Sé	Harps
Rakes AA		Whole Band (F#)
Verse 3	Seán Ó Sé	Harps
Oró AA		Whole Band
Verse 4	Seán Ó Sé	Harps
Rakes A		Whole Band
Verse 5	Seán Ó Sé	Harps
Verse 5	Seán Ó Sé	Whole Band
	Big rall on end	

Raedh Chnoc Mná Duibhe

Version # 1

Intro		Harps
Verse 1	Seán Ó Sé	Harps
Verse 2	Seán Ó Sé	3 Fiddles
Verse 3	Seán Ó Sé	3 Whistles
Verse 4	Seán Ó Sé	Box
Verse 5	Seán Ó Sé	Box, Fiddles
Verse 6	Seán Ó Sé	Pipes
Verse 7	Seán Ó Sé	Whistle
Verse 8	Seán Ó Sé	Whole Band
AAAA		Whole Band

Version # 2 (slow minor Melody)

Verse 1	Seán Ó Sé	Harps
Verse 2	Seán Ó Sé	Harps, Fiddle, Pipes
Verse 3	Seán Ó Sé	Whole Band

Version # 3 (for Reacaireacht)

Verse 1	Seán Ó Sé	Harps
Verse 2	Seán Ó Sé	Whole Band
Verse 3	Seán Ó Sé	3 Fiddles
Verse 4	Seán Ó Sé	Whole Band
Verse 5	Seán Ó Sé	Flute, Whistle
Verse 6	Seán Ó Sé	Whole Band
Verse 6	Seán Ó Sé	Pipes
Verse 8	Seán Ó Sé	Whole Band
AAAA	Seán Ó Sé	Whole Band

Version # 4
Intro		Harps
Verse 1	Seán Ó Sé	Harps
Verse 2	Seán Ó Sé	Fiddles
Verse 3	Seán Ó Sé	Pipes
Verse 4	Seán Ó Sé	Whole Band & Box Chords
Verse 5	Seán Ó Sé	Whole Band & Box Chords

                          Box Chords: D G A D
                                                      D A A D
                                                        D A G A D
                                                        DG G GA D

Raghadsa ar an Aonach

Verse 1	Seán Ó Sé	Harps
Verse 2	Seán Ó Sé	Fiddle Pizz, Flute, Pipes
Verse 3	Seán Ó Sé	Whole Band

Raghadsa is mo Cheaití (Slow air)

Verse	Solo accordion (melody)
Verse	Whistle, Flute. Chanter, Box Chords
Verse	Whole Band, Box Chords

                Box Chords: (Verse 2) Single Bass: E A <u>D</u> <u>E</u>
                                           E A E   G D G D
                                           E A E G D A <u>D</u> (hold)
                                           E A D E
                             (Verse 3) Bass Chords: Emin = (Ebass, GB treb)
                           A E A D Emin A Emin
                           Emin A D G DGD
                           Emin   A Emin A D A D
                         <u>D</u> Emin A D Emin A Emin

An Raibh tú ar an gCarraig

Intro		Box drone E
	AB	Whistle, Box drone E
	AB	Harps
	ABAB	Whole Band
	Pause	

Jig – 3 Little Drummers

	AABB	Whole Band (Fiddles Chords A G)

	AABB	Whole Band
	AABB	Whole Band
(Éamon's notes): DCAA	ACCDD	
	DEFF E	
	DCAGA DEFF	
	EDEE DCADD	
	CDED FED	
	CAGABA FEDCA	
	GEDC DEFF	
	DCADG GGEDD	
	CDEDD	

Ráiteachas na Tairingreacht (G)
    Verse 1   Seán Ó Sé   Box Chords
    Verse 2   Seán Ó Sé   Box Chords, Flute, Fiddle
    Verse 3   Seán Ó Sé   Whole Band

Raithineach a Bhean Bheag
Chorus   Seán Ó Sé   Whole Band
    Verse 1   Seán Ó Sé   2Whistles, Flute (contra-melody), Fiddles pizz
    Chorus   Seán Ó Sé   Whole Band
    Verse 2   Seán Ó Sé   2 Whistles, Flute, Fiddles Pizz
    Chorus   Seán Ó Sé   Whole Band
    Verse 3   Seán Ó Sé   2 Whistles, Flute, Fiddles Pizz
    Chorus   Seán Ó Sé   Whole Band
    Verse 4   Seán Ó Sé   2 Whistles, Flute, Fiddles Pizz
    Chorus   Seán Ó Sé   Whole Band
    Verse 5   Seán Ó Sé   2 Whistles, Flute, Fiddles Pizz
    Chorus   Seán Ó Sé   Whole Band
    Chorus   Seán Ó Sé   Whole Band
(during Verses band plays lines 1–6, 7 is silent with 8 starting with AAAs)

Rakes of Clonmel
    AABBCC   Whole Band
    AABBCC   Whistle, Flute, Chanter
    AABB   Fiddles

	CC	3 Whistles
	AABBCC	Whole Band

Reddigan's

	AB	Flute
	AB	Box
	AB	Whistle, Chanter
	AB	Whole Band
	AB	Fiddle
	AB	Whole Band
	AB	Flute, 2 Whistles
	ABAB	Whole Band

Reddigan's / Abbey Reel & Golden Keyboard

Abbey R	ABAB	Whole Band
	AB	Whole Band (leave out notes at end of 2nd bar)
	ABABAB	Fiddles, Chanter Break
	ABABAB	Whole Band Break
Golden Key	AABB	Fiddle (Golden Keyboard)
	AABB	Whistles, Flute, Fiddle
Abbey R	AABB	Whole Band
	AABB	Whole Band

Red-Haired Boy

Intro		Fiddle Plucked
	AABB	Whistle, Flute G
	AABB	Pipes in A
	AA	Fiddles Octaves in D
	BB	Fiddle Solo, Fiddle Plucked
	AA	Box in G
	AABB	Whole Band in D
	AABB	Whole Band in G
		End: B G G long
		Sharp ending G (short) and Bass

Réice Luimnighe

Version # 1

    Intro notes E, E, A on fiddle, flute, Whistle chant and accordions

Verse 1	Seán Ó Síocháin	Whole Band sings 'agus fágfaigmíd siúd mar atá sé'

    Intro (repeated as above)

Verse 2	Seán Ó Síocháin	Whole Band sings 'agus fágfaigmíd siúd mar atá sé'

    Intro (repeated as above)

Verse 3	Seán Ó Síocháin	
		Whole Band plays from 'Rí Soloman trá'
		Whole Band plays & sings 'agus fágfaigmíd siúd mar atá sé'

Version #2

Intro		Harps
Verse 1	Seán Ó Sé	Harps
Sister Jig	AABB	Whole Band
Verse 2	Seán Ó Sé	Harps
Contentment is wealth	AABB	Whole Band
Verse 3	Seán Ó Sé	Harps
Sister Jig	AABB	Whole Band
Verse 4	Seán Ó Sé	Whole Band
Reice Luimnighe	AB	Whole Band in tempo

Box Chords during Verses: A E D G A E A / A G A (Box Bass)

    D G A E A 3rd Verse only

    After 3rd Verse Band play – Box Bass

    Intro: Whistle EEA, Flute EEA, Fiddle EEA, Box EEA

Repeal of the Union

AABB	Flute
AABB	Fiddle, Chords AD CE
AA	Whistle, Chanter
BB	Whistle, Chanter, Flute
AABB	Whole Band
AABB	Whole Band

Rights of Man (4:00)
Version # 1

AABB	Harps
AABB	Harps, 3 Fiddles
AABB	Harps, Chanter
AABB	Harps, 3 Whistles
AABB	Whole Band

Version # 2

Intro	Drones E – 4 bars (Box!), Percussion
AABB	Flute, Whistle
AABB	Pipes, Viola
AABB	2 Fiddles, Harps
AABB	Boxes, Whole Band, Drones E
AABB	Whole Band, Harps

Ril Mhór Bhaile an Chaladh (3:45)

	Intro	Fiddle or Viola pizz (FGABCDEF)
Ríl Mhór	ABAB	Whole Band
Callaghan's	AB	Flute, Bodhrán
Callaghan's	AB	Fiddle & Fiddle plucked
Shaskeen	AABB	Harps
Ríl Mhór	AB	Harps, Chanter
Ríl Mhór	AB	Whole Band
Callaghan's	AB	Flute
Callaghan's	AB	Fiddle & Fiddle plucked
	A lines 1+2	Whole Band Singing (*Gheall sí, do gheall sí*)
	A Lines 3+4	Harps
	B	Whole Band
	AB	Whole Band
	AB	Whole Band

Do gheall sí is do gheall sí,
Gheall sí go dtiocfadh sí
Poll a bhí 'na bróigín
'S dó' dob é a cnoinnibh í

Rocky Road to Dublin
Version # 1

AABB	Flute
AABB	Flute, Whistle
AABB	Flute, Whistle, Fiddles
AABB	Flute, Whistle, Fiddles, Chanter
AABB	Flute, Whistle, Fiddles, Box
AABB	Whole Band
AABB	Whole Band Bass A + Low note A on Box
AABB	Whole Band Bass A + Low note A on Box
AABB	Whole Band Bass A + Low note A on Box
AABB	Whole Band Bass A + Low note A on Box

Version # 2 (Alleliú #5) (A minor)

Intro	Bones
AB	Flute
AB	Flute, Whistle
AB	Flute, Whistle, Fiddles
AB	Flute, Whistle, Fiddles, Chanter
AB	Flute, Whistle, Fiddles, Chanter
AB	Flute, Whistle, Fiddles, Chanter, Box
AB	Whole Band
ABABABAB	Whole Band, A drones on Box

Rógaire Dubh

AABB	Whole Band
AABB	Box, Fiddle (Sonny & John Kelly)
AABB	Whole Band
AABB	3 Whistles
AABB	Whole Band

Rogha Beethoven
Version # 1

Band open with Rogha Beethoven after interval and the follow with:

Reel Jenny's wedding   AA   Whole Band
                        BB   Whole Band

John Kelly and Sonny play tune 3 times
Remainder of group plays series as follows:

1   Series   D A C E,   D D F B   twice each note per a bar

		D E D C	D C A D	twice each note per a bar
2		As above, play each note per 1/2 bar and play each line once		
3		As above, play each note per 1/4 bar and play each line once		

Then whole Band play series No. 3 twice
Chanter plays special series
Whole Band 'breaking down' series DDFDA – DDFDA, etc.
Fiddle   Martin's version 4 times
Whole Band   AACA – CCEC EEGE A – 4 times
Whistles in harmony
Whole Band   DDFDA, DDFDA, etc. to A second time and hold A until cue
Fiddle   AA BB (whole Tune)
Whole Band   AABB

Version # 2

	Intro		Harps
		AABB	Whole Band (played as a reel)
		AABB (taken in phrases)	Flute – whistle – chanter – fiddle
		March played 6 times	
Girl I left behind A/2			Box
Jig + Triplets – twice			Whole Band
Girl I left behind AB			Box
		AABB (Reel)	Whole Band
O'Donnell Abú AABB			Flute, Chanter, Whistle
		AABB (Reel)	Whole Band

Rogha an Riadaigh

   Box Chords: G D G G D G D D
                     G D G G G C D G
                     G G C C C A D D G D G G

Róisín Dubh (A)

Intro	Harps, Flute (1st notes of tune)
Verse	Harps, Flute, Chords on Box & Fiddles
Verse	Harps, Flute, Chords on Box & Fiddles
Verse	Harps, Flute, Chords Box & Fiddles (Forte-lines 1&2)
	Flute, Chords Box & Fiddles (softly – lines 3&4)

			Drop out flute finishing with fiddle softly
Chords: Line 1			A E D A E
Harmony			E G F# E G# E
Line 2			A D E A
			E F# G# E
Line 3			A D E D
			E F# G# A
Line 4			E A E D A E A
			G# E G# F# E G# E
	Box Chords (Softly):		A E D A E, A
			A A D A E, A
			A – A – D – A – E, A
			E A E D A E, A

Rolling in the Rye Grass (6:03)

Rolling	AABB		Chanter (slowly)
		pause	
	AABB		Fiddle (normal tempo)
		pause	
	AABB		3 whistles (very fast tempo)
		pause	
Mazurka	AABB		Box (Sonny Brogan), finishing tutti loud
laugh			
		pause	
	AABB		Whole Band (normal tempo)
	BB		Whole Band silent until playing last 2 bars second B
Barn dance			Fiddle (John Kelly) + Whistle (Paddy Moloney)
		pause	
	AABB		3 Whistles (very fast tempo)
		pause	
Mazurka	AABB		Box (Sonny) very slowly
		pause	
Rolling	AABB		Whole Band (normal tempo)
	AABB		Whole Band

	B	Whole Band silent except for last 2 bars

Rolling on the Rye Grass (For **Playboy** *Ballet)*

Rolling	AABB	Chanter, Pause
	AABB	Fiddle, Pause
	AABB	Whistles, Pause
Mazurka	AABB	Box (Sonny Brogan),
	AABB	Whole Band – last 2 bars 4 times
Polka	AABB	Fiddle, Whistle
	AABB	Whistles – quicken tempo
Mazurka	AABB	Box (Sonny Brogan)
	AABB	Whole Band
	AABB	Whole Band (Tempo quickens, last 4 bars after counting 4)

Rolling Wave (5:00)

	AABB	Harps, with Pipes & Box Drones (D)
	AABB	Harps, 3 Whistles
	AABB	Harps, 2 fiddles, Viola
	AABB	Harps, Whistle, Flute, Chanter
	AABB	Harps, Fiddles, Chanter,
	AABB	Whole Band
	AABB	Whole Band

Ruadhraí Ó Mórdha (Máirseáil Rí Laoise)

Version # 1

	AABB	Pipes, Drones, Bodhrán
	AABB	3 Fiddles, Drones, Bodhrán
	AABB	Harps, Bodhrán
	AABB	Whole Band

Version # 2

	A	Harps
	A	Whole Band
	B	Harps
	B	Whole Band
	A	Chanter
	A	Whole Band

		B	Chanter
		B	Whole Band
		AABB	Whole Band

Saighdiúirín Singil

Verse 1	Seán Ó Sé	Harps
Verse 2	Seán Ó Sé	Harps, Fiddles
Verse 3	Seán Ó Sé	Harps, Fiddles, Whistle, Flute, Box Chords
Verse 4	Seán Ó Sé	Harps, Fiddles, Whistle, Flute, Chant, Box Chords
Verse 5	Seán Ó Sé	Whole Band, Box Chords

Box Chords: Emin A Emin A D
A Emin A Emin A
A Emin A A D
G A Emin A D

Salamanca

Salamanca	AABB	Pipes
	AABB	Whole Band
	AABB	Fiddle
Love in America	AABB	Flute
	AABB	Flute, Whistle
Salamanca	AABB	Whole Band
Love in America	AABB	Whole Band

Sceilpín Draighneach

Intro		Harps
Verse 1	Seán Ó Sé	Harps
Verse 2	Seán Ó Sé	Fiddles
Verse 3	Seán Ó Sé	Whole Band

Seachrán Cairn tSaoghail

Intro		Fiddles & Harps
Verse 1	Seán Ó Sé	Whistle & Harps
Verse 2	Seán Ó Sé	Whistle & Harps Flute
Verse 3	Seán Ó Sé	Whistle & Harps Flute Chanter
Verse 4	Seán Ó Sé	Whole Band
Repeat Chorus	Seán Ó Sé	Whole Band

Seán a' Bhríste Leathair
Version # 1

Intro		Harps
Verse 1	Seán Ó Sé	Harps
Chorus	Seán Ó Sé	Whole Band
Verse 2	Seán Ó Sé	Fiddles
Chorus	Seán Ó Sé	Harps, Flute, Box
Verse 3	Seán Ó Sé	Harps, Flute, Box
Chorus	Seán Ó Sé	Whole Band
Verse 4	Seán Ó Sé	Whole Band
Chorus	Seán Ó Sé	Whole Band

Version # 2

Intro		Harps
Verse 1	Seán Ó Sé	Harps
Chorus	Seán Ó Sé	Whole Band (Tooraloora laddie)
Polka	AB	Whole Band
Verse 2	Seán Ó Sé	Harps, Pipes, Box
Chorus	Seán Ó Sé	Whole Band
Polka	AB	3 Whistles
Verse 3	Seán Ó Sé	Whole Band
Chorus	Seán Ó Sé	Whole Band
Polka	ABB	Whole Band

Seán Ó Díghe

Intro		Harps (Mozart Phrasing)
Verse 1	Seán Ó Sé	Harps
Intro		Harps
Verse 2	Seán Ó Sé	Harps, Fiddle, Whistle, Flute
Intro		Harps
Verse 3	Seán Ó Sé	Harps, Whole Band
Intro		Harps

Seán Ó Duibhir a' Ghleanna
Version # 1

Verse 1	Seán Ó Sé	Harps
Verse 2	Seán Ó Sé	Harps
Verse 3	Seán Ó Sé	Whole Band

Version # 2 (Old Version)

Verse 1	Seán Ó Sé	Harps
Verse 2	Seán Ó Sé	Harps, Whistle, Flute Chanter, Fiddle
Verse 3	Seán Ó Sé	Whole Band

'

'Sé Fáth mo Bhuartha

Verse 1	Seán Ó Sé	Whistle, Box Chords
Verse 2	Seán Ó Sé	Harps
Verse 3	Seán Ó Sé	Whole Band

Box Chords: A D A Bmin G D A
D A Bmin G A D
D C D GA
D Bmin Emin A D

Seoladh na nGamhna

Intro		Harps
Verse 1	Seán Ó Sé	Harps
Verse 2	Seán Ó Sé	Harps, 3 Whistles
Verse 3	Seán Ó Sé	Whole Band

Shaskeen Reel

AABB	Whole Band
AA	Flute
BB	Flute, Whistle, Chanter
AA	Box
BB	Fiddles, Chanter
AA	Whistle
BB	Whistle, Flute
AABB	Whole Band
AABB	Whole Band

A Shíle Ní Ghadhra

	Intro		Harps
Síle	Verse 1	Seán Ó Sé	Harps, 2 Whistles, Flute
	Chorus	Seán Ó Sé	Whole Band
	Oró Bog Liom	Seán Ó Sé	Whole Band
Síle	Verse 2	Seán Ó Sé	Harps, 2 Whistles, Flute
	Chorus	Seán Ó Sé	Whole Band

Bould Thady Quill		Seán Ó Sé	Whole Band
Síle	Verse 3	Seán Ó Sé	Harps, 2 Whistles, Flute
	Chorus	Seán Ó Sé	Whole Band
Mo Thaighleach		Seán Ó Sé	Whole Band
Síle	Verse 4	Seán Ó Sé	Harps, 2 Whistles, Flute
	Chorus	Seán Ó Sé	Whole Band
Cnocáinín Aerach		Seán O Sé	Whole Band
Sile	Chorus	Seán Ó Sé	Whole Band
	Chorus	Seán Ó Sé	Whole Band

Ships are Sailing (reel)

A	Box
A	Whole Band
B	Box
B	Whole Band
AABB	Whole Band
A	Chanter
A	Whole Band
B	Flute
B	Whole Band
AB	Fiddle
AABB	Whole Band
AABB	Whole Band

Ships in Full Sail (3:10) (See counter-melodies at end of book)

A	Flute
A	Flute, Bodhrán
BB	Flute, Bodhrán, Whistle
AABB	Whole Band
A	Box, Bones
A	Fiddles, Bodhrán
B	Box, Bones
B	Fiddles, Bodhrán
AABB	3 Whistles (2 playing harmony), Bodhrán
A	Boxes, Fiddles

	A	Boxes, Fiddles, Bodhrán
	BB	Whole Band
	AABB	Whole Band

Sí Beag, Sí Mór
Version # 1

AA	Harps
BB	Harps, Fiddles
AA	Harps, Flute, Whistle
BB	Whole Band

Version # 2

A	Harps
A	Whole Band
B	Harps
B	Whole Band
A	Harps, Fiddles
A	Harps, Flute, Whistle, Chanter
BB	Whole Band

Box Chords: A DD DE FG AA BC# BA BA
G F# G AG F E F E D CE DD C#
A A A A

Sí Bhean Locha Léin

Intro		Harps
Verse 1	Seán Ó Sé	Harps, 3 fiddles
Tune		3 Fiddles
Verse 2	Seán Ó Sé	3 Fiddles, 2 whistles, Box-drone Emin
Tune		3 Fiddles, 2 whistles, Box-drone Emin
Verse 3	Seán Ó Sé	3 Fiddles, 2 whistles, Box-drone Emin, Flute
Tune		3 Fiddles, 2 whistles, Box-drone Emin, Flute
Verse 4	Seán Ó Sé	Whole Band
Tune		Whole Band
Verse 5	Seán Ó Sé	Whole Band (without Drone)
Tune	Seán Ó Sé	Lilting
Tune	Seán Ó Sé	Lilting, Whole Band

Since Boney is Down

Verse 1	Seán Ó Sé	Harps
Verse 2	Seán Ó Sé	Harps
Verse 3	Seán Ó Sé	Harps
		Whole Band on second Half

Since Mary's heen went to Bonane (Ceo Draíochta)

Intro		Harps
Verse 1	Seán Ó Sé	Harps
Verse 2	Seán Ó Sé	Harps, Box
Verse 3	Seán Ó Sé	Harps, Whistle Flute, chanter
Verse 3	Seán Ó Sé	Whole Band

An Síoda 'tá id' bhfhallait (in G)

Intro		Harps
Verse 1	Seán Ó Sé	Harps
Chorus		Whole Band
Chorus		Whole Band
Gander in the Pratie Hole AABB		Whole Band
Verse 2	Seán Ó Sé	Harps
Chorus		Whole Band
Chorus		Whole Band
Gander	AABB	Whole Band
Verse 3	Seán Ó Sé	Harps
Chorus		Whole Band
Chorus		Whole Band

Sláinte Bhreá Hewlett

Intro		Harps
AB		Whole Band
A		Harps, Chanter
B Line	1	Harps
	2	Harps, Fiddles
	3–4	Whole Band
A		Harps, Flute, Whistle
B	1	Harps Flute, Whistle Chanter
	2	Harps, Fiddles

	3–4		Harps, Fiddles, Flute, Whistle
	AB		Whole Band

Slán agus Beannacht le Buairibh an tSaoil (G)

Verse 1	Seán Ó Sé	Harps
Verse 2	Seán Ó Sé	Whole Band
Verse 3	Seán Ó Sé	Whole Band, Box Chords
Verse 4	Seán Ó Sé	Whole Band, Box Chords

                Box Chords: G D G C D D G ---- C G
                                          G D G C G-D G G ---- C G
                                          G C G C G D G ---- C G
                                          G C G C G D G ---- C G

Sliabh na mBan (5:20)
Version # 1

Verse 1	AB	Seán Ó Sé	Harps
Verse 2	A	Seán Ó Sé	Harps, Pipes
	B		Harps, Pipes, Whistle
			Whole Band in on last line
Verse 3	AB	Seán Ó Sé	Whole Band

Version # 2

Verse 1	Seán Ó Sé	Harps
Verse 2	Seán Ó Sé	Whole Band

Version # 3

A	Harps, Chanter.
B	Harps, Chanter, Whistle, Flute
AB	Whole Band

Slide
Version # 1 Gaiety

A	Flute, Bodhrán
A	Flute, Bodhrán, Whistle
B	Flute, Bodhrán, Whistle, Fiddles
B	Whole Band

Version # 2 Gaiety

A	Flute, Bodhrán
A	Flute, Bodhrán, Whistle
B	Flute, Bodhrán, Whistle, Fiddles

	B	Whole Band
	C	Fiddles in Octaves
	C	Whole Band
Version # 3 Gaiety		
	AABBC	Whole Band – go beo! (Lively)

Spailpín a Rúin

Version # 1

Spailpín	AA BA	Box, Pipes
	AABA	Whole Band, Box chords
	Pause	
Blackbird	A	Flute, Bodhran
	A	Whole Band
	B	Flute, Bodhrán
	B	Whole Band
	AABB	Whole Band
	Pause	
Spailpín	BA	Whole Band & Box Chords

Box Chords: G A D G A D A D
G A D G A D A D
D D D G A <u>D</u> A D
C AD G A D A D

Version # 2

Blackbird	A	Flute (very plain)
Spailpín verse	AABB	Pipes, 2 Accordions
	AABB	Whistle, Flute Pipes, Fiddles, Box chords
Blackbird	A	Flute
	A	Whole Band
	B	Flute
	B	Whole Band

Spailpín Fánach

Version # 1

Intro		Bodhrán
Verse 1	Seán Ó Sé	Bodhrán
Traveller	AABB	Whole Band, Bones, Bodhrán

Spailpín Verse 2	Seán Ó Sé	Bodhrán
Little Beggarman	AABB	Whole Band, Bones, Bodhrán
Spailpín Verse 3	Seán Ó Sé	Bodhrán
Traveller	AA	Whole Band
Spailpín Verse 4	Seán Ó Sé	Bodhrán
Traveller	BB	Whole Band
Spailpín Verse 5	Seán Ó Sé	Whole Band
Verse 5	Seán Ó Sé	Whole Band

Version # 2

Intro		Bodhrán
Verse 1	Seán Ó Sé	Bodhrán
Traveller	AABB	Whole Band
Spailpín Verse 2	Seán Ó Sé	Bodhrán
Little Beggarman	AABB	Whole Band
Spailpín Verse 3	Seán Ó Sé	Bodhrán
Verse 3	Seán Ó Sé	Whole Band

An Spealadóir

Version # 1

Intro		Harps
	Pause	
Cuckoo's nest	AA	Flute
	BB	Flute, Whistle
	CC	Flute, Whistle, Chanter
	AA	Fiddles
	BB	Boxes
	CC	Fiddle, Fiddle plucked
Leitrim's Fancy	AABB	Whole Band
Cuckoo's Nest	AABB	Whole Band

Version # 2   (For Aililiú – tv series)

Intro		Harps
Verse 1	Seán Ó Sé	Harps of what?
Plains of Boyle	A	Whole Band
Verse 2	Seán Ó Sé	Harps
Plains of Boyle	B	Whole Band
Verse 3	Seán Ó Sé	Harps

Plains of Boyle	A	Whole Band
Verse 4	Seán Ó Sé	Harps
Plains of Boyle	B	3 Whistles
Plains of Boyle	B	Whole Band
Verse 5	Seán Ó Sé	Whole Band
Version # 3		
Intro		Harps
Verse 1	Seán Ó Sé	Harps
Verse 2	Seán Ó Sé	Whole Band
Version # 4		
Spealadóir Verse 1	Seán Ó Síocháin	(Singing)
Verse 1		Whole Band
Verse 2	Seán Ó Síocháin	(Singing)
Plains of Boyle	AA	Whole Band
Version # 5		
Verse 1	Seán Ó Sé	Flute Whistle, Chanter, Bodhrán
	A	Whole Band
Verse 2	Seán Ó Sé	Flute Whistle, Chanter, Bodhrán
Pains of Boyle	A	Whole Band, Bodhrán
Verse 3	Seán Ó Sé	Flute Whistle, Chanter, Bodhrán
Pains of Boyle	B	Flute Whistle, Chanter, Bodhrán
Verse 4		
Line 1	Seán Ó Sé	Bodhrán
Line 2	Seán Ó Sé	Whole Band
Line 3–4	Seán Ó Sé	Whole Band
Speic Seoigheach		
	A	Harps
	A	Fiddles (in Octaves)
	B	Harps
	A	Chanter
	A	Flute, Whistle
	B	Chanter
	A	Whole Band
	A	Harps, Fiddles (Octaves)
	B	Whole Band

An Spéir Bhean Mhilis

Intro		Harps
Verse 1	Seán Ó Sé	Harps
Verse 2	Seán Ó Sé	Harps, Pipes, Fiddles in Octaves
Verse 3	Seán Ó Sé	Whole Band

Sporting Paddy

Version # 1

AB	Flute
AB	Flute, Whistle
AB	Flute, Whistle, Pipes
ABAB	Whole Band
AB	Fiddles in D
AB	Whole Band
AB	Boxes
ABAB	Whole Band

Version # 2 (3.20)

AB	Flute
AB	Harps
AB	Flute, Whistle (in after 8 bars), Harps
AB	Flute, Whistle, Harps, Pipes
AB	Flute, Whistle, Harps, Pipes, Fiddles
ABAB	Whole Band
BBAB	Whole Band
AB	Whole Band

End on long A (Count of 8 Beats)

Stácadh an Mhargaigh (Ag Taisteal na Blárnan) (3:20)

Version # 1

Intro		Harps
Verse 1 (AAB)	Seán Ó Sé	Harps
Verse 2	Seán Ó Sé	Whole Band
Verse 3	Seán Ó Sé	Whole Band

Version # 2

AAB	Chanter, Box Chords
AAB	3 Fiddles, Box (with tune), Harps

			AAB	Whole Band, Box Chords

Box Chords: D G D G D G C D G F C G C G
D G G G D G G G G D G C G →
D G C D G D G D F C G C G

Stad Airiú Rógaire

	Intro		A bass note on Box
	Verse 1	Seán Ó Sé	Box (Single Bass notes) Bodhrán
Jig: Rakes of Clonmel		AA	Whole Band
	Verse 2	Seán Ó Sé	Box, Bodhrán, Whistle, Flute
Rakes		BB	Whole Band
	Verse 3	Seán Ó Sé	Box, Bodhrán, Whistle, Flute, Fiddles
Rakes		CC	Whole Band
	Verse 4	Seán Ó Sé	Whole Band

Box Chords: A E A E A A E E
A E A D A E A A

Curfá: A E C C C E A A
A E A E A E A A

Staicín Eornan
Version # 1

Intro		Harps
	AA	Harps, Flute
	BB	Harps, Flute, Whistle
	AA	Pipes
	BB	Box, Fiddles, Viola
	AB	Harps
	ABAB	Whole band

Version # 2 (4.40)

Intro		Harps
	AABB	Whole Band
	A	Flute, Whistle
	A	Pipes
	B	Flute, Whistle
	B	Pipes

A		Harps
A		Fiddles
B		Harps
B		Fiddles
AABB		Whole Band

Star of Munster (5.30)

Version # 1

Air	AABB		Harps
		Pause	
Reel	AABB		Pipes (played slowly)
		Pause	
	AABBAABB		Whole Band (normal Tempo)
	AABB		Box (Sonny in C – G minor)
	AABB		Fiddle (John in C)
	AA		Flute (A min)
	BB		Pipes, Whistle (A min)
	AABB		Whole Band (A min)
	AABB		Whole Band (end A Maj chord A on Flute)
		end	Harps

Version # 2

AABB		Whole Band (in A min)
AABB		Whole Band (A min)
AABB		Box (G min)
AABB		Fiddles (G min)
AA		Chanter, Flute (A min)
BB		Chanter, Whistle (A min)
AABB		Whole Band (A min)

Steam Packet

Version # 1

Steam Packet	AB	Whistle, Pipes, Flute
	AB	Whole Band
Limestone Rock	AB	Flute
	AB	Whole Band

Deisiú na Líonta		AB	Pipes
		AB	Whole Band
Steam Packet		AB	Fiddle
		AB	Whole Band
Limestone Rock		AB	Box
		AB	Whole Band
Deisiú na Líonta		AB	Pipes
		AB	Whole Band
Version # 2			
Steam Packet		AB	Flute
		AB	Flute, Whistles
		AB	Flute, Whistles, Fiddles
		AB	Flute, Whistles, Fiddles, Box
		AB	Flute, Whistles, Fiddles, Box, Pipes
		AB	Flute, Whistles, Fiddles, Box, Pipes, Harps
		AB	Whole Band, Bones
Limestone Rock		ABAB	Whole Band
Steam Packet		ABAB	Whole Band
Version # 3			
Steam Packet		A	Whistle, Pipes, Flute
		B	Whole Band
		AB	Whole Band
		AB	Box
		AB	Whole Band
Limestone Rock		AB	Whistle, Pipes, Flute
Steam Packet		AB	Whole Band
Jig		AB	Fiddle
		AB	Whole Band
		A	Whistle, Pipes, Flute
		AB	Whole Band
Version # 4 (3:00) (Playboy)			
1st	4 Bars	A	Whistle
	4 Bars		Silence
2nd	4 Bars	A	Flute
	4 Bars		Silence

3rd	4 Bars	A	Whistle
	4 Bars		Silence
4th	4 Bars	A	Chanter
	4 Bars		Silence
1st	4 Bars	A	Whistle
	4 Bars		Silence
2nd	4 Bars	A	Flute
	4 Bars		Silence
3rd	4 Bars	A	Whistle
	4 Bars		Silence
4th	4 Bars	A	Chanter
	4 Bars		Silence
		A	Whistle, Flute, Chanter, Bodhrán
1st	4 Bars	B	Whistle
2nd	4 Bars	B	Flute
3rd	4 Bars	B	Whistle
4th	4 Bars	B	Chanter
		B	Whistle, Flute, Chanter, Bodhrán
		AB	Whole Band
		AB	Box
		AB	Whole Band
		AB	Fiddle
		AB	Whole Band

Mock finish – Silence while counting 4 beats

1st	4 Bars	A	Whistle
	4 Bars		Silence
2nd	4 Bars	A	Flute
	4 Bars		Silence
3rd	4 Bars	A	Whistle
	4 Bars		Silence
4th	4 Bars	A	Chanter
		AB	Whole Band

End prolong note A

Version # 5

| Steam Packet | | AB | | Fiddle (Seán) |

	AB	Whole Band
	AB	Fiddle (John)
	AB	Whole Band
	AB	Whistle, Fiddle (Martin)
	AB	Whole Band
Limestone Rock	AB	Harpsichord
	AB	Whole Band
	AB	Flute
	AB	Whole Band
Steam Packet	AB	Chanter
	AB	Whole Band

Version # 6

Steam Packet	AABB	Whole Band
	AABB	Whole Band
Limestone Rock	AABB	Flute
	AABB	Whole Band
Sixpenny Money	AABB	Chanter
	AABB	Whole Band
Steam Packet	AABB	Whole Band
	AABB	Whole Band
Limestone Rock	AABB	Flute
	AABB	Whole Band
Sixpenny Money	AABB	Chanter
	AABB	Whole Band

Pause before last 4 bars

Strawberry Blossom

	AB	Flute, Whistle
	AB	Chanter
	AB	Boxes
	AB	Fiddles
	AB	Flute, Whistle, 2 Fiddles, Chanter
	ABAB	Whole Band

An Súiste Geal Beag Bán (Casadh an tSugáin)

| | Verse 1 | Seán Ó Sé | Box, Bones |
| | Verse 2 | Seán Ó Sé | Box, Bones |

Verse 3	Seán Ó Sé	Whistle, Flute, Chanter
Verse 4	Seán Ó Sé	Whistle, Flute, Chanter
Verse 5	Seán Ó Sé	Whistle, Flute, Chanter, Fiddles
Verse 6	Seán Ó Sé	Whole Band

An Súiste Buí/The Yellow Flail

	AABBCC	Whole Band
	A	Pipes
	A	Whole Band
	B	Pipes
	B	Whole Band
	C	Pipes
	C	Whole Band
Humours of Ennistymon	A	Fiddle
	A	3 Fiddles
	B	Fiddle
	B	3 Fiddles
	C	Fiddle
	C	3 Fiddles
The Day of the Thrashing	AABB	Harps
An Súiste Buí	AABBCC	Whole Band

Sunshine Hornpipe

	AABB	Fiddle (John) Whistle (contra-melody), Bones
	AABB	Fiddle, Fiddle Pizz, 3 Whistles, Bones
	AABB	Whole Band

Swallow's Tail/The Sligo Maid

Swallow's Tail	AABB	Box (Sonny)
	AABB	Whole Band
	AABB	Fiddle
	AABB	Whole Band
Sligo Maid	AABB	Pipes
	AABB	Whole Band
	AABB	Flute

| | | AABB | Whole Band | End on A |

Sweet Boney (will I n'ere see you more) (4:15)

Intro		Harps
Verse 1	Seán Ó Sé	Harps
Verse 2	Seán Ó Sé	Harps, Flute, Whistle, Fiddle
Verse 3	Seán Ó Sé	Whole Band
		Stop before last few notes

Sweet William Craig's Dragoons

	Intro		Harps (Rule Britannia)
	Verse 1	Seán Ó Sé	Whole Band.
Sash			3 Whistles, Box Base, Bodhrán
	Verse 2	Seán Ó Sé	Whole Band
Rule Britannia			Harps
	Verse 3	Seán Ó Sé	Whole Band
Sash			3 Whistles, Box Base, Bodhrán
	Verse 4	Seán Ó Sé	Whole Band
	Verse 5	Seán Ó Sé	Whole Band

Tabhair dom do Láimh

Version # 1 (3:24)

AB	Harps
AB	Harps, 3 Fiddles
AB	Harps, Chanter
AB	Whole Band, Bodhrán

Version # 2

AB	Harps
AB	Fiddles
AB	Chanter
AB	Whole Band
AB	3 Whistles
AB	Whole Band

Tá Gaeghil Bhocht Cráite

| Intro | | Harps |
| Verse 1 | Seán Ó Sé | Harps |

Verse 2	Seán Ó Sé	Harps, Whistle, Flute, Pipes
Verse 3	Seán Ó Sé	Whole Band

Tailliúr Aerach (Ding Dong Dedaró)

Intro (Loop/Riff)　　　x 4　　　beat on Bodhrán, Beat on tin Box, Staccato A on Chanter, beat on Bottle. This riff continues throughout

AB	Seán Ó Sé	Riff, Harps
A	Seán Ó Sé	Riff, Harps, Flute, Whistle
interlude		Harps, Riff
BA	Seán Ó Sé	Harps, Riff, Flute, Whistle
interlude		Harps, Riff
BA	Seán Ó Sé	Riff, Flute, Whistle, Fiddles

Finish clattering/banging, Trill/n D (Flutter tongue Flute, Whistles)

A = Chorus   B = Verse

Táim Breoite go Leor

Version # 1

Intro		Harps
Verse 1	Seán Ó Sé	Harps
Verse 2	Seán Ó Sé	Harps, Whistle, Fiddle
Verse 3	Seán Ó Sé	Whole Band
Verse 4	Seán Ó Sé	Whole Band

Version # 2

Intro		Harps
Verse 1	Seán Ó Sé	Harps
Verse 2	Seán Ó Sé	Harps
Verse 3	Seán Ó Sé	Harps, Whistle, Fiddle
Verse 4	Seán Ó Sé	Harps, Whistle, Fiddle
Verse 5	Seán Ó Sé	Whole Band
Verse 6	Seán Ó Sé	Whole Band

Box Chords: A D G A D
　　　　　　 A D G C D
　　　　　　 A D G C D
　　　　　　 C D GD A D

Táimse ar an mBaile seo

Verse 1	Seán Ó Sé	Harps,
Verse 2	Seán Ó Sé	Harps, Box Chords
Verse 3	Seán Ó Sé	Harps, Box Chords, Fiddles octaves
Verse 4	Seán Ó Sé	Whole Band, Box Chords

        Box Chords: G G D D G D G
                                    G C D D Amin Amin D
                                      G C D D Amin Amin D
                                    G G D D G D G

Táimse in Arrears

Verse 1	Seán Ó Sé	Harps
Chorus	Seán Ó Sé	Whole Band (Verse Tempo)
Chorus		Whole Band (up to tempo)
Verse 2	Seán Ó Sé	Harps
Chorus	Seán Ó Sé	Whole Band (Verse Tempo)
Chorus		Whole Band (up to tempo)
Verse 3	Seán Ó Sé	Harps
Chorus	Seán Ó Sé	Whole Band (Verse Tempo)
Chorus		Whole Band (up to tempo)
Verse 4	Seán Ó Sé	Harps,
Chorus	Seán Ó Sé	Whole Band (Verse Tempo)
Chorus		Whole Band (up to tempo)
Verse 5	Seán Ó Sé	Harps
Chorus	Seán Ó Sé	Whole Band (Verse Tempo)
Chorus	Seán Ó Sé	Whole Band (up to tempo)

        Box Chords: G D G, D G C, D G D, G D G
        Chorus: G C D, G C D, GCD, G D G

Táimse Im' Chodhladh
Version # 1

Verse 1	A	Seán Ó Sé	Box Chords
	B	Seán Ó Sé	Flute, Whistle, Fiddle (Octavo) (in at ba bhacalach)
Verse 2	AB	Seán Ó Sé	Whole Band, Box Chords

Version # 2 (Instrumental)

        AB   Chanter

			Whole Band in on last line
	AB		Whole Band (with harmonies)

Version # 3

Verse 1	AB	Seán Ó Sé	Harps
Verse 2	AB	Seán O Sé	Whole Band

Version # 4

Verse 1	AB	Seán Ó Sé	Harps
Verse 2	AB	Seán O Sé	Whole Band
Verse 3	A	Seán Ó Sé	Harps
	B	Seán Ó Sé	Whole Band (1st 2 lines)
		Seán Ó Sé	3rd line with Harps
		Seán Ó Sé	Whole Band in on last line (Táimse im' chodhladh)

Box Chords: D G D G C D   G D C G
                     D G D G C D   G D C G
                     C D ---- G D D   G D C G
                     D G C G C D   G D C G

(Alternative 2nd half of Verse

                     D .... G ...   D G C D G
                     D G C G D   G D C G

Tá 'na Lá

Version # 1

Key of D	Verse 1	Seán Ó Síocháin	Box Chords
Chorus		Seán Ó Síocháin	Whole Band, Box Chords
	Verse 2	Seán Ó Síocháin	Box Chords
Chorus		Seán Ó Síocháin	Whole Band, Box Chords
	Verse 3	Seán Ó Síocháin	Box Chords
Chorus		Seán Ó Síocháin	Whole Band, Box Chords
Key of G	Verse 4	Seán Ó Síocháin/ Seán Ó Sé	Whole Band
Chorus		Seán & Seán	Whole Band, Box Chords
	Verse 5	Seán & Seán	Whole Band, Box Chords
Chorus		Seán Ó Síocháin	Whole Band, Box Chords

Version # 2

Verse 1	D		Seán Ó Sé	Box Chords
Chorus			Seán Ó Sé	Whole Band, Box Chords
	D		Seán Ó Sé	Box Chords
Chorus Verse 2			Seán Ó Sé	Whole Band, Box Chords
Verse 3	D	Seán Ó Sé		Box Chords
Chorus			Seán Ó Sé	Whole Band, Box Chords
Verse 4	G		Seán Ó Sé	Whole Band, Box Chords
Chorus			Seán Ó Sé	Whole Band

Version # 3

Verse 1	D	Seán Ó Sé	Box Chords
Chorus		Seán Ó Sé	Whole Band, Box Chords
Verse 2		Seán Ó Sé	Box Chords
Chorus		Seán Ó Sé	Whole Band, Box Chords
Verse 3		Seán Ó Sé	Box Chords
Chorus		Seán Ó Sé	Whole Band, Box Chords
Verse 4	G	Seán Ó Sé	Whole Band
Chorus		Seán Ó Sé	Whole Band, Box Chords
Verse 5		Seán Ó Sé	Whole Band, Box Chords
Chorus		Seán Ó Sé	Whole Band, Box Chords

Version # 4

Verse 1	D	Seán Ó Sé	Box Chords
Chorus		Seán Ó Sé	Whole Band, Box Chords
Verse 2	D	Seán Ó Sé	Box Chords
Chorus		Seán Ó Sé	Whole Band, Box Chords
Verse 3	D	Seán Ó Sé	Box Chords, Box Chords
Chorus		Seán Ó Sé	Whole Band. Box Chords
Verse 4	G	Seán Ó Sé	Whole Band. Box Chords
Chorus		Seán Ó Sé	Whole Band

Box Chords: Key D D G D A D G DAD
Key G G C G D G CG D G

Version # 5 (Alleliú)

Intro			Harps
Verse 1	D	Seán Ó Sé	Harps
Chorus		Seán Ó Sé	Whole Band, Box Chords

	Verse 2	D	Seán Ó Sé	Harps
	Chorus		Seán Ó Sé	Whole Band, Box Chords
	Verse 3	D	Seán Ó Sé	Harps
	Chorus		Seán Ó Sé	Whole Band, Box Chords
	Verse 4	G	Seán Ó Sé	Whole Band
	Chorus		Seán Ó Sé	Whole Band, Box Chords

Tá mo mhadra, Níl mo Mhadra (1:42)

Intro		Long 'Agus'	Sung by all as intro
	Chorus	Seán Ó Sé	Whole Band, Box Chords
	Verse 1	Seán Ó Sé	Whistle, Flute, Box Chords
Chorus		Seán Ó Sé	Whole Band, Box Chords
	Verse 2	Seán Ó Sé	Whistle, Flute, Box Chords
	Chorus	Seán Ó Sé	Whole Band, Box Chords
Caileach a'Túirne			♪♪♪♪♪
		A	2 Whistles, Flute, Fiddle, Bodhrán Bones
		A	Whole Band
	Chorus	Seán Ó Sé	Whole Band, Box Chords
	Verse 3	Seán Ó Sé	Whistle, Flute, Box Chords
	Chorus	Seán Ó Sé	Whole Band, Box Chords
Caileach a'Túirne		A	Fiddles, Flute
Caileach a'Túirne		A	Whole Band ending with long A to long 'Agus' Sung by all into
Fast Chorus		Seán Ó Sé	Whole Band, Box Chords

Box Chords: D A D E D A D E A
A E A A
D A E A D D D E

Tap Room

Version # 1

	A	Whistle
	A	Whistle, Flute
	B	Whistle, Flute, Pipes
	B	Whistle, Flute, Pipes, Fiddles

	AABB		Whole Band
	AA		Whistle, Fiddle
	BB		Pipes
	AA		Box, 3 fiddles
	BB		Flute
	AABB		Whole Band

Version # 2

Tap Room	AABB		Whole Band
	AABB		Whole Band
Liffey Banks	AABB		Whole Band
	AABB		Whole Band
Tap Room	A		Whistle
	A		Whistle, Fiddle
	B		Whistle
	B		Whistle, Fiddle
	AABB		Whole Band

Tarring go Ciúin

Verse 1 & Chorus (AB)	Seán Ó Sé	Harps
AABB		Whole Band
Verse 2	Seán Ó Sé	Harps
AABB		Whole Band
Verse 3	Seán Ó Sé	Harps
AABB		Whole Band
Verse 4	Seán Ó Sé	Harps
Chorus	Seán Ó Sé	Whole Band (4 times)

Tatter Jack Walsh

Version # 1

A	Chanter (Slowly)
B	Box, Verse read
B	Chanter
B	Box, Verse read
AABB	Whole Band
A	Fiddle
A	Box
B	Fiddle

			Box
	B		
	AB		Pipes Drone and Verse read
	AABB		Whole Band Correct Tempo
	AABB		Whole Band
	AABB		Whole Band

Version # 2
	Intro		Harps, with Pipes drones
	AABB		Chanter and Drones
	AABB		Harps
	AABB		Fiddle
	AABB		Box
	AABB		Flute Whistle Fiddle (Plucked)
	AABB		Fiddle (Seán) & Low Fiddle (Martin – Viola)
	AABB		Whole Band

Teetotaller
	AABB		Whole Band
	AABB		Fiddle
	AABB		Whole Band
	AABB		Whistle, Flute, Pipes
	AABB		Whole Band
	AABB		Whole Band

Tell Her I Am / *An síoda 'tá id' bhfallait?*

Tell Her		AA		Whole Band
An Síoda	Verse 1	AB	Seán Ó Síocháin	Flute Whistle, Box
Tell Her		BB		Whole Band
An Síoda	Verse 2	AB	Seán Ó Síocháin	Flute Whistle, Box
Tell Her		CC		Whole Band
An Síoda	Verse 3	AB	Seán Ó Síocháin	Flute Whistle, Box
Tell Her		AABBCC		Whole Band
An Síoda	Verse 4	A	Seán Ó Síocháin	Flute Whistle, Box
		B		Whole Band

There was a Lady
	Intro		Harps
	Verse 1	Seán Ó Sé	Harps
	Verse 2	Seán Ó Sé	Harps, Box

| Verse 3 | Seán Ó Sé | Harps, Box |
| Verse 4 | Seán Ó Sé | Whole Band |

Three Little Drummers

AABB	Pipes
AABB	Harps
AABB	Fiddles – Octaves
AABB	Whistle, Flute, Fiddle – Martin (Octaves)
AABB	Whole Band
AABB	Whole Band

Three Sea Captains

Version # 1

AABB	Harps
A	Pipes
A	Fiddles, Viola
B	Pipes
B	Fiddles, Viola
A	Box, Fiddles, Viola
A	3 Whistles
B	Box, Fiddles, Viola
B	3 Whistles
AB	Whistles
AB	Whole Band

Ending Flute, Whistles G D E G the rest on G

Version # 2 (7:00)

AABB	Harps
A	Pipes
A	Fiddles
B	Pipes
B	Fiddles
AB	3 Whistles
AABB	Whole Band

Thugamar féin an Samhradh Linn (2:55) (C)

| Chorus | Harps, 2 Whistles, Flute, Fiddle – Octaves (Martin) |

Verse 1	Seán Ó Sé	Harps
Chorus	Seán Ó Sé	Whole Band, Box Chords
Verse		Harps, 2 Whistles, Flute, Fiddle – Octaves (Martin), Box Chords
Verse 2	Seán Ó Sé	Harps
Chorus	Seán Ó Sé	Whole Band, Box Chords
Verse		Harps, 2 Whistles, Flute, Fiddle – Octaves (Martin), Box Chords or just C?
Verse 3	Seán Ó Sé	Harps, Box Chords
Chorus	Seán Ó Sé	Whole Band, Box Chords
Verse		Harps, 2 Whistles, Flute, Fiddle – Octave (Martin), Box Chords or just C?
Verse 4	Seán Ó Sé	Harps, Box Chords
Chorus	Seán Ó Sé	Whole Band, Box Chords
Chorus		Whole Band, Box Chords
		Fade out

Box Chords: C, G, C, G, C, G, C, G, C, G, C, G, C, G, G, C

Tiarna Mhuigheo

AABB	Harps
AABB	Harps, 3 Fiddles (Martin – Octaves)
AABB	Harps, Chanter
AABB	Harps, Chanter, Whistle, Flute
AABB	Whole Band

Tiocfaigh an Samhradh

Seán Ó Sé	Harps
Seán Ó Sé	Harps
Seán Ó Sé	Harps, Fiddles
Seán Ó Sé	Whole Band
Seán Ó Sé	Whole Band

Tommy Cohen's Reel

AA	Chanter
BB	Fiddles (Octaves)
CC	Whistles, Flute
AA	Harps

	BB	Fiddles
	CC	Whistles, Flute
	AA	Harps
	BB	Fiddles (Octaves)
	CC	2 whistles, Flute
	AABBCC	Fiddle, Flute
	AABBCC	Whole Band

Tons of Bright Gold (see An Capaillín Bán)

Intro		Harps
Verse 1	Seán Ó Sé	Harps
Verse 2	Seán Ó Sé	Harps
Verse 3	Seán Ó Sé	Harps
Verse 4	Seán Ó Sé	Harps, Whole Band (softly)
Verse 5	Seán Ó Sé	Whole Band

Box Chords: G C G C G
G D G C D
G D G Emin C D
G C G C G

Torramh an Bharraile / Humours of Ennistymon

Version # 1

	A	Seán Ó Síocháin	Harps
	A		Whole Band
	B	Seán Ó Síocháin	Whole Band
	B		Whole Band
Humours	AABB		Whole Band
Torraimh Verse 2	A	Seán Ó Síocháin	Harps
	A		Whole Band
	B	Seán Ó Síocháin	Whole Band
	B		Whole Band
Humours	CC		Whole Band
	A	Seán Ó Síocháin	Harps
	A		Whole Band
	B	Seán Ó Síocháin	Whole Band
	B		Whole Band

Version # 2

	Verse 1	A	Seán Ó Sé	Whole Band
		A		Whole Band
		B	Seán Ó Sé	Whole Band
		B		Whole Band
Humours		AABB		Whole Band
	Verse 2	A	Seán Ó Sé	Whole Band
		A		Whole Band
		B	Seán Ó Sé	Whole Band
		B		Whole Band
Humours		BB		Whole Band
	Verse 3	A	Seán Ó Sé	Whole Band
		A		Whole Band
		B	Seán Ó Sé	Whole Band
		B	Seán Ó Sé	Whole Band

Toss the Feathers

AB	Box (Sonny)
AB	Whole Band
AB	Fiddles, Drones, Bodhrán
AB	Whistle, Flute, Pipes Riff, Bodhrán
AB	Box, Pipes Riff, Bodhrán
AB	Fiddles, Pipes Riff, Bodhrán
AB	Bodhrán, Bones, Pipes Riff
AB	Whole Band

End with long D

Trím Rachaigh Subhail

Verse 1	Seán Ó Sé	Harps
Verse 2	Seán Ó Sé	Harps, Whistle, Flute
Verse 1	Seán Ó Sé	Whole Band

Trip to Durrow

AABC	Whole Band
AABC	Whole Band
AA	Harps

B		Harps, Flute
C		Harps, Flute Whistle
AABC		3 Fiddles
AABC		Chanter, Flute, Whistle
AABC		Whole Band
AABC		Whole Band

Tripping to the Well

AABB		Box
AABB		Whole Band

Ma Ma will buy me a

AB		Fiddles
AB		Whole Band

Girl I left behind

AABB		Flute, Whistle
AABB		Whole Band

Kiss the Girl Behind the Door

AABB		Box, Fiddle
AABB		Whole Band

An tÚll

Verse 1	Seán Ó Sé	Harps

Portláirge

		Whole Band
Verse 2	Seán Ó Sé	Harps

Leather away

		Whole Band
Verse 3	Seán Ó Sé	Harps

Dashing White Sergeant

		Whole Band
Verse 4	Seán Ó Sé	Whole Band

The Union of Macroom

Intro		Harps
Verse 1	Seán Ó Sé	Harps
Verse 2	Seán Ó Sé	Harps, Box Chords
Verse 3	Seán Ó Sé	Harps, Box Chords, Fiddles
Verse 4	Seán Ó Sé	Harps, Box Chords, Fiddles, Whistle, Flute
Verse 5	Seán Ó Sé	Harps, Box Chords, Whole Band

Box Chords: C G C G

                                      D5 G C D (full)
                                        D5 G C G
                                        C G C G

Valley of Knockanure (4:03)

Intro		Harps (1st line of verse)
Verse 1	Seán Ó Sé	Harps
Verse 2	Seán Ó Sé	Harps, Viola, Box Chords
Verse 3	Seán Ó Sé	Harps, Viola, Whistle, Flute Pipes, Box Chords
Verse 4	Seán Ó Sé	Whole Band, Box Chords

                Box Chords: Amin Dmin Amin, Dmin Emin Dmin, Amin
                          Amin Fmaj. Cmaj. Cmaj. Dmin Dmin Emin
                          Amin Fmaj. Cmaj. Cmaj Dmin Dmin Emin
                Amin Dmin Amin, Dmin Emin Dmin, Amin

Wearing of the Green (3:10)

Verse 1	Seán Ó Sé	Harps or Box Chords
Verse 2	Seán Ó Sé	Harps or Box Chords
Verse 3	Seán Ó Sé	Harps or Box Chords, Whistle, Flute Chanter
Verse 1	Seán Ó Sé	Whole Band

Wexford Hornpipe (Medley)

Version # 1

Wexford	AABB	Harps (in G) layout?
Cork	AABB	Chanter (D)
Liverpool	AABB	Fiddles (G)
Plains of Boyle	AABB	Flute (D)
Stack of Wheat	AABB	Flute, Box (G)
Rights of Man	AABB	Whistle (E min)
Wexford	AABB	Whole Band (G)

Version # 2

Wexford	AABB	Harps (in G)
Cork	AABB	Chanter (D)
Liverpool	AABB	Fiddles (G)
Liverpool	AABB	Fiddles
Stack of Wheat	AABB	Box

Rights of Man	AABB	Whistles
Wexford	AABB	Whole Band

The Whinney Fields of Leitrim (2 jigs played simultaneously)

AB (a)	Whistle, Bodhrán (in after 4 bars), Bones (in after 8 bars)
AB (a)	Whole Band
AB (b)	Whistle, Bones, Bodhrán, with Flute (counter-melody)
AB (b)	Whistle, Fid, Bones/ Bodhrán, Flute (Contra) Fiddle Contra
AB (b)	Whole Band, with Flute (Contra) Fiddle Contra
AB (a)	Whole Band
AAAA (a)	Whole Band with Long Drone D on Box

Ending on long D

(a) is straight playing of melody

(b) is melody with counter-melody against it.

Counter-melody is for A each turn:

FAB, FAB AFD, FAB, FAB D'—, FAB, FAB, AFD, F'G'F', E'D'C', B–A

FAB, FAB AFD, FAB, FAB D'—, FAB, FAB, AFD, F'G'F', E'D'C', B–A

F'G'F', E'F'E', D'-E', F'G'F', E'F'G' A'–G', F'G'F', E'F'E', D'–B, BAF, DFA, B–A

F'G'F', E'F'E', D'-E', F'G'F', E'F'G' A'-G', A'F'D', G'E'C, D–B, BAF, DFA, B–A

Followed by B as in the straight tune.

The White Cockade (An Coileachóg Bán) (Mo Ghille m'fhear) (LP Battle of Aughrim)

AB	Harps, D Drone on all instruments
AB	Harps, Chanter & Drones, Fiddles, Whistle
AB	Whole Band, Bodhrán
A	Whole Band, Bodhrán

Fade

Wife of the Bold Tennant Farmer

Intro		Harps
Verse 1	Seán Ó Sé	Harps
Verse 2	Seán Ó Sé	Harps, Whistle

Verse 3	Seán Ó Sé	Harps, 2 Whistles
Verse 4	Seán Ó Sé	Harps, 3 Whistles
Verse 5	Seán Ó Sé	Harps, 3 Whistles, Fiddles
Verse 6	Seán Ó Sé	Whole Band
	repeat 2nd Verse 6	

William Tell
Gaiety

Intro		Harps
	A	Whole Band
	B	Pipes, Harps
	C	Fiddle
	A	Whole Band (without Pipes)

Oró Bog Liom í

	A	Harps, Fiddle, Flute, Whistle
	B	Whole Band

Willie Dear (key G)

Intro		Harps
Verse 1	Seán Ó Sé	Harps, Box Chords
Verse 2	Seán Ó Sé	Harps, Box Chords
Verse 3	Seán Ó Sé	Harps, Viola (Counter-melody)
Verse 4	Seán Ó Sé	Harps, Viola, Flute
Verse 5	Seán Ó Sé	Harps, Viola, Flute, Chanter
Verse 6	Seán Ó Sé	Whole Band
Verse 7	Seán Ó Sé	Harps Lines 1+2
	Pause	
		Whole Band in at lines 3/4

Counter-melody: ABD GAG F# ED
GABCDE F# EDCB
GABCDE F# EDCB
ABDGAG F# ED

Box Chords: G C G G C G G C G G C G

Wind the Shakes the Barley
Version # 1

	AB	Fiddle Solo, Fiddle Chords
	AB	Fiddle Box

	AB	Fiddle, Box, Flute
	AB	Fiddle, Box, Flute, Whistle
	AB	Fiddle, Box, Flute, Whistle, Pipes
	AB	Fiddle, Box, Flute, Whistle, Pipes, Box notes
Version # 2		
	AB	Whistle, Flute
	AB	Fiddles, Pipes
	AB	Box
	AB	Whole Band
	AB	Whole Band
Version # 3		
	Intro	Whistles (Thrills on 2 A & F#), Flute (Thrill D)
	4 Beats of Rhythm	Fiddle (Martin)
	AB	Fiddle (John) Fiddle (Rhythm)
	AB	Fiddle (John), Box, Fiddle (Rhythm)
	AB	Fiddle (John), Box, Flute, Fiddle (Rhythm)
	AB	Fiddle, Box, Flute, Chanter, Fiddle (Rhythm)
	AB	Whole Band, Fiddle (Rhythm)
	AABB	Harps
	AB	Whistle, Flute, Chanter Drones
	AB	Fiddles
	AB	Boxes
	ABAB	Whole Band
	Ending	2 Whistles (Thrills on 2 A & F#) Flute (Thrill D)
		2 Whistles (Thrills F#) Flute (Thrill A)

Woman of the House (3:30)

	AABB	Flute
	AABB	Fiddle
	AABB	Chanter (Old Version) (2nd D'TLD, TLS)
	AABB	Whistle & Flute
	AABB	Whole Band
	AABB	Whole Band

Discography

Vinyl and Digital releases of Seán Ó Riada and Ceoltóirí Chualann
GL 1 Seán Ó Riada – Saoirse!
GL 2 Seán Ó Riada, Seán Ó Sé agus Ceoltóirí Chualann – An Poc ar Buille
GL 3 Seán Ó Riada, Seán Ó Sé agus Ceoltóirí Chualann – Neillí
GL 5 Seán Ó Riada, Seán Ó Sé agus Ceoltóirí Chualann – Mo Chailín Bán/Tá mo Mhadra
CES 004 Seán Ó Riada, Seán Ó Sé agus Ceoltóirí Chualann – Príosún Chluain Meala/Valley of Knockanure (1968)
CEF 081 Seán Ó Riada Aifreann 2
CEF 074 Claisceadal Chúil Aodha – Ceol is Cibeal
CEF 076 Seán Ó Sé, Seán Ó Riada and Ceoltóirí Chualann – Na Céirníní 45

CBC 3 Ceol an Aifrinn

CEFCD 001 Radio Éireann Light Orchestra/ Tomás Ó Súilleabháin accompanied by Seán Ó Riada (1958)
CEFCD 010 Seán Ó Riada, Ceoltóirí Chualann agus Darach Ó Catháin – Reacaireacht an Riadaigh
CEFCD 012 Seán Ó Riada, Ceoltóirí Chualann – Playboy of the Western World
CEFCD 015 Seán Ó Riada, Ceoltóirí Chualann agus Seán Ó Sé – Ceol na nUasal (1967)
CEFCD 016 Seán Ó Riada, Ceoltóirí Chualann agus Seán Ó Sé – Ding Dong
CEFCD 027 Seán Ó Riada, Seán Ó Sé agus Ceoltóirí Chualann – Ó Riada Sa Ghaiety (1970)
CEFCD 032 Seán Ó Riada, Ceoltóirí Chualann agus Seán Ó Sé – Ó Riada
CEFCD 080 Seán Ó Riada – Mise Éire, Saoirse?, An Tine Bheo (1979)

ORIADACD01 remastered Ó Riada sa Gaiety +3 trks
ORIADACD02 Seán O Riada Ceol an Aifrinn / Aifreann 2
ORIADACD03 Seán Ó Riada – Mise Éire (2006)
ORIADACD04 Seán Ó Riada – Pléaráca an Riadaigh 93cds: 2008 includes CEF 010,015, and 016)
ORIADACD06 Seoda an Riadaigh (a 3 cd compilation from previous albums) including Playboy of the Western World, A selection of Ceoltóirí Chualann Recordings and the Gael Linn recorded film music including Mise Éire, Saoirse?, Tine Bheo and Ceol na Laoi
ORIADACD7 Port na bPucaí. 25 tracks from various recordings of Seán Ó Riada playing piano or harpsichord. (2014)

List of Fleadh Cheoil an Radio Progammes
Venues
　　GG　　　　　　　　Galloping Green (Seán Ó Riada's house)
　　FXH　　　　　　　Francis Xavier Hall
　　OCH　　　　　　　O'Connell Hall
　　PBS　　　　　　　 Portobello Studio
　　PXH　　　　　　　Phoenix Hall
　　9&10　　　　　　　Rooms 9 and 10 Radio Éireann Studios, Henry Street, Dublin

Early rehearsals and recordings:
Date	Type	Programme	Location
06/11/1960	Rehearsal		GG
13/11/1960	Rehearsal		GG
13/11/1960	Rehearsal		GG
17/11/1960	Rehearsal		GG
11/12/1960	Rehearsal		GG
01/01/1961	Rehearsal		GG
08/01/1961	Rehearsal		GG
14/01/1961	Recording	Reacaireacht an Riadaigh	PDS
12/02/1961	Rehearsal	Reacaireacht an Riadaigh	GG
26/02/1961	Rehearsal	Reacaireacht an Riadaigh	GG
12/03/1961	Rehearsal	Reacaireacht an Riadaigh	GG
12/03/1961 – 8:00 p.m.	Broadcast	Reacaireacht an Riadaigh	Radio Éireann
15/03/1961	Repeat Broadcast		Radio Éireann
19/03/1961 – 8:00 p.m.	Broadcast	Reacaireacht an Riadaigh	Radio Éireann

Fleadh Cheoil an Raidio

Prog No.	Broadcast date	Recorded	Location
Winter 1962–63			
1	25/12/1962	12/12/1962	FXH
2	03/01/1963	05/12/1962	FXH
3	10/01/1963	05/12/1962	FXH
4	17/01/1963	12/12/1962	FXH
5	24/01/1963	19/12/1962	FXH
6	31/01/1963	19/12/1962	FXH
7	07/02/1963	17/01/1963	FXH
8	14/02/1963	17/01/1963	FXH
9	21/02/1963	24/01/1963	FXH
10	28/02/1963	24/01/1963	FXH
11	07/03/1963	31/01/1963	FXH
12	14/03/1963	31/01/1963	FXH
13	21/03/1963	08/02/1963	FXH
14	28/03/1963	08/02/1963	FXH
15	04/04/1963	10/02/1963	FXH
16	11/04/1963	10/02/1963	FXH

17	18/04/1963	17/02/1963	FXH
18	25/04/1963	17/02/1963	FXH
19	02/05/1963	21/04/1963	FXH

Winter 1963–64

1	21/10/1963	12/10/1963	OCH
2	28/10/1963	12/10/1963	OCH
3	04/11/1963	13/10/1963	OCH
4	11/11/1963	13/10/1963	OCH
5	18/11/1963	09/11/1963	OCH
6	28/11/1963	09/11/1963	OCH
7	05/12/1963	10/11/1963	OCH
8	12/12/1963	10/11/1963	OCH
9	19/12/1963	07/12/1963	OCH
10	25/12/1963	07/12/1963	OCH
11	26/12/1963	08/12/1963	OCH
12	09/01/1964	08/12/1963	OCH
13	16/01/1964	04/01/1964	OCH
14	23/01/1964	04/01/1964	OCH
15	30/01/1964	05/01/1964	OCH
16	06/02/1964	05/01/1964	OCH
17	13/02/1964	08/02/1964	OCH
18	20/02/1964	08/02/1964	OCH
19	27/02/1964	09/02/1964	OCH
20	05/03/1964	09/02/1964	OCH
21	12/03/1964	29/02/1964	OCH
22	19/03/1964	29/02/1964	OCH
23	26/03/1964	02/03/1964	OCH

Winter 1964–65

1	02/11/1964	11/10/1964	OCH
2	9/11/1964	11/10/1964	?
3	16/11/1964	11/10/1964	?
4	23/11//1964	11/10/1964	?
5	30/11/1964	08/11/1964	OCH
6	7/12/1964	05/12//1964	OCH
7	14/12/1964	5/12//1964	OCH
8	21/12/1964	5/12/1964	OCH
9	25/12/1964	6/12/1964	OCH
10	31/12/1964	6/12/1964	OCH
11	7/1/1965	2/1/1965	OCH
12	14/1/1965	2/1/1965	OCH
13	21/1/1965	3/1/1965	OCH
14	28/1/1965	3/1/1965	OCH

15	4/2/1965	16/1/1965	PBS
16	11/2/1965	16/1/1965	PBS
17	18/2/1965	17/1/1965	PBS
18	25/2/1965	17/1/1965	PBS
19	4/3/1965	13/2/1965	PBS
20	11/3/1965	13/2/1965	PBS
21	18/3/1965	14/2/1965	PBS
22	25/3/1965	14/2/1965	PBS
23	1/4/1965	13/3/1965	PBS
24	unknown	13/3/1965	PBS
25	8/4/1965	14/3/1965	PBS

Winter 1965–66

Prog No.	Broadcast date	Recorded	Location
1	28/10/1965	26/9/1965	OCH
2	4/11/1965	26/9/1965	OCH
3	11/11/1965	9/10/1965	PBS
4	18/11/1965	9/10/1965	PBS
5	25/11/1965	9/10/1965	PBS
6	2/12/1965	9/10/1965	OCH
7	9/12/1965	6/11/1965	OCH
8	16/12/1965	6/11/1965	PBS
9	23/12/1965	4/12/1965	PBS
10	30/12/1965	4/12/1965	PBS
11	6/1/1966	4/12/1965	PBS
12	13/01/1966	4/12/1965	PBS
13	20/1/1966	1/1/1966	OCH
14	27/1/1966	1/1/1966	OCH
15	3/2/1966	2/1/1966	OCH
16	10/2/1966	2/1/1966	OCH
17	17/2/1966	5/2/1966	OCH
18	24/2/1966	5/2/1966	OCH
19	4/3/1966	6/2/1966	OCH
20	11/3/1966	6/2/1966	OCH
21	17/3/1966	12/3/1966	OCH
22	24/3/1966	12/3/1966	Special for Easter

Winter 1966–67

1	6/12/1966	19/11/1966	OCH
2	13/12/1966	19/11/1966	OCH
3	20/12/1966	17/12/1966	OCH
4	27/12/1966	17/12/1999	OCH

5	3/1/1967	18/12/1966	OCH
6	10/1/1967	18/12/1966	OCH
7	17/1/1967	21/1/1967	OCH
8		21/1/1967	OCH
9		22/1/1967	OCH
10		22/1/1967	OCH
11		18/2/1967	OCH
12		18/2/1967	OCH
13		19/2/1967	OCH
14		19/2/1967	OCH
15		18/3/1967	OCH
16		18/3/1967	OCH
17		19/3/1967	OCH

Winter 1967–68

Prog No.	Broadcast date	Recorded	Location
1		21/1/1968	OCH
2		21/1/1968	OCH
3		17/2/1968	OCH
4		17/2/1968	OCH
5		18/2/1968	OCH
6		18/2/1968	OCH
7		30/3/1968	PBS
8		30/3/1968	PBS
9		31/3/1968	PBS
10		31/3/1968	PBS
11		27/4/1968	OCH
12		27/4/1968	OCH
13		28/4/1968	OCH
14		28/4/1968	OCH

Winter 1968–69

1		19/10/1968	OCH
2		19/10/1968	OCH
3		20/10/1968	OCH
4		20/10/1968	OCH
5		9/11/1968	OCH
6		9/11/1968	OCH
7		10/11/1968	OCH
8		10/11/1968	OCH
9		30/12/1968	OCH
10		30/12/1968	OCH

11	4/1/1969	OCH
12	4/1/1969	OCH
13	5/1/1969	PBS
14	5/1/1969	PBS
15	25/1/1969	PBS
16	25/1/1969	PBS
17	26/1/1969	PBS
18	26/1/1969	PBS
19	8/2/1969	PBS
20	8/2/1969	PBS
21	9/2/1969	PBS
22	9/2/1969	PBS
23	22/3/1969	PBS
24	22/3/1969	PBS
25	23/3/1969	PBS
26	23/3/1969	PBS

Reacaireacht an Riadaigh Programmes

Prog No.	Broadcast date	Recorded	Location
Series 1 (Winter 1961–62)			
1	12/3/1961	14/1/1961	PBS
2	16/7/1961	13/5/1961	PBS
3	6/8/1961	29/7/1961	FXH
4	26/12/1961	1/12/1961	FXH
5	19/2/1962	14/1/1962	FXH
6	26/12/1962	21/7/1962	FXH
7 (/2)	—	4/8/1962	FXH
7 (/2)	5/1/1963	3/11/1962	FXH
8	19/1/1963	5/1/1963	FXH
9	2/2/1963	12/1/1963	OCH
10	16/2/1963	19/1/1963	PBS
11 (/2)	—	19/1/1963	PBS
11 (/2)	30/3/1963	5/3/1963	OCH
12	2/3/1963	2/2/1963	PBS
13	16/3/1963	16/2/1963	FXH (PBS?)
14	13/4/1963	1/3/1963	OCH (Foxchase)
15	21/9/1963	1/9/1963	OCH
16	5/10/1963	1/9/1963	OCH
17	19/10/1963	1/9/1963	OCH
18	2/11/1963	1/9/1963	OCH
19	16/11/1963	1/9/1963	OCH

Series 2 (Satharn)

Prog No.	Broadcast date	Recorded	Location
1	22/8/1964	13/6/1964	OCH
2	29/8/1964	13/6/1964	OCH
3	5/9/1964	13/6/1964	OCH
4	12/9/1964	14/6/1964	OCH
5	19/9/1964	14/6/1964	OCH
6	26/9/1964	14/6/1964	OCH

Series 3 (Satharn)

Prog No.	Broadcast date	Recorded	Location
1	14/8/1965	17/7/1965	PBS
2	21/8/1965	17/7/1965	PBS
3	28/8/1965	17/7/1965	PBS
4	4/9/1965	18/7/1965	PBS
5	11/9/1965	18/7/1965	PBS
6	18/9/1965	18/7/1965	PBS

Series 4

1	20/8/1966?	23/7/1966	OCH
2	27/8/1966?	23/7/1966	OCH
3	3/9/1966?	23/7/1966	OCH
4	10/9/1966?	24/7/1966	OCH
5	17/9/1966?	24/7/1966	OCH
6	24/9/1966?	24/7/1966	OCH

Series 5

1	26/8/1967?	14/8/1967	PBS
2	2/9/1967?	14/8/1967	PBS
3	9/9/1967?	14/8/1967	PBS
4	16/9/1967?	15/8/1967	PBS
5	23/9/1967?	15/8/1967	PBS
6	30/9/1967?	15/8/1967	PBS

Series 6

1	11/9/1968?	6/7/1967	PBS
2	18/9/1968?	6/7/1967	PBS
3	25/9/1968?	6/7/1967	PBS
4	2/10/1968?	7/7/1967	PBS
5	9/10/1968?	7/7/1967	PBS
6	16/9/1968?	7/7/1967	PBS

Aililiú Television Programmes

Prog No.	Broadcast date	Recorded	Location
1 (Harvest)	7/10/1965	25/9/1965	RTÉ, Montrose
2 (Napoleon)	21/10/1965	10/10/1965	RTÉ, Montrose
3 (Ainmithe)	4/11/1965	10/10/1965	RTÉ, Montrose
4 (The Hunt)	18/11/1965	7/11/1965	RTÉ, Montrose
5 (Travellers)	2/12/1965	7/11/1965	RTÉ, Montrose
6 (The Sea)	16/2/1965	16/5/1965	RTÉ, Montrose
7 (Unknown)	30/12/1965	5/12/1965	RTÉ, Montrose

List of Ceoltóirí Chualann Concerts:

10/9/1961	Shelbourne Hotel
16/9/1961	Marion Hall, Milltown, Dublin, Recorded music for Cork Ballet Company
12/11/1961	Recorded film music for Playboy of the Western World
13/3/1962	Coirm Ceoil na Féile, Phoenix Hall, Dublin
13/8/1962	Marion Hall, Milltown, Dublin, Recorded music for Cork Ballet Company
25/10/1962	Mansion House, Dublin – for Oireachtas na Gaeilge
2/12/1962	South County Hotel (Stillorgan). Played during charity dance
3/3/1963	Abbeyfeale, Co. Limerick (Glór na nGael, With B/W archive footage extant)
19/3/1963	Gaiety Theatre, Dublin
6/4/1963	Scarriff, Co. Clare
7/4/1963	Ennis, Co. Clare
4/8/1963	Kilrush, Co. Clare
5/8/1963	Kilrush, Co. Clare (Fleadh Ceoil?)
??/8/1963	Recorded music for the West Cork Ballad for Irish Theatre Company
25/12/1963	RTÉ TV programme, Fionn Mc Cumhail agus An Bhean Níocháin ó Éireann
22/2/964	Carnegie Library, Kenmare, Co. Kerry (with Paddy Bán Ó Broin dancing)
23/2/1964	Town Hall Millstreet, Co. Cork (with Paddy Bán Ó Broin dancing)
24/2/1964	BBC TV play Peter Hunt's Studio (some of the group)
8/3/1964	Aula Maxima, UCC, Cork
15/3/1964	Gaiety, Dublin
14/11/1964	Rupert Guinness Hall, Dublin
17/4/1966	Aula Maxima, UCC, Cork
13/3/1966	Gaiety Theatre, Coirm Ceoil na Féile
30/7/1966	BBC recording in Cúil Aodha (some of the group), Director Peter Luke
14/11/1966	Queens University, Belfast
15/11/1967	Provost's House, Trinity College, Dublin.
19/11/1967	Queens University, Belfast
13/12/1967	UCD, Dublin
17/3/1968	Gaiety Theatre, Dublin
19/5/1968	Recording in RTÉ for BBC Radio 3 programme

8/3/1969	Recorded film music for Gael Linn ('Pobal', directed by Louis Marcus)
30/3/1969	Gaiety theatre, Dublin, Peadar Ó Doirnín concert (Ó Riada sa Gaiety LP)
29/8/1969	Ennis Co Clare, Cumann Merriman (Annual school)
28/6/1970	Cork City Hall, O'Carolan Tercentenary Concert (basis of Ó Riada LP)
27/11/1971	UCC, Commemoration Concert (Commemorating Seán Ó Riada RIP)
16/1/1972	Gaiety Theatre, Dublin, Commemoration Concert (Commemorating SÓR)

List of Ceoltóirí Chualann Records
All released on Gael Linn label.

LPs

Reacaireacht an Riadaigh	Peter Hunt Studio	CEF 010	1961
Playboy of the Western World	Phoenix Hall	CEF 012	1961
Ceol na nUasal	Ardmore Studios	CEF 015	1963
Ding Dong	Peter Hunt Studio	CEF 016	1967
Ó Riada sa Gaiety	rec live (É. de Buitléar Studio)	CEF 027	1969
Ó Riada	rec live (É. de Buitléar Studio)	CEF 032	1971
Seán Ó Riada	Compilation	CEF 076	1978

45s – 4 songs

An Poc ar Buile	Marianella	GL2	1962
Neillí	De la Salle, Churchtown	GL3	1964
Bruach na Carraige Báine	St Joseph's Orphanage	GL5	1966

45s – 2

Táimse 'mo Chodhladh	CES 003	1968
Príosún Chluain Meala	CES 004	1968
An Poc ar Buile	CES 011	1971
Do Bhí Bean Uasal	CES 012	1971

Clár/programme of various concerts:
29/8/1969 Ennis Co. Clare, Cumann Merriman (Annual school)
Carolon's Concerto
Castle Kelly
An Mac Alla (Seán Ó Sé)
Lord Inchiquin
Marcshlua Uí Néill
An Buachaill Caol Dubh (Seán Ó Sé)
Beidh Aonach Amáireach (Seán Ó Sé)
Bonapart's Retreat
Gander in the Pratie Hole
Raghadsa ar an Aonach (Seán Ó Sé) Harps accomp. alone
The Rolling Wave
Break …

The Ewe Reel
Ace and Deuce of Piping
Iníon an Phailitínigh (Seán Ó Sé)
Rights of Man
Marnabh Luimnigh/Limerick's Lamentation
Boys of Kilmichael (Seán Ó Sé)
Barry's Column (Seán Ó Sé)
Repeal of the Union
Craigs Dragoons
Port na bPucaí
Ril Mhór Bhaile an Chaladh
Táimse 'mo Chodhladh (Seán Ó Sé)
Encore – Níl 'na Lá (Seán Ó Sé)

3/3/1963 Abbeyfeale, Co. Limerick (Glór na nGael) With B/W archive footage extant)
Soldiers Song
Speech
Murphy's Reel
Song – Nicolás Tóibín
Newport Lass
Táimse 'mo Chodhladh
Dance (Sporting Paddy) – Paddy Bán Ó Broin dancing
Caoineadh an Spailpín
Story – Éamon Kelly
Carraig Donn
Barney McKenna
Song – Nicolás Tóibín
Galbally Farmer
Break …
Old Tipperary
Story – Éamon Kelly
Dance – Paddy Bán
Song – Nicolás Tóibín
Cath Chéim an Fhia
Seán Maguire
Barney McKenna
Cnocáinín Aerach Chill Mhuire
Song – Nicolás Tóibín
Toss the Feathers
Story – Éamon Kelly

Dingle Regatta
Shaskeen
Spailpín

Programme running order for series 6 of Reacaireacht an Riadaigh for Radio Éireann 1968
Programme 1
Planxty Johnson
An Cailín Deas Rua
The Longford Collector
Marbhna Eoghain Uí Néill
The Miners of Wicklow
Cois na Siúire

Programme 2
Planxty Irwin
Eibhlín Gheal Chiúin
Drowsey Maggie
An Cóta Caoin
Since Marysheen Went to Bonane
Job of Journeywork

Programme 3
Geaftaí Bhaile Bhuí
The Gimlet
Tighearna Mhuigheo
Castle Kelly
Réidh Chnoc Mná Duibhe
The Teetotaller

Programme 4
An Ghaoth Aneas
Dunmore Lassies
An Goirtín Eornan
Langstrom's Pony
Garden of the Daisies

Programme 5
An Chúilfhionn
Lord Inchiquin
An Banbh
Flogging Reel
Draighneán Donn

Programme 6
Repeal of the Union
Buachaill Caol Dubh
Gorman's
Harpsichord Solo
An Chéad Mháirt den Fhomhair
Kerry Jig Set

Running order for Fleadh Cheoil an Raidio Programmes 1968–69

19–20/10/1968
Programme 1
Rights of Man
Craig's Dragoons
Story – Éamon Kelly
Chief O'Neill
Competition
Barry's Column
Dingle Regatta

Programme 2
Castle Kelly
Boys of Kilmichael
Story – Éamon Kelly
Chase me Charlie
Competition
A Dhruimín Donn Dílis
Rolling Wave

Programme 3
Fylmore Races
Trip to Durrow
Story – Éamon Kelly
Tighearna Mhuigheo
Competition
Tá 'na Lá

9–10/11/1968
Programme 5
An Speic Seigheach
Races of Cahersiveen
Story – Éamon Kelly
Solo John Kelly
Competition
Carolan's Concerto
Ar an Loing seo Phaidí Loinsigh

Programme 6
Ruadhairí Ó Mórdha
Bean Dubh a' Ghleanna
Story – Éamon Kelly
Solo Michael Tubridy
Gather 'Round the Fireplace Boys
Competition
Moirín Ní Chuilleanán

Programme 7
Raca Breagh mo Chinn
Bumper Squire Jones
Story – Éamon Kelly
Solo Martin (Fay)
Longford Collector
Competition
Comharaigh mo Leabaigh, táim breoite go leor

Programme 8
An Bínsín Luachra
Marcshlua Uí Néill
Solo Paddy (Moloney)
Story – Éamon Kelly
Port na bPucaí
An Spailpín Fánach
Competition
Sporting Paddy (as filler)

30/11/1968
Programme 9
Cnocáinín Aerach Chill Mhuire
Tommy Cohen
Story – Éamon Kelly
Sídhe Beag, Sídhe Mór
Competition
Seán Keane Solo
Raghadsa ar an Aonach
Planxty Drury

Programme 10
Nách fada an Lá
Repeal of the Union
Story – Éamon Kelly
Muircheartach MacAnna
Solo Seán Potts
Réidh Chnoc Mná Duibhe
Competition
George Brabazon

4–5/1/1969
Programme 11
The Red-Haired Man's Wife
Fead an Iolair (of the Donoghue's of Glenflesk)
Story – Éamon Kelly
Solo John Kelly (Concertina)
Gleann Cam
Competition
Boy in the Gap

Programme 12
An Gamhanaichín
Brian O'Lynn
Story – Éamon Kelly
Competition
Solo – Éamon (de Buitléar)
Caitlín Triail
Polka Set

Programme 13
An Habit Shirt
Leitrim Fancy
Story – Éamon Kelly
An Gaoth Anaia Aneas
Competition
Solo – Seán Ó Riada
An Carraig Aonair
Dunmore Lassies

Programme 14
An Saighdiúirín Singil
Carolan's Concerto
Story – Éamon Kelly
Maguire's March

Solo – John Kelly (Fiddle)
Cath Chéim an Fhia
Competition
Steam Packet

25–26/1/1969
Programme 15
Cois a' Ghaorthaigh
Boy in the Boat
Story – Éamon Kelly
Steam Packet
Solo – Michael Tubridy
The Airy Batchelor
Competition
Three little Drummers

Programme 16
Máire Bheag na Gruaige Báine
Woman in the House
Story – Eamon Kelly
Solo – Seán Potts
Limerick is Beautiful
Competition
Three Sea Captains

Programme 17
Plúirín na mBan Donn Ó
Planxty Irwin
Story – Éamon Kelly
Solo – Paddy (Moloney)
Geaftaí Bhaile Bhui
Competition
Lady on the Island

Programme 18
By the bright silvery Light of the Moon
Ace and Deuce of Piping
Story – Éamon Kelly
Solo Martin (Fay)
An Chéad mháirt den Fhomhair
Competition
Conaught Heifers

8–9/2/1969
Programme 19
Gáirdín an Rí
Eilí Gheal Ciúin
Story – Éamon Kelly
Bumper Squire Jones
Bard of Armagh
Competition
Shaskeen

Programme 20
Maid of the Sweet Brown Know
An Cóta Caol
Story – Éamon Kelly
Planxty Maguire
Competition
Aithrighe Chathail Buí
Kid on the Mountain

Programme 21
Peeler and the Goat
The Groves
Story – Éamon Kelly
The Laurel Bush
Solo John Kelly
Buachaill Caol Dubh
Competition
Ewe Reel

Programme 22
Pléaráca na Ruairceach
Blackbird
Story – Éamon Kelly
Solo – Seán Ó Riada
Seán Ó Dighe
Competition
Cailleach an Túirne

22–23/3/1969
Programme #23 – #26 unavailable
Cathaoir an Phíobaire
Libretto Devil to Pay

Scores

Not in the score is the extended intro on Harpsichord (it is referred to in the end note i.e. 'A'). It is unique in it's approach and was an experiment using the new concept of a traditional Irish Music ensemble – Ceoltóirí Chualan – as a European Classical Chamber Ensemble, with the inherent rules of counterpoint and harmony associated with it's classical culture and model.

The first are a series of tunes. etc., in Seán's hand. One can see the distinctive clear style he scored with. He also was pretty succinct with his transcribing and one can see this in the way he allocated time values – crochets, quavers etc. to the notes of a melody line.

An unpublished recording exists of this piece.

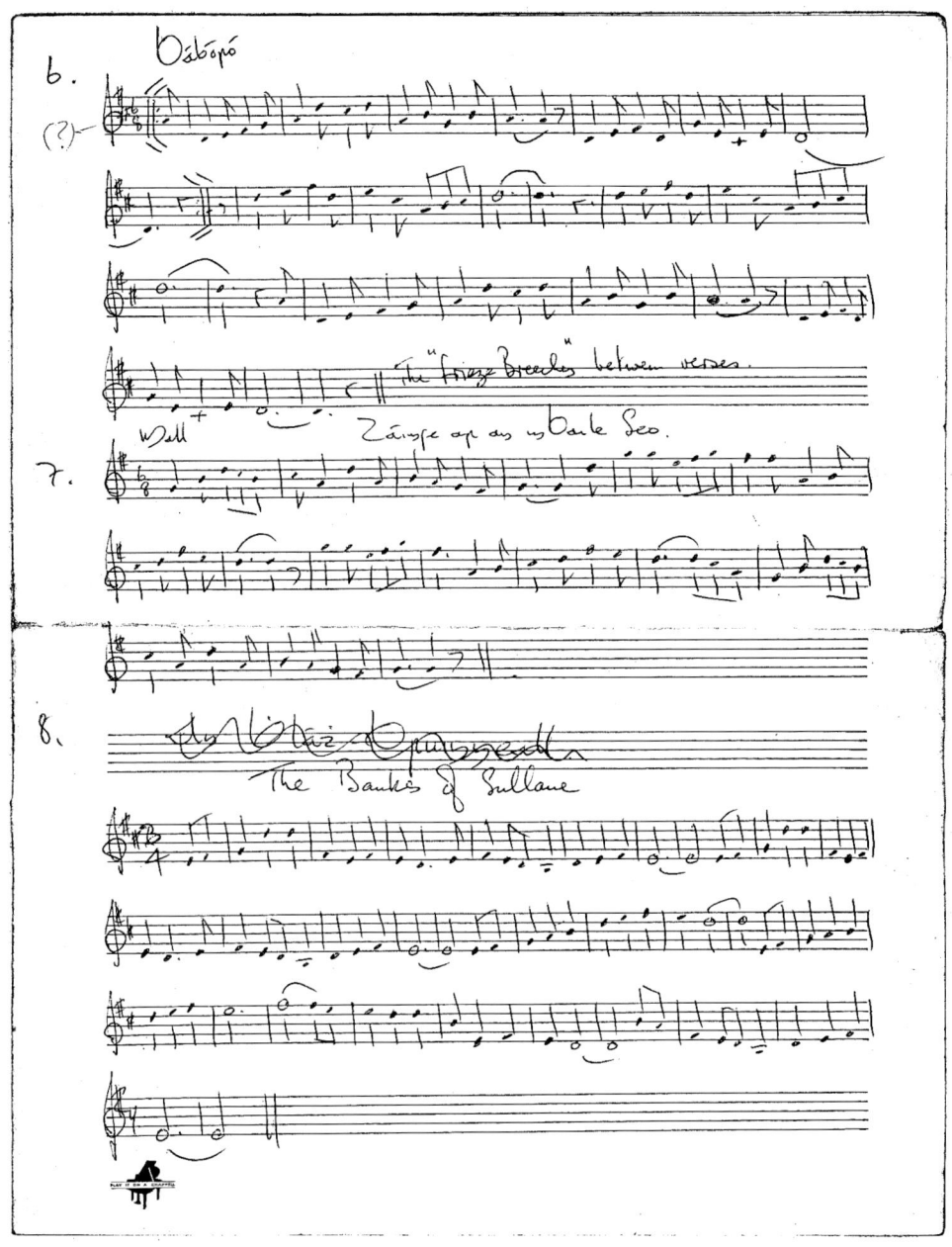

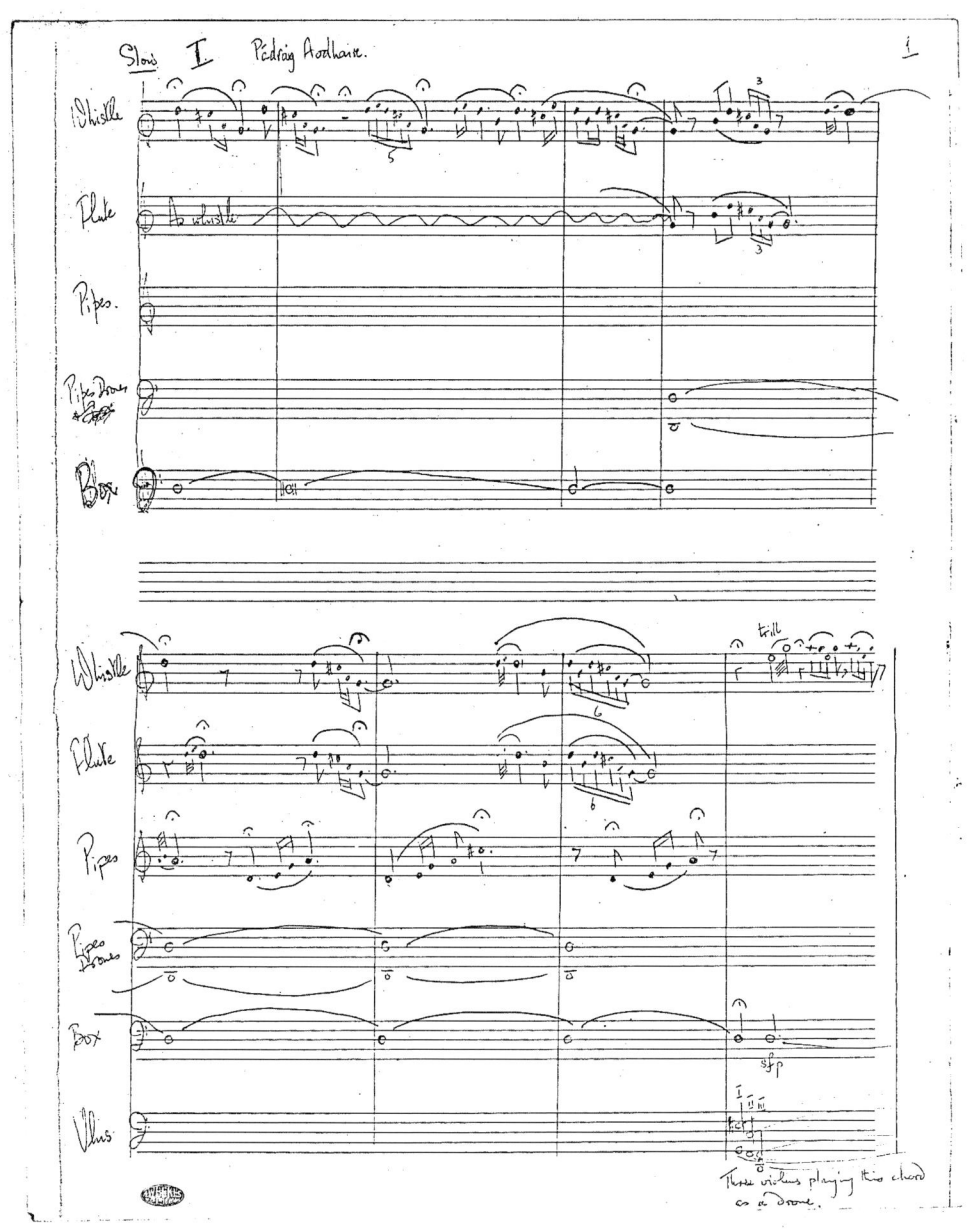

Miscellaneous pieces

DUBLIN THEATRE FESTIVAL
10th — 24th September, 1961

"Reacaireacht an Riadaigh"
IN THE
SHELBOURNE HOTEL
on Sunday September 10th at 8 p.m.
AN EVENING OF TRADITIONAL GAELIC ENTERTAINMENT

ADMISSION — — — 5/-

Bá onóir le Seán Ó Riada agus le Coiste Fhéile Amharclainne Átha Cliath.

a theacht chun Óstán Shelbourne i mBaile Á'Cliath Dé Domhnaigh an 10ú Meán Fómhair 1961, le haghaidh Reacaireacht an Riadaigh.

7·45 i.n. fá choinne 8 i.n.   R/S.V.P.

Carrolls Number 1
an tSlat Tomhais

QuikPrint Shop, 23 Anglesea St., Dublin 2. Telephone 775963

PEADAR Ó DOIRNÍN

AMHRÁIN

Breandán Ó Buachalla

díol anocht 10/- An Clóchomhar tta.

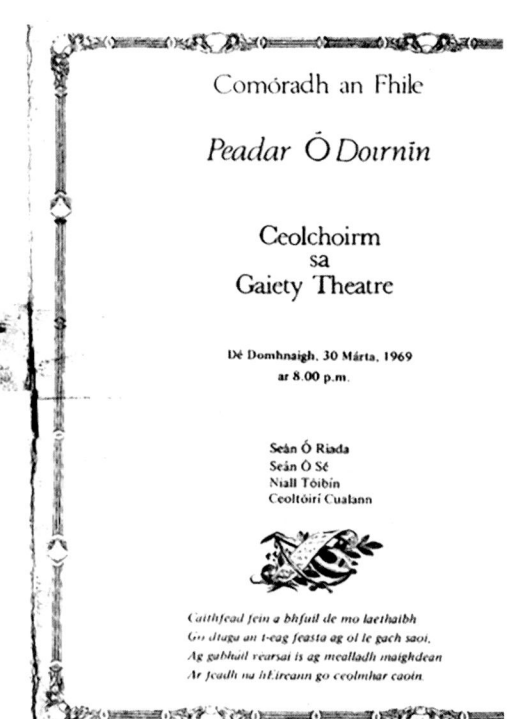

Comóradh an Fhile

Peadar Ó Doirnín

Ceolchoirm
sa
Gaiety Theatre

Dé Domhnaigh, 30 Márta, 1969
ar 8.00 p.m.

Seán Ó Riada
Seán Ó Sé
Niall Tóibín
Ceoltóirí Cualann

Caithfead féin a bhfuil de mo laethaibh
Go dtaga an t-eag feasta ag ol le gach saoi,
Ag gabhail reursai is ag mealladh maighdean
Ar feadh na hÉireann go ceolmhar caoin.

Bheidhlíní:
Máirtín Fay
Seán Ó Ceallaigh
Seán Ó Catháin

Píob:
Paidí Moloney

Feadóg:
Seán Potts

Fliúit:
Mícheál Ó Toibride

Bosca Ceoil:
Éamon de Buitléir

Bodhrán:
Peadar Mercier

Cruitchorda:
Seán Ó Riada

Coiste Comórtha Pheadair Uí Dhoirnín:
An tAthair Diarmuid Mac Íomhair, S.P.; Breandán Ó Buachalla; An tAthair Tomás Ó Fiaich;
Proinsias Mac Cana; Ríobard Mac Góráin; Aodán Ó hAnluain; Donnchadh Ó Súilleabháin; Séamus Ó
Néill; Séamus P. Ó Mórdha.
Gach eolas ó: Breandán Ó Buachalla, Telefón: 887676.

Peadar Ó Doirnín

éad bliain ann ó cailleadh
l a d'fhágfadh ina 'nuafhile'
íocht. Is file Nua-Ghaeilge
rímid bearna idir sinn
am ar dhóbair dúinn an
illiúint, cailleadh tuairisc

e a dhéanamh ní mór is
anteacht faoi shaol Uí
nd sách cinnte faoi dháta
eán 1769 – agus tá a fhios
il sé curtha sa seanreilig
orainn Lú agus Árd
s cár rugadh é ach is in
Jladh a chaith sé formhór
ian linn Ó Doirnín a
: dúiche agus dúchas is é
chéad áit go mba fhile
hairis sin go mba fhile

ease peacaí fáillí lucht na
go bhfuil dearmad déanta
oh na Gaeilge ainneoin
:anga saol ar fud an
as go dtí aimsir na
. Chuir imeachtaí na

staire néal ar shaothar Mhic Cuarta agus Mhic Cobhthaigh agus Mhic a Liondain thar mar a chuir ar dhéantús na Muimhneach fiú.

Maidir le Ó Doirnín níl ach aon amhrán amháin dá chuid atá ag an bpobal, mar atá Úr-Chnoc Chéin Mhic Cáinte; maidir leis an gcuid eile, dánta grá is mó atá iontu, más fíor. Ní fheadar féin an grá nó gean nó machnas coirp nó aigne faoi deara iad. Is cuma liom. Tá siad ann mar atá siad: aistí file narbh aon de fhilí móra Éireann é ach go mba file Éireannach ina dhiaidh sin é, chomh maith le bheith ina fhile Ultach. Agus tá sé tabhachtach go n-aithneoimis an méid sin.

Is í an Ghaeilge ár n-eochair chun na hÉireann, inné agus inniu. An Ghaeilge — agus éigse na Gaeilge a léiríonn éagsúlacht ré agus réigiúin ach a léiríonn thairis agus tríd an éagsúlacht sin, aontas traidisiúin agus oidhreachta. Teacht i seilbh cuid den oidhreacht sin dúinne is ea ár gcuid féin a dhéanamh de dhéantús Pheadair Uí Dhoirnín.

Seán Mac Réamoinn.

Peadar Ó Doirnín
[1684 - 1769]

Biographical detail on Ó Doirnín is very scanty. He was born near the Louth/Armagh border, became a familiar figure throughout the South East corner of Ulster and when he died was buried in the little cemetary at Urney in North Louth. Apart from this very little is known.

In the 17th, 18th and 19th centuries this part of Ulster produced a remarkable group of poets, scholars and scribes. Ó Doirnín was perhaps the finest lyric poet of this school and his best work has always had an honourable place in anthologies of modern Irish literature. No complete edition of his work has been available, however, but this deficiency has now been rectified by the publication of Breandán Ó Buachalla's "Peadar Ó Doirnín: Amhráin".

Other events in this year's commemoration will include a special study weekend, Scoil Éigse Uí Dhoirnín, in Dundalk (11th – 13th April) and the unveiling of a memorial in Urney graveyard at 3.30 p.m. on Sunday 29th June.

By honouring the bi-centenary of Peadar Ó Doirnín's death the organising committee hope to awaken a greater interest in his work and also to direct attention to historic Ulster's contribution to the Irish cultural tradition.

AN DAMER

Cóta Bán Chríost
le CRÍOSTÓIR Ó FLOINN

Ag tosú Máirt, 8/4/69, 8p.m.

Áirithint: 776624

Tabhair dom do Lámh	15. Dánta le Peadar Ó Doirnín: Niall Tóibín
Uileachán Dubh Ó: Seán Ó Sé	16. Planxty Johnson
Marcshlua Uí Néill	17. Do Bhí Bean Uasal: Seán Ó Sé
Mná na hÉireann (Peadar Ó Doirnín/Seán Ó Riada): Seán Ó Sé	18. The Whinny Hills of Leitrim
Tiarna Mhuigheo	19. Geaftaí Bhaile Bhuí: Seán Ó Sé
An Beinnsín Luachra: Seán Ó Sé	20. Píosaí Aonair ar an gCruitchorda: Seán Ó Riada
Máirseáil Uí Dhonnchadha/Fead an Fhiolair	*An Chéad Mháirt den Fhomhar*
A Ghaoth ó nEas	*Na Gamhna Geala*
Máirseáil Rí Laighean/Ruairí Ó Mórdha	21. Sídhe Beag is Sídhe Mór
An Spéirbhean Mhilis (Peadar Ó Doirnín/Seán Ó Riada): Seán Ó Sé	22. Gardaí an Rí: Seán Ó Sé
Planxty Maguire	23. Bumper Squire Jones
Pléaraca na Ruarcach: Seán Ó Sé	24. Binn Luisín Aerach a Bhrogha: Seán Ó Sé
Marbhna Luimní	25. The Rights of Man
Thugamar Féin an Samhradh Linn: Seán Ó Sé	26. Iníon an Phailítínigh: Seán Ó Sé
SOS 15 Nóiméid	27. Rú Mhór Bhaile an Chalaidh

Fáilte chuig na Gaiety Bars ar gach urlár !!

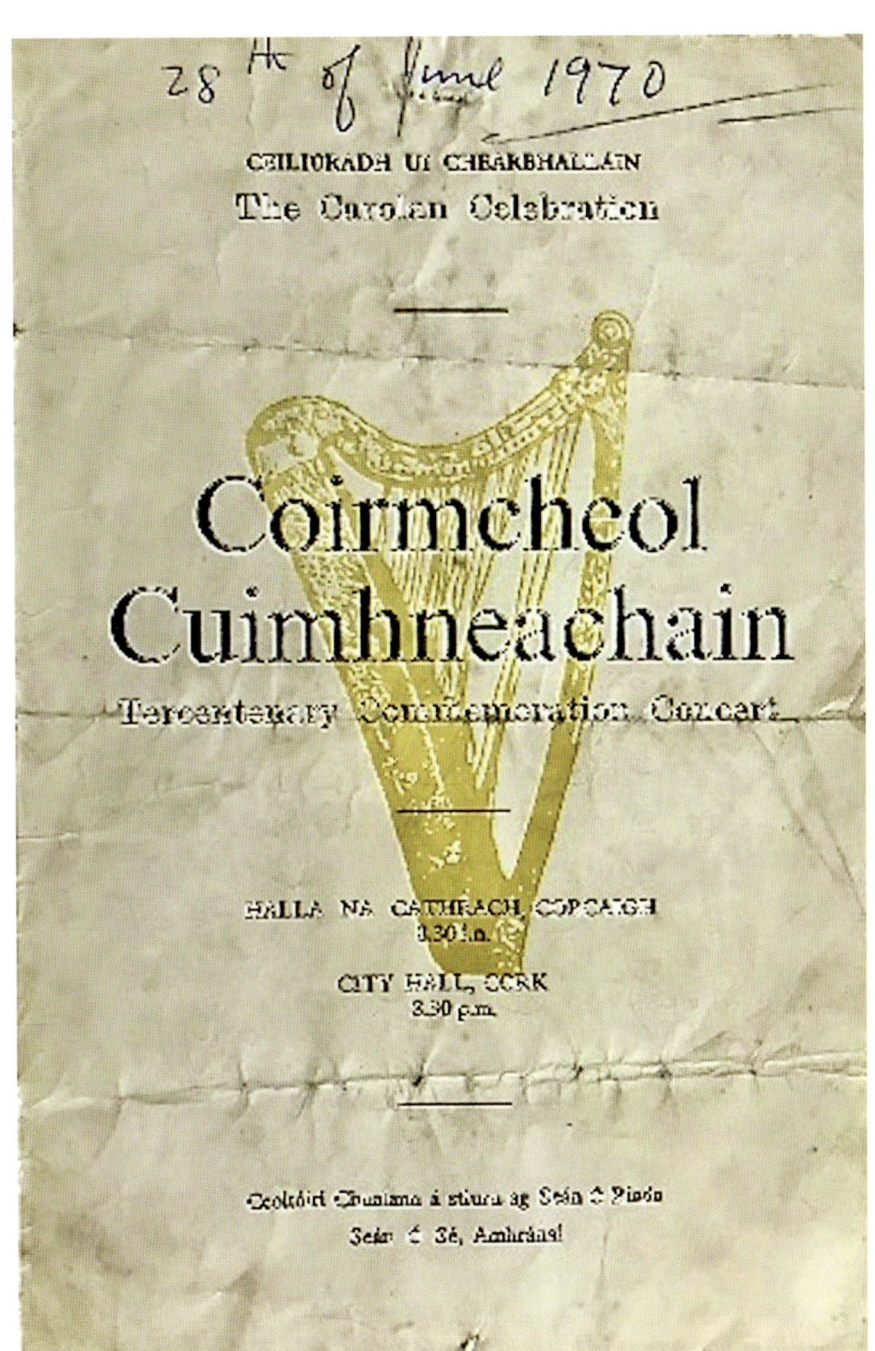

Personal programme of last concert dated in Seán Ó Riada's own hand.

Last Ceoltóirí Cualann concert City Hall Cork 1970. Left to right: Seán Ó Riada at harpsichord, Peadar Mercier, Éamon de Buitléar, Martin Fay hidden behind Seán Ó Sé standing, Seán Keane, John Kelly, Michael Tubridy, Seán Potts, Paddy Moloney

Recording of Ding Dong album (Dublin Feis Ceol Hall, 37 Molesworth Street) – left to right: Seán Ó Riada, Seán Ó Sé, John Kelly behind Martin Fay, Paddy Moloney, Michael Tubridy, Seán Potts, Ronnie McShane, Éamon de Buitléar, Sonny Brogan, Seán Keane and Peter Hunt engineer. Notice the placing of microphones to adjust the sound levels of the different instruments.

Index

Symbols

1916 Mar do Cumadh an Aisling 42, 46

A

Abbeyfeale 43, 219, 221
Abbey Reel 15, 55, 62, 67, 171
Abbey Theatre 10, 11, 15, 18, 19, 27
Ace and Deuce 55, 67, 221, 223
A Collection of Irish Traditional Step Dances 18
Adare 9
A Druimfhionn Donn Dílis 106
After Aughrim's Great Disaster 68
A Ghrá Luí Laimh Liom 68
Ag Scaipeadh na gCleití 16, 33
Ag Taisteal na Blárnan 39, 68, 188
Aililiú na Gamhna 55, 69
Aithrighe Chathail Buí 69, 224
All around my Hat 43
Amharclann an Damer 11, 21
Amhrán an Taé 33
Amuigh Faoin Spéir 13
An Bothánín íseal gan Fáltas 82
An Brianach Óg 84
An Buachaill sa Bhád 33
An Cailín Rua 87
An Caipilín Bán 90
An Ceannaí Glic 12
An Chéad Mháirt den fhomhair (Na Gamhna Geala) 96
An Chúilfhionn 38, 97, 221
An Dord Féinne 42
An Droighneán Donn 105
An Drúcht Gheal Cheoigh 42
An Gaoth Aniar Aneas 122, 223
An Ghaoth Aneas 124, 221
An Long Faoi Lán-tSeol 33
An Lon is an Chéirseach 140
An Mhóin (Cleaganna) 145
An Phis Fliuch 30
An Poc ar Buile 39, 40, 163, 220
An Raibh tú ar an gCarraig 46, 169
An Réaltan Leanbach 42
An Síoda 'tá id' bhfallait? 183, 202
An Spailpín Fánach 40, 222
An Spealadoir 186
An Spéir Bhean Mhilis 188
An Súiste Geal Beag Bán 193
An tAmhráinín Síodraimín 42
An tAthair Jack Walsh 71
An té a mholas an éigse 33
An tÚll 207
A Phlúirín na mBan Donn Óg 160
Ard Oileán (High Island) 46
Ar Éirinn ní n'eosfainn cé hí 70
A Shíle Ní Ghadhra 180

B

Baile Mhuirne 27
Bakerswell 17
Barrel of Porter & Seán Buí 74
Barry, Garrett 14
Battle of Aughrim 144
BBC Third Programme 46
Beidh Aonach Amáireach 76, 220
Beidh Spórt Againn & Off She Goes 76
Bell, Derek 44
Bhíosa Lá 'bPort Láirge 78, 144
Bímse i gConaí 'Radaireacht 79
Bínn Lisín Aerach a Bhrogha 77
Bodley, Seoirse 42
Bonapart's Retreat 220
Brídín Deas Uí Néill 84
Brogan, Harry 10
Brogan, Sonny 7, 12, 14, 15, 25, 26, 30, 31, 122, 176, 177
Browne, Gareth 43, 44, 45
Buitléar, Éamon de 7, 12, 13, 15, 26, 28, 29, 30, 53, 85
Bunting, Edward 32, 37
By Sandymount Strand 44
By the Bright Silvery Light of the Moon 86

C

Cailleach an Airgid 89
Cailleach a'Túirne 56, 89
Caint na n-éan 33
Caiptín Ó Máille 33
Caitlín Triall 90
Caoineadh an Spailpín 57, 90, 221
Caoineadh na hÓige 42
Caoine Bhean Choinn Uí Laoire 42
Capel Street, Dublin 14
Carolon's Concerto 220
Carrigaholt, Co. Clare 12, 128
Casaim Araon na Géanna Romhainn 92
Cathaoir an Phíobaire 57, 94, 224
Cath Chéim an Fhiaidh 42, 93
Ceannaí Glic 12, 21
Cearta an Duine 35
Ceol an Aifrinn & Aifreann 2 49, 212
Ceol a' Phíobaire (also Pósfaidh mé an t-Iascaire) 95
Ceol is Cibeal 212
Ceol na nUasal 36, 212, 220
Ceolta Éireann 41
Ceoltóirí Laighean 13
Chase Me Charlie 96
Chieftains, The 16, 17, 18, 21, 44, 47, 49
Ciarraíoch Mallaithe 98
Cill na Martra 9, 28
Claddagh label 44, 45
Clancy, Willie 44
Clare 9, 12, 13, 14, 20, 21, 219, 220
Cleggan 45
Cleverdon, Douglas 46
Clifford, Len 49, 51, 52
Cnocáinín Aerach Chill Muire 42
Cois a' Ghaorthaigh 100, 223
Cois na Siúire 101, 221
Coláiste Íosagáin 39
Comhaltas Ceoltóirí Éireann 27
Comhsheinm Uí Chearbhalláin 38
Concept Album 33
Conneally, Marie 21
Connemara 21, 47
Cór Cúil Aodha 47, 49

Cork 9, 13, 23, 24, 25, 28, 31, 39, 41, 43, 51, 52, 208, 219, 220
Cork School of Music 24
Cóta Caoin 102, 221
Cóta Caoin Caol 102
Craig, Jeffrey 45
Croke Park 23
Cronin, Bess 27
Crow 44
Cuaichín Ghleann Néifinn 42
Cú-cú-ín 42
Cúil Aodha 13, 20, 23, 27, 39, 164, 219
Cúm Thóla, Cork 23
Cusack, Cyril 46

D

Day-Lewis, Cecil 46
de Brún, Garach (Gareth Browne) 44, 45
de Buitléar, Éamon 12, 13, 25, 31, 38, 48, 49, 51, 122
Deora Áille 44
de Valera, Pres. Éamon 43, 49, 50
Devlin report 47
Dí -i-dí á dí (An Puirtín) 104
Dineen, Pat and Kit 30
Ding Dong 13, 34, 35, 36, 196, 212, 220
Domhnal na Gréinne 105
Domhnal Ó Mulláin 39
Donegal 18
Donnycarney 16
Doran, Johnny 14
Drimnagh 20
Drops of Brandy 58, 106
Drowsie Maggie 106
Dublin 9, 12, 14, 15, 16, 17, 19, 20, 21, 24, 28, 40, 47, 51, 174, 213, 219, 220
Duff, Arthur 42
Dunmore Lassies 107

E

Eibhlín a Rúin 108
Eilí Gheal Chiúin 58, 108
Emigrants Jig 109
Ennis 21, 219, 220

Ennis, Seámus 27
Ennistymon 21, 128, 194, 205

F

Fáinne an Lae 42
Fair Eleanor O Christ Thee Save 44
Farrington, Conor 43
Fay, Martin 18, 21, 25, 26, 31, 38, 48, 51, 122, 130, 145
Feadóg an Iolair 111
Fenians of Cahersiveen 111
Fiach an Mhadra Ruaidh 112
Fleadh Cheoil an Radio 20, 27, 35, 40, 41, 43, 213
Fleischmann, Aloys 9, 31
Fornocht a Chonac Thú 42
France 10
Frank Roche's Favourite 117
Fuaireasa Cuireadh chun dul ar an bPósadh 119
Fylemore, You're the Place 119

G

Gaelic Nation 23, 24, 25, 46, 48
Gael Linn 8, 13, 25, 26, 34, 39, 41, 42, 43, 46, 49, 50, 51, 212, 220
Gaeltacht 9, 21, 22, 25, 26, 27, 47, 50
Gaeltarra Éireann 47
Gaiety 18, 41, 43, 49, 51, 52, 93, 125, 156, 164, 184, 185, 210, 219, 220
Gáirdín an Rí 224
Galloping Green 16, 19, 24, 31, 213
Galvin, Nell 14
Galway 12, 45, 120
Gander in the Pratie Hole 121, 183, 220
Gardaí an Rí 122
Garden of Daisies 122, 129
Garrett Barry's Favourite 123
Gather around the Fireplace 59, 123, 124
Geary, Patsy 14, 69
George, Brian 27
Gille mo Chroí 125
GlenLea 125
Glór na nGael 43, 219, 221

Gneeveguilla 27
Golden Keyboard 171
Gorman's/Callaghan's 126
Gorman's /The Hut in the Bog 126
Gort a Choirce, Donegal 18
Gráinne Mhaol 157
Graves, Robert 44

H

Hamilton, Diane 27
Hayes, Pat 49
Heaney, Séamus 44
He's not Guilty My Lord 40
Hide an Go Seek 127
Hilliard, Frances 14
Horne, John T. 24
Hughes, Ted 44, 46
Hunt, Peter 42, 219, 220
Hyde, Douglas 13

I

Icnhees 30

Index of Arrangements
I'll sing you a song of peace and love 43
Abbey Reel (Redican's) 55
Ace and Deuce of Pipering 55
After Aughrim's great disaster 55
Ag Taisteal na Blárnain (Stácadh an Mhargaidh) 55
Ag Taisteal na Sléibhte 55, 68
Aililiú na Gamhna (Amhrán) (Fonn Mall) 55
Airéir is mé go hUaigneach 55, 68
Aithrí Chathal Bhuí (He is not Guilty My Lord) 55
A Lady Stood 60, 137
Amhráinín Síoduimín 40, 55
Anach Cuan 46, 55, 69
An Banbh 55, 73, 221
An Bínsín Luachra 56, 77, 222
An Londubh is an Chéirseach 60
An Raibh tú ar an gCarraig 55
An Spealadóir 40, 63

An t-Athair Walsh (see tatter) 55
An t-Úll 64
Anything for John Joe 55, 70, 138
Arabia 55, 70
Ar an Loing Seo Pad Uí Loinsigh 55
Ar Éirinn ní n'eosfainn cé hí 55
Ar Maidin Dé Máirt 55, 72
Babaró 55, 72
Bacach Buí na Léige 55, 72
Bán Chnoic Éireann Ó 55, 73
Banks of Sullane 55, 73
Banna Strand 55, 74
Bard of Armagh 55, 224
Barley Grain 55, 74
Barrel of Porter + Seán Buí (Sweet Biddy or Paddy Clancy) 55
Barry's Column 55, 75, 221, 222
Battering Ram (Blackthorn Stick) 55
Bean a' Tí 55, 75
Bean Dubh a' Ghleanna 55, 75, 222
Beggarman 55, 76, 139, 186
Beidh Aonach amáireach i gCo. an Chláir 56
Beidh Sport Againn + Off She Goes 56
Bhí Bean Uasal 56, 78, 220
Bhíosa lá 'bPort Láirge 56
Bhíosa Lá i gCill Áirne 56, 79
Bill Harte's Jig (Newport Lass) 56
Bímse i gcónaí Radaireacht 56
Bín Lisín Aerach a Bhrogha (Air – Ar Éirinn ní n'eosfainn cé hí) 56
Blackbird, The 56
Blackthorn Stick 55, 56, 80
Bold Thady Quill 56, 81, 167
Bonaparte's Retreat 56, 81
Bonnie Bunch of Roses Oh 56, 82
Botháinín Íseal gan Faltas 56
Boy in the Boat 56, 82, 223
Boy in the Gap 44, 56, 82, 145, 146, 223
Boyne Hunt 56, 83, 115, 116, 143
Boys of Kilmichael 35, 56, 83, 221, 222
Boys of the Loch 56, 83
Brennan on the Moore 56, 83
Briannach Óg, An 56
Brian O'Lynn 56, 84, 223

Bruach na Carraige Báine 56, 84, 220
Buachaill Caol Dubh 56, 84, 220, 222
Buck in the Wood 56, 85
Bucks of Oranmore 56, 85
Bumper Squire Jones 56, 85, 222, 224
Butcher's March 56, 124, 159, 160
By the Light of the Silvery Moon (Tune Curragh of Kildare) 56
Cailín Bán 56, 86
Cailín Deas Donn 56, 86
Cailín Deas Rua 56, 87, 221
Cailíní an Fhactory 56, 88
Cailíní Deasa Mhuigheo 56, 88
Cailín Rua, An 56
Cailleach an Airigid 56
Cailleach a' Túirne (Maid at the Spinning Wheel) 56
Caitlín Triail 38, 57
Cáit Ní Dhuibhir 42, 56, 90
Callaghan's Reel 57
Caoineadh an Spailpín 57, 90
Capaillín Bán 57, 205
Carolan's Concerto 57, 91, 222, 223
Carraig an Aoibhnis 57, 91
Carraig Aonair 57, 92, 223
Carraig Donn 57, 92, 221
Casadh an tSúgáin 57, 92, 193
Casaim Araon na Géanna Romham 57
Castle Kelly 57, 93, 220, 221, 222
Cath Chéim an Fhiadh 57
Cat in the Corner (The Hag with the Money) 57
Ceol a' Mhála 57, 95
Ceol an Phiobaire 57
Charles O'Connor 57, 96
Chase me Charlie 57, 133, 222
Chase me Charlie/Walshe's Hornpipe/Limerick Lasses 59
Chéad Mháirt an Fhomhair, An 57
Cherish the Ladies 57, 96
Chief O'Neill 57, 97, 222
Chúilfhionn, An 57
Ciarraíoch Mallaithe 57
Clár Bog Déil 57, 99

Cnocáinín Aerach Chill Mhuire 57, 99, 221, 222
Cois an Ghaorthaidh 57
Cois na Siuire 57
Collier's Reel 57, 101
Comhcheadal a h-aon 57
Connaught Heifers 57, 101
Contentment is Wealth 57, 84, 102, 148
Cóta Caoin Caol 57, 224
Craig's Dragoons (Sweet William Craig's Dragoons) 57
Cruiscín Lán (Maidin Áluinn Gréinne) 57
Cuan Bhéilínse 57, 103
Cuckoo's Nest + Leitrim Fancy 57, 103
Cup of Tea (and Ashplant) 57
Diarmuid Ó Dubhda 57, 104
Dí Eidí Dí a Dí (An Puirtín) 57
Dingle Regatta 58, 104, 221, 222
Diver the Dancer 58, 105
Domhnail na Gréinne (Leg of a Duck/Loan of my bellows) 58
Droighneán Donn, An 58
Drowsey Maggie 58, 221
Dunmore Lassies 58, 71, 221, 223
Dwyer's Hornpipe 58, 108
Éamon Magháine 58, 108
Eibhlín a Riúin 58
Eilí Gheal Chiúin Ní Cearbhaill 58
Emigrant's Jig (Port a' Deoraí) 58
Eochaill 58, 109
Ewe Reel, The 58
Faill Mór 58, 110
Fanny Power 58, 110
Farewell to Connaught 58, 110
Farewell to Erin 58, 110
Fead an Fhiolair (O'Donoghue's March – of Glen Flesk) 58
Fenians of Cahirsiveen (to air of My Beauty of Limerick) 58
Fiach an Mhadra Rua 58
Flannel Jacket / Heather Breeze / Sheehan's 58, 113
Flogging Reel 58, 221
Foggy Dew 58, 114

Fox Chase 58, 114
Frank Roche's Favourite 58
Frieze Breeches 58, 118
Frost is all Over 58
Fuaireasa Cuireadh Chun dul ar an bPósadh 58
Fylemore you're the Place 58
Galbally Farmer (Rakes of Kildare) 58, 120
Galway Races 20, 58, 120
Gamhnaichín 58, 121
Gander at the Pratie Hole 58
Gaoth Aniar Aneas, An 58
Gardaí an Rí 58
Garden of the Daisies 58, 221
Garret Barry's Jig 58
Gather around the Fireplace + Colliers 59
Gather around the Fireplace (played as a jig) 59
Geaftaí Bhaile Bhuí 59, 124, 221
George Brabazon 59, 124, 223
Ghaoth Aniar Aneas, An 59
Gile mo Chroí 59
Gimlet, The Munster 59
Gleann Cam 59, 61, 125, 155, 223
Glen Lee 59
Goirtín (Eornan) 59
Gorman's /The Hut in the Bog 59
Habit Shirt 59, 126, 223
Hewlet 59, 127
Hide and Go Seek 59
High Caul Cap 59, 127
Humours of Ballyconnell 59, 127
Humours of Carrigaholt 59, 128
Humours of Ennistymon (Coppers and Brass) 59
Hunting the Hare 58, 59, 117
Im' Aonar Seal 59, 129
Iníon an Fhaoit ó' nGleann 59
Irish Molly 59, 129
Irish Rag 59, 129, 130
Irish Washerwoman 59, 130
Is Trua gan Gáirdín Úll agam 59, 130
Ivy Leaf 59, 96, 131
Jackson's Grove Hornpipe 59

Jackson's Morning Brush 59, 145
Jenny Picking Cockles/Jenny's Welcome to Charlie 59
Jenny's Wedding 59, 132
Jig Set in A (For Fleadh Cheoil 196–'69) 59
Jig Set in A (For Reacaireacht) 59, 133
Job of Journey Work 59, 77, 134
Kerry Harriers 59, 134, 135
Kerry Hornpipe 59, 135
Kid over the Mountain 60
Kitty Come Down (The Gimble) 60
Lady of the Island 60
Langstrom's Pony 60, 115, 137, 221
Laurel Bush 60, 224
Leather away the Wattle Oh 60
Leg of the Duck (Dónal na Gréinne) 60
Leitrim Fancy (See Cuckoo's Nest) 60
Little Beggerman, The (Rigadoon – Red-Haired Boy) 60
Longford Collector, The 60
Lord Inchiquin 60, 141, 220, 221
Mabel Kelly (Máible Ní Cheallaigh) 60
Madame Bonaparte 60, 141
Madcap (Sixpenny Money) 60
Maguire's March 60, 141
Mahony's Frolics (Cat in the Corner) 60
Maid at the Spinning Wheel 56, 60, 89, 142, 166
Maidin Aluin Gréinne 60
Maid of the Sweet Brown Knowe 60, 142
Maidrín Ruadh 60, 110, 112, 113, 115, 116, 143
Máiréad de Róiste 60
Máire Bheag na Gruaige Báine (Cois na na Bríghde Thiar) 60, 144
Máire (Móirín) Ní Chuileanáin 60
Marbhna Eoghain Uí Néill 60, 144, 221
Marc Shlua Ui Néill (Marcaiocht Uí Néill) 60
Mhóin, An – see Na Cleaganna 60
Miller's Daughter 60
Miners of Wicklow 60, 146, 221
Miss McLeod's Reel 60
Mná Dé hAoine 60, 147

Moladh an Athair Séamus Máinséal 60
Molloy's Jig 60, 148
Molly Bán 60, 149
Molly Saint George 61
Mo Mhuirnín Bán 61, 149
Money from America 61, 124
Morrison's Jig 61, 150
Mo Thaighleach (Mo Thúirnín Línn) 61
Mount Phoebus' Hunt 61, 143, 151
Mug of Brown Ale (Old Man Dillon) 61, 152
Muileagán Dubh Ó 61
Munster Gimlet 61, 152
Murphy's Hornpipe 61, 153
Murphy's Reel (Mulvihill's Reel) 61
My Love in the Morning 61, 153
Ná beadh buachailín deas ag Síle 61
Nách Fada an Lá 61
Na Cleaganna (an Mhóin) 57
Napper Tandy (Wearing of the Green) 61
Newport Lass (Trip to Athlone) 61
Nuair a ghabhaimhse tríd an mBaile seo (Gleann Cam) 61
Old Joe's Jig + Sixpenny Money 61
Old Tipperary 61, 155, 221
O'Mahony's 61, 156
O'Mahony's Frolics (The Cat in the Corner) 61
One Day for Recreation 61, 156
Ó Neillí, Neillí 61, 154
Ó Riada's Favourite 61, 157
Oró nách é siúd an seó 61
Óró Sé do Bheatha 'bhaile (Dord Féinne) 61
Outlaw of the Hill 61, 159
Paddy Clancy (Sweet Biddy Daly or the Barrel of Porter) 61
Páirc an Fhoghmhair 61
Peeler and the Goat 59, 61, 133, 134, 159, 224
Peeler and the Goat /Chase me Charlie/ Walshes' 59
Peigín Leitir Mór 61
Píce an tSúgaire 61
Piper's Chair 61

Plains of Boyle 61, 161, 186, 187, 208
Planxty Drury 61, 161, 222
Planxty Irwin 61, 162, 221, 223
Planxty Johnson 61, 162, 221
Pléaráca na Ruaircach 62, 224
Poc ar Buile, An 62
Polka 62, 95, 145, 147, 164, 177, 179, 223
Pósadh (Fuaireasa Cuireadh chun dul ar an bposadh) 62
Pretty Girls of Mayo 62, 166
Priest and his Boots 62
Pup Came Home from Claoideach 62
Ráca Breagh mo Chínn 62
Races of Cahirciveen 62
Raedh Chnoc Mná Duibh 62
Raghadsa ar an Aonach 62, 169, 220
Raghadsa 's mo Cheataí ag Bhalcaoireacht 62
Raibh tú ar an gCarraig? 62
Ráiteachas na Tairingreacht 62, 170
Raithineach a Bhean Bheag 62, 170
Rakes of Clonmel 62, 170, 189
Reddington's 62
Red-haired Boy (Reel) 62
Redican's (Abbey Reel) 62
Réice Luimní 62
Repeal of the Union 62, 172, 221, 222, 223
Rights of Man 62, 173, 208, 209, 221, 222
Ril Mhór Bhaile an Chaladh 62, 173, 221
Rocky Road to Dublin 62, 174
Rógaire Dubh 62, 174
Rolling Wave 62, 177, 220, 222
Ruadhraí Ó Mórdha (Máirseáil Rí Laoise) 62, 177
Saighdiúirín Singil 62, 178, 223
Salamanca 62, 178
Sceilpín Droighneach 62
Seachrán Carn tSaoghail 62
Seán Buí – see Barrell of Porter 63
Seán Ó Dighe 63, 224
Seán Ó Duibhir/Éistíg Liomsa Sealad 63
Seán's a Bhríste Leathair 62
'Sé fáth mo Bhuartha 63
Seoladh na Gamhna sa bhfásach 63
Shaskeen Reel 63, 180

Shíle Ní Ghadhra, A 63
Ship in Full Sail 63
Ships are Sailing 63, 181
Sí Beag, Sí Mór 63, 182
Sí-Bhean Locha Léin 63
Since Bonie is Down 63
Since Mary she went to Bonnán 63
Sioda 'tá id' Bhfalleit, An 63
Sláinte Bhreá Hewlett 63, 183
Slán agus Beannacht le Buaireamh an tSaoghail 63
Sliabh na mBan 63, 184
Slide 63, 184
Spailpín a Rúin 33, 63, 185
Spailpín Fánach 40, 63, 185, 222
Speic Seoigheach 63, 187
Spéir Bhean Mhilis, An 63
Sporting Paddy 63, 188, 221, 222
Stáca an Mharagaigh (Ag Taisteal na Blárnan) 63
Stad Airiú Rógaire 63, 189
Staicín Eornan 63, 189
Star of Munster 63, 190
Steampacket 63
Strawberry Blossom 63, 193
Suisín Geal Beag Bán (air of Casadh an tSugáin) 63
Súiste Buí, An (Yellow Flail) 63
Sunshine Hornpipe 63, 194
Swallow's Tail – Sligo Maid 63
Sweet Bonie will I ne'er see you more? 63
Sweet William Craigs Dragoons 63
Tabhair Dom do Lámh 63
Tá Gaidhil Bhocht Cráidhte 63
Táiliúr Aerach – see Ding Dong 64
Táim Breoite go Leor 64, 196
Táimse ar an mBaile Seo 64
Táimse Im' Chodhladh 64, 197
Táimse in Arrears 64, 197
Tá mo Mhadra, Níl mo Mhadra 64
Tá 'na Lá 64, 198, 222
Tap Room 64, 200, 201
Tarraing go ciúin, go ciúin 64
Tatter Jack Walsh – see an tAthair Walsh 64

Teetotaller 64, 202
Tell her I am 64
The Airy Bachelor 55
The Ashplant 55, 71
The Light of the Moon (melody like The Curragh of Kildare) 60, 139
There was a Lady 64, 202
The White Cockade (An Coileachóg Bán) 64, 209
Three little Drummers 64, 223
Three Sea Captains 64, 203, 223
Tiarna Mhuigheo 64, 204
Tiocfaigh an Samhradh 64, 204
Tons of Bright Gold 64, 205
Torramh an Bharraile 64, 205
Toss the Feathers 16, 64, 206, 221
Trím' Rachaidh Siubhail 64
Tripping to the well 64
Trip to Athlone – see Newport Lass 64
Trip to Durrow / Up against the Buachalán's 64
Union of Macroom 64, 207
Wearing of the Green – see Napper Tandy 64
Wexford Hornpipe 64, 208
Whinney Fields of Leitrim 64, 209
Wife of the Bold Tenant Farmer 64
William Tell 64, 210
Willie Dear 64, 210
Wind that Shakes the Barley 64
Woman of the House 64, 211

Iníon an Fhaoit ón nGleann 129
Iníon an Phailitínigh 42, 59, 129, 221
Inish Boffin 45
Iremonger, Valentine 44
Irish Nation 33, 34, 37, 47

J

Jackson's Grove Hornpipe 131
Jackson's Morning Brush 131
Japan 18
Jazz 9, 29, 31, 59, 130, 132
Jenny Picking Cockles 59, 132
Jig – 3 Little Drummers 169

K

Kealkill 23
Keane, James 20
Keane, Sarah & Rita 44
Keane, Seán 7, 8, 20, 38, 48, 51, 54, 137, 222
Keane, Tom 14
Kelly, Celine 18
Kelly, Éamon 27, 221, 222, 223, 224
Kelly, John 7, 12, 13, 14, 15, 20, 25, 26, 31, 38, 48, 51, 81, 97, 110, 122, 128, 133, 137, 152, 153, 174, 176, 222, 223, 224
Kenmare Carnegie Hall 30
Kennedy, Peter 27
Kentucky Derby 47
Kerry 10, 24, 25, 40, 134, 135, 219, 222
Kid on the Mountain 136, 224
Kilgarvan 30
Killarney 27, 52
Kinsella, Thomas 44
Kitty come down 136
Knocknaheeny, Cork 23
Kubrick, Stanley 19, 20

L

Lady on the Island 137, 223
Lamb, Charles 12
Lamb, Lally (de Buitléar) 12, 17, 31
Lamb, Mary 52
Langstrom's Pony 151
Larchet, JF 42
Leather away the Wattle O 138
Leeds, England 22, 26
Leg of the Duck 60, 89, 105, 129, 130, 139, 160, 161
Leitir Mór 21
Leitrim Fancy 57, 60, 103, 104, 139, 223
Liberties, Dublin 17
Limerick 9, 86, 133, 219, 221, 223
Ar an Loing Seo Pheadí Loingsigh 70
Listowel 10
London 47, 52
Longford 20, 140, 221, 222
Long, Paddy 10

Lorient Festival 47

M

Mac an Ailí (Fhailí), Reamonn 10
Mac Anna, Tomás 10
Mac Cafraidh, Seamus 10
Mac Cionnaith, Tomás P. 10
Mac Góráin, Roibard 25, 39
Mac Leid, Pádraig 10
MacLochlainn, Fonnuala 43
MacMahon, Bryan 10, 12, 15
MacMahon, Dolly 43, 44
Mac Mathúna, Séamus 27
Mac Piarais, Pádraig 42
Macra na Feirme 30
Mac Réamoinn, Seán 43, 52
Mac Seáin, Raghnall 10
Mahony's Frolics 60, 61, 141
Máible Ní Cheallaigh 60, 142
Maidin Áluinn Ghréinne (Crúiscín Lán) 143
Maidin Luain Chinchíse 42
Maidrín Ruadh 143
Máire (Mairead) de Róiste 144
Máire Ní Chuilleanáin 144
Mansion House Dublin 43, 219
Marbhna Luimní 144
Marbhna Luimnighe 46, 60
Marcshlua Uí Néill 46, 220, 222
Marc Shlua Uí Néill 145
Mayo 45, 166
McCormack, Gertie 18
McGann, Nuala 21
McKenna, Siobhán 26
McShane, Ronnie 13, 19, 20, 25, 26, 28, 31, 113, 119, 120, 121, 130, 143, 149, 154
Meascra Ríleanna 42
Meath 21
Mercier, Mel 21
Mercier, Peadar 21, 51
Merrion Street, Dublin 17
Miller, Liam 52
Miller's Daughter 145, 146
Millstreet 30, 219

Mise Éire 19, 26, 212
Miss McLeod's & Callaghan's 146
Mná na hÉireann 49, 60, 147
Mo Chailín Bán 40, 60, 147, 212
Mo Chailín Bán/Tá mo Mhadra 40, 212
Mo Ghile, m'Fhear 33
Mo Ghille Mear 46, 60, 148
Moladh don Athair Máinséal 148
Molly St George 149
Moloney, Paddy 16, 25, 26, 38, 44, 47, 48, 51, 122
Moloney, Rita 31
Molony, Paddy 18
Mo Mhúirnín Bán 42
Money From America 149
Monjarret, Polig 47
Montague, John 44
Mooney, Ria 10
Moscow 47, 49
Mosney 18
Mo Thuirnín Línn 150
Muileagán Dúbh Ó 152
Muirceartach MacAnna 152
Murphy, Denis agus Julia 44
Murphy, Richard 44, 45, 46
Murphy's Reel 61, 153, 221
Murtagh, Michael 29
Múscraí 27

N

Ná béadh buachaillín deas ag Síle 153
Nách Fada an Lá (Dorian Mode) 154
Na Cleaganna (an mhóin) 99
Náisiún Gaelach/Gaelic Nation 12, 23, 24, 25
Na Píobairí Uilleann 17
Neillí 40, 154, 212, 220
Newport Lass 56, 61, 64, 154, 155, 221
Ní Bhearain, Caitlín 10
Ní Bhrolcháin, Ester 10
Nic Dhonnachadha, Máire Áine 44
Ní Chatháin, Máire 11
Ní Cheallaigh, Eadaoin 11
Ní Dhomhnaill, Máire 11

Ní Laoghaire, Máire Bhuí 42
Ní Liodáin, Eithne 11
Níl na Lá 28
Ní Mhurchú, Fidelma 11
Ní Nuamain, Aingeal 11
Nioclás Tóibín 221
Ní reacaireacht gan reacaire 33
Nuair a Ghabhaimse tríd an mBaile seo 155

O

Ó Bhean a'Tí cad é an bhuairt sin ort 42
Ó Briain, Micheál 11
Ó Broin, Paddy Bán 30, 219, 221
Ó Buachalla, Breandán 50
O'Carolan, Turlough (Toirdhealbhach Ó Cearbhalláin) 33, 37, 38, 51, 220
Ó Catháin, Darach 21, 22, 23, 24, 25, 26, 27, 33, 34, 89, 135, 136, 160, 212
Ó Catháin), Ruairí Dall 39
Ó Ceallaigh, T.C. 42
O'Connell Hall 28, 213
O'Connor, Desi 30
O'Connor, P.J. 29
Ó Cróinín, Seán 27
Ó Doirnín, Peadar 48, 49, 220
Ó Dubhlainn, Uinsionn 11
Ó Dúill, Breandán 43
Ó Fiaich, Tomás 48
Ó Floinn, Philib 11
Ó Foghludh (Foghlú), Liam 11
Ó Frighil, Éamonn 42
Ó Gallchobhair, Éamonn 42
Ó Goilidhe (Ó Goilí), Seathrún 11
Ó Grianna, Séamas 42
Ó Guaillí, Éamonn 10
Ó hAnnracháin, Fachtna 42
Ó hAonghusa, Micheál 11
Ó hÉanaí, Seosamh 41
Oireachtas na Gaeilge 47, 219
Oireachtas na nGael 47
Old Joe's Jig 61, 155, 156
Ó Longáin, Micheál Óg 42
Ó Luain, Peadar 11

Once I Loved 44
O'Neill, Fr Charles 42
Ó Raghallaigh, Liam 33
Ó Raifteirí, Antoine 42
Ó Rathaille, Aogán 24
Ó Riada, Ruth 20, 24, 47, 50, 52
Ó Riada sa Gaiety 48, 212, 220
Ó Riada's Farewell 44
O'Riordan, Mick 47
Oró Bog Liom í 81, 111, 159, 180, 210
Óró Nach é siúd an Seó 158
Oró Sé do Bheatha 'Bhaile 157
Ó Síocháin, Seán 27, 28, 69, 70, 71, 99, 100, 138, 139, 166, 172, 187, 198, 202, 205
Ó Súilleabháin, Eoghan Rua 12, 24, 25, 39
Ó Súilleabháin, Tomás 41, 43, 212
O'Sullivan, Clara 11
Our Musical Heritage 53

P

Páirc an Fhomhair 159
Peaití Tadhg Pheig 13, 27
Pearse Street, Dublin 19
Peigín Leitir Mhóir 26, 160
Petrie, George 32
Phoenix Hall 213, 219, 220
Píce an tSúgaire 160, 161
Pickow, George 27
Pipers Chair 161
Planxty Maguire 38, 61, 162, 224
Playboy of the Western World 26, 212, 219, 220
Pléaráca na Ruarcach 38, 163
Port an Deoraí 33
Port Laoise 29
Port na bPucaí 43, 62, 164, 212, 221, 222
Portobello Studio 213
Pósadh 165
Potts, Bernie 12, 31
Potts, Seán 17, 18, 25, 26, 38, 48, 51, 68, 105, 223
Potts, Tommy 44
Priest in his Boots 166

Príosún Chluain Meala 40, 62, 166, 212, 220
Pup Came Home from Claodach 167
Purcell, Henry 46

Q

Queen's Royal Theatre 19
Quimper 47, 49

R

Ráca Breagh mo Chínn 35, 167
Races of Cahirsiveen 167
Radio Éireann 10, 12, 24, 26, 27, 30, 42, 43, 212, 213, 221
Raghadsa is mo Cheaití 169
Raithneach a Bhean Bheag 35
Rath Chairn 21, 22
Rathcoole 21
Reacaireacht an Riadaigh 16, 24, 25, 26, 27, 33, 34, 43, 91, 94, 126, 133, 168, 212, 213, 217, 220, 221
Reddigans 171
Red-Haired Boy 60, 139, 171
Redmond, Avice 11
Reel of Bogey 71
Réice Luimnighe 172
Richie, Jean 27
Ril Mhór Bhaile Chaladh 36
Rí na bPíobairí 44
Robertson, Margaret 46
Roberts, Robin 27
Rogha an Riadaigh 62, 175
Rogha Beethoven 62, 174
Rogha Liatroma 35
Róisín Dubh 62, 175
Rolling in the Rye Grass 62, 176, 177
Rolling on the Rye Grass (Ballet) 62
Ros Muc 47
Rowsome, Leo 16, 44
Ryan, Patricia 11

S

Sail Óg Rua 33
Sanfey, Bernie 17
Saor Radió Chonamara 47
Scattery 14
Sceilpín Draighneach 178
Scoil Lorcáin 26
Seachrán Cairn tSaoghail 178
Séamus 'ac Murchaidh 42
Seán a' Bhríste Leathair 179
Seán Ó Díghe 39, 179
Seán Ó Duibhir a' Ghleanna 42, 63, 179
Sefauch Farewell 46
Seoladh na nGamhna 180
Shelbourne Hotel, Dublin 24, 219
Ships in Full Sail 181
Sí Bhean Locha Léin 182
Since Boney is Down 183
Slán agus Beannacht le Buairibh an tSaoil 184
Slán le Máigh 42
Sliabh Luachra 24, 27
Song of the Anvil, The 10, 15
Song of the Whiteboys 42
Soviet Union 47
Spillane, John 27
Stácadh an Mhargaigh 188
Star Above the Garter 44
Steam Packet 190, 191, 192, 193, 223
St Francis Xavier Hall 28, 213
Swallow's Tail 63, 194
Sweet William Craig's Dragoons 57, 195

T

Tabhair dom do Láimh 39, 195
Tá Gaeghil Bhocht Cráite 195
Tailliúr Aerach 196
Táimse ar an mBaile seo 35, 197
Táimse im' Chodladh 40, 221
Tá mo Mhadra 40, 212
Tá mo Mhadra, Níl mo Mhadra 200
Tarring go Ciúin 201
Tatter Jack Walsh 64, 201
Taylor, Paddy 44
Tell Her I Am 202
The Airy Batchelor 68, 223
The Battle of Aughrim 44, 45

The Blackbird 80
The Boy in the Gap 44
The Boys of Kilmichael 35
The Drones and the Chanters 44
The Ewe Reel 109, 221
The Green Sailed Vessel 44
The Holy Streets of Dublin? 43
The Liffey Banks 44
The Little Beggarman 139
The Longford Collector 140, 221
The Northern Muse 44
The Pipering of Willy Clancy 44
The Sligo Maid 194
The Testament of Freedom 42
The Yellow Flail 194
Three Little Drummers 203
Thugamar féin an Samhradh Linn 39, 42, 64, 203
Tóibín, Niall 43, 46, 49, 50
Tóibín, Nicolás 43, 221
Tommy Cohen's 64, 204
Torramh an Bharaile 40
Trím Rachaigh Subhail 206
Trinity College 11, 219
Tripping to the Well 70, 207
Trip to Athlone 61, 64, 154, 155
Trip to Durrow 64, 206, 222
Tubridy, Michael 7, 17, 25, 26, 28, 30, 38, 48, 51, 53, 54, 66, 222, 223

U

University College Cork 9, 31, 43, 54, 219, 220
Úr-chnoc Chéin Mhic Cainte 42
USA 13, 47, 49

V

Valley of Knockanure 35, 40, 64, 208, 212
Vertical Man 45

W

Walsh, Edward 42
Waterford 13
Wearing of the Green 61, 64, 154, 208
Wesleyan church, Portobello 28
Wexford 17, 208, 209
Wicklow 14
Wife of the Bold Tennant Farmer 209
Wind the Shakes the Barley 210
Woodtown 44, 45